WARNING!

**This Product
Contains Nuttiness**

OTHER BOOKS BY SAM VENABLE

WARNING!

This Product Contains Nuttiness

**A Fun Look
at the
Bizarre World
in Which
We Live**

SAM VENABLE

ILLUSTRATIONS BY TOMMY SMITH

THE UNIVERSITY OF TENNESSEE PRESS / KNOXVILLE

Copyright © 2013 by The University of Tennessee Press / Knoxville.
All Rights Reserved. Manufactured in the United States of America.
First Edition.

The paper in this book meets the requirements of American National Standards Institute
/ National Information Standards Organization specification Z39.48-1992 (Permanence
of Paper). It contains 30 percent post-consumer waste and is certified by the Forest
Stewardship Council.

Library of Congress Cataloging-in-Publication Data

Venable, Sam.
[Essays. Selections]
Warning! this product contains nuttiness: a fun look at the bizarre world in which we
live / Sam Venable; illustrations by Tommy Smith. — First edition.
        pages cm
Edited essays that originally appeared as Sam Venable's columns in the Knoxville news
sentinel.
ISBN 978-1-62190-006-1 (pbk.)
   I. Smith, Tommy, 1974– illustrator.
   II. Title.

PN4874.V46A25 2013
741.6092—dc23
2013018589

FOR MY SWEET GRANDDAUGHTER LUCY

CONTENTS

Acknowledgments

Most of these essays originally appeared as Sam Venable's columns in the *Knoxville News Sentinel*. They have been edited for book use and may differ somewhat from their original form. The author gratefully acknowledges permission from the *Knoxville News Sentinel* to reprint this material. He also thanks illustrator Tommy Smith and cover photographer Paul Efird for their excellent graphics contributions to this effort, along with Scot Danforth and the entire staff of the University of Tennessee Press for their continued help and guidance. And, as always, the author is ever-appreciative of his sainted wife, Mary Ann—not only for lovingly and patiently abiding his nuttiness for more than four decades, but also for her incomparable computer skills, without which this book would have remained nondescript boxes of newspaper clippings in the upstairs closet. She thanks him for finally getting rid of them.

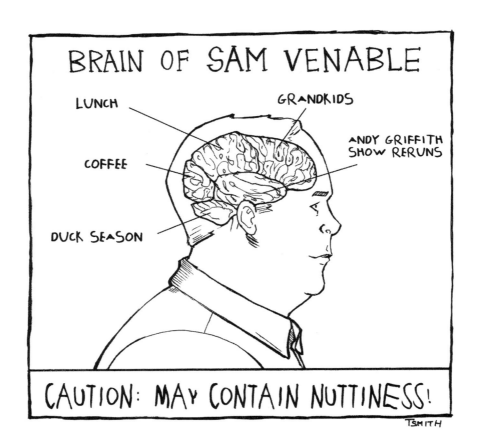

INTRODUCTION
DOES SAM VENABLE EVEN EXIST?

As proof of the fleeting significance of a historic event, I once left a Super Bowl party and within five days had completely forgotten the final score of the game. Now, years removed from that moment, I can't even tell you who played whom. Or where.

I can, however, tell you about an item I removed from the host's house. (Removed with permission, I hasten to point out. Odd as it may seem, journalists do occasionally have ethics, if not manners.) It's a ten-ounce can that once was filled with "deluxe mixed nuts." Says so in big block letters, right there on the label.

Also on the label are two color illustrations: one a drawing, the other a photograph.

The drawing features the company's logo—a smiling, yellow peanut character with skinny black arms and legs. He is wearing white gloves, has a monocle on his right eye, and is carrying a curve-handled cane in his left hand while his right hand executes the courteous tip of his black top hat. You know who I'm talking about, of course. With the possible exception of a certain oblong "'em&'em" character covered with chocolate and protected from melting by a thin candy shell, this guy is the most famous peanut in junk-food advertising history.

The photograph shows the "new nut blend" waiting inside the can. Included in this vast array are cashews, Brazil nuts, macadamia nuts, hazelnuts, and peanuts. The picture is so inviting, my mouth waters as my fingers tickle these computer keys.

But it was neither the drawing nor the photograph that caught my attention and prompted me to take post-party possession of the can. Instead, it was three itty-bitty words below the nutrition facts, serving size, total fats, cholesterol, and other data that nobody, except strange newspaper columnists, would inspect:

"May contain peanuts."

"Imagine that!" I spoke aloud to no one in particular at the party (only to be *ssshhhushed!* by several radical fans hovering around the television). "You reach into a can of deluxe mixed nuts and might actually find a peanut!"

OK, I know. Peanuts are not nuts, botanically or dietarily. They are legumes. They grow underground, not on a tree. What's more, peanut allergies are quite common—and I have no further to look than my adult son, Clay, who has suffered this potentially life-threatening condition since he was a toddler.

Nonetheless, I chuckled then—and chuckle now while holding the can—at the notion that a peanut company, with an iconic peanut on all its commercials, has to warn consumers they might buy its peanut products and—*tah-dah!*—find a peanut inside.

Oh, well. Such is life in this nutty world. And more power to it. Without nutty events, nutty circumstances, and nutty people, I wouldn't have a job. At least not a real one.

I think about this weird situation every year when winners of the "Wacky Warning Label Contest" are announced. This event, sponsored by a Detroit organization called Michigan Lawsuit Abuse Watch, attempts to underscore the more egregious labels in our midst. Some are so bizarre, they leave a single word echoing in my head: "Why?"

Such as one recent champion—a one-thousand-degree industrial heating gun affixed with a label telling users not to attempt drying their hair with it. In second place was this cautionary note on a certain brand of kitchen cutlery: "Never try to catch a falling knife." Third was the fine print on a cocktail-napkin image of waterways in North Carolina: "Not to be used for navigation."

This nuttiness has become so pervasive, I now actively seek it. My wife hates for me to grocery-shop with her because I spend most of the time strolling up and down aisles at random and yanking packages off the shelf, just to read their details. Herewith a few gems I've discovered:

Cigarette lighter fluid that cautions, "Do not use near fire or flame." Huh? How, then, does it work? Are you supposed to douse two Marlboros with fluid and rub them together like sticks at a Boy Scout camping contest?

A one-ounce bottle of "imitation" brandy extract, with emphasis on "imitation." Once more, I stress this stuff is "imitation" brandy extract and, therefore, permissible for purchase by Southern Baptists. The first item listed in the ingredients? "Alcohol 35 percent." Meaning this fake brandy is 70-proof. Whoo-hoo! Football stadium, here we come!

A rectal thermometer that warns, "Do not use a rectal thermometer to take an oral temperature." I suspect this is a mistake you only make once—after the thermometer has been, uh, "broken in," if you catch my drift. Sorta runs along the line of legalistic fine print that always comes with chainsaws: "Never attempt to stop moving chain with your hand."

These zany things are everywhere, I tell you. In my garage is a stepladder virtually layered with safety stickers. One says to "always face ladder while climbing up or down."

I had never considered climbing a ladder backward until I read a stern label instructing me not to do it . . .

Yikes! Trust the voice of experience: Backward laddering may or may not be dangerous, but it is exceedingly difficult. In fact, it gives the arms and legs such a strenuous workout, I'm surprised someone hasn't patented a backward-ladder exercise machine, complete with a label warning users not to attempt frontal ascent.

Now consider this: Not long ago I traded in my old bass boat. The new one came with a ream of official writs, documents, warnings, precautions, and admonitions heavy enough to double as an anchor. Verily, I attempted to read them. By the third or fourth page, however, my eyes were all but glazed over with highlighted, bold-faced, exclamation-pointed paragraphs *WARNING!* and *CAUTIONING!* me about one potential crisis after another.

If I hadn't owned boats and outboard motors for four decades, I probably would have said heck with it and forsaken marine recreation altogether. To hear those labels tell it, boating is too risky for a rank amateur like me. Far better left to graduates of the U.S. Naval Academy.

In fact, by the time I set the safety manuals aside, my head was aching. A real cranial-crusher. So I popped three ibuprofens. (Sure, the label said to only take two. But what does it know?)

Which brings us to the pages that follow. They contain nuttiness, foolishness, craziness, goofiness, silliness, weirdness, and wackiness. I can't help it. That's how I've made my living for more than forty-five years. Hey, if readers and bosses are willing to put up with a charade like this, who am I to argue with their brilliant judgment?

As incredible as it seems in this era of layoffs, cutbacks, closures, and aborted careers, I've spent almost half a century—first at the (old) *Knoxville Journal,* then the *Chattanooga Free Press,* but the vast majority at the *Knoxville News Sentinel*—having the journalistic time of my life. The first three years were as a police reporter and feature writer, followed by fifteen as outdoors editor, the rest as an anything-goes humor columnist. All of these assignments have allowed me to showcase the one and only job skill I've ever had.

I'm a natural-born smart-ass.

Who else do you know—I triple-dog swear on a stack of Harbrace manuals this is true—breezed through collegiate English courses with easily earned As and Bs and then managed to fail the University of Tennessee's once-required-and-always-feared Junior English Exam *on the very day* he was inducted into the student chapter of Sigma Delta Chi, the journalism honorary society?

Normal people aren't blessed with gifts, or timing, like that.

And now imagine getting paid all these many years later for clowning around as my fingertips tap idly on a keyboard. In some circles this is known as larceny.

To be sure, the tools of the newspaper trade certainly have changed. When I entered this business, stories were created the same way they had been for more than a century. They were composed on sheets of coarse paper in noisy manual typewriters, edited with the deft use of a pencil, scissors, and paste, then re-created into line slugs of molten lead on an even noisier Linotype machine. Compared with the high-tech, high-speed, wireless operations of today, those quaint tasks seem downright prehistoric.

And the speed of changes will only increase in the months and years to come.

In 2009, I discussed this evolution in a commencement speech for UT's College of Communication and Information. (Imagine that, Junior English Exam profs of yore! Neener-neener!) I felt like an antique standing before all those young faces—the way a doughboy from World War I might feel addressing the current crop of cadets at West Point.

No way could I impress them with technology because what I consider cutting edge is the stuff they learned in high school. In fact, there were only three words of wisdom I could impart about this shaky field in these economically perilous times: "I don't know."

I don't know what's going to happen to newspapers or to the news-gathering and news-dissemination business—except that people are always going to read. In some form.

I just hoped somewhere in that audience was another natural-born smart-ass who can find a way to parlay this single skill into a career as rewarding as the one I've enjoyed—and hope to enjoy for many years to come—even if I'm not 100-percent certain of who I am in the first place.

You see, when you own an odd name like "Venable," people are forever trying to track down your lineage. One was a *News Sentinel* reader named Judy Wilson.

While digging through her own family's history, Judy came across Sir Roger Venables of Kinderton, Chesire, England.

The way Judy had it figured, Sir Roger was my twenty-sixth great-grandfather. He was born in 1220 and died forty-one years later, making him somewhat of a graybeard given the relatively short life span of that era.

According to what Judy was able to unearth—high-brow research is easy when others do it for you—clans named "Venables," with an "s," came from France into England around 1066 during the Battle of Hastings. (No doubt the natives are still talking about how the neighborhood has gone straight to hell ever since.) Somewhere along the line, the "s" was dropped—perhaps our way of losing weight—and the name became simply "Venable." More on that in a moment.

Judy also found reference to Thomas Venables, who was registered at the University of Oxford in 1616. There was no mention of when ol' Tom might have graduated, but surely this earns him the family record for longest collegiate career. I wonder if he was a natural-born smart-ass who majored in journalism and riotous living, like certain of his descendants?

Then I saw another line in Judy's research, and my baby blues poked out on stems. To wit: "The name 'Venable' is derived from the Latin word 'venabulum' or 'hunting ground'—a derivative of the verb 'venari,' meaning 'to hunt.'"

Holy moly! That's a DNA match if I ever saw it! I just hope Sir Roger was successful at riding the family name into a lifetime of outdoor adventures on the company dole. It's a good gig.

About that time another subscriber, Ruth Riggs, added even more intrigue. Seems that some time ago, Ruth mailed one of my columns to a writer friend, Boyd Stone, in her native Coquille, Oregon. Lo and behold, scribe Stone had heard of my family's name, too—this doesn't happen to the Smiths, Joneses, and Johnsons, does it?—and sent back the following nugget of history: "Venable isn't a very common name, but an early Coos County gold miner (circa 1853) named Venable was murdered by Indians six miles below Coquille while going down the river in a canoe."

You can't argue with DNA or nautical history in these matters. Given my bent toward the outdoors, I simply *must* be kin to both of these characters.

There's one way to tell absolutely: Find out if gold miner Venable was going down the river in his canoe backward—which is usually the way I wind up traveling in whitewater, thanks to my superb paddling "skills." What do you bet this smart-ass clown majored in journalism and riotous living, too?

Actually, you need not even delve into history to start connecting the dots between "Venable" and "nuts." There's plenty of evidence in the here and now.

Not long ago, a multimillion-dollar theft of walnuts and almonds occurred during shipment in California. Every time there was a update on this crime, reporters and broadcasters would quote the official spokeswoman for the Almond Board of California. Her name? Marsha Venable.

Several readers contacted me to see what relationship, if any, existed. Hate to disappoint, I told them; I have first cousins in California all right, but they are Spencers, not Venables.

Oh, you don't know how I would love to have claimed Miss Marsha as one of my own! Since she's an expert on nuts, ours would have been a kinship made in heaven, if not Madison Avenue.

But while all this enjoyable name-gaming was playing out in the papers, I suddenly got dope-slapped. My cover was blown to smithereens by a reader named Charles E. Cardwell.

Charles had done some Venable research of his own. Forget that alleged France-to-England loss of the "s" on my surname, he said; it's all a bunch of Battle of Hastings historical bull.

Noting that the first word of my company-mandated email address (last name, first letter) comes out to "venables," Charles squinted his eyes, pointed a practiced trigger finger like an Old West sheriff, and snarled the question I've dreaded since January 3, 1968, the day I walked into my first newspaper office: *"Just how many Venables are you?"*

Gulp. Sigh. My long-held secret was out.

So since Charles pierced this balloon, I must confess: Sam Venable isn't real. He is a fictitious person, a collage, a jumble, the result of a horrible and cruel journalistic experiment gone awry. Just check "my" photo on the cover of this book. Bogus City, eh? It's nothing more than the computer-connected ears, nose, eyes, hair, and mouth from a variety of people plucked out of bus stations and police identification lines. Ain't no way any one person can be *that* ugly.

Consider yourself warned.

Chapter 1
WHO NEEDS FICTION?

Dave Barry, Pulitzer Prize–winning humorist for the *Miami Herald,* came to Knoxville in September 2002 to entertain at a corporate awards ceremony. Since the *News Sentinel* carried his popular syndicated column at the time, the suits in our front office decided to throw a fancy reception for him.

Fine by all us po' folks in the newsroom. Anytime there's a combination of free food, free liquor, and an excused absence from work, the motion carries unanimously.

Fortunately, the audience was limited to personnel from the newspaper; otherwise the crowd would have spilled onto the street. The guy was mobbed. Not surprisingly, Barry proved to be just as warm and witty as he is in print. He had everyone laughing. When I finally was able to get in a few words one-on-one, I said something I'd been wanting to tell him ever since I discovered a hilarious story of his in *Rolling Stone* many years earlier: "Dave, I am not making this up. I was writing 'I am not making this up' before you were writing 'I am not making this up.'"

Could be, we agreed. There wasn't time for either of us to search through a few kazillion columns right there on the spot and compare numbers—especially since the free food was approaching crumb status and the free liquor had nearly evaporated. (Cheap-ass front-office suits and their stingy budgets.)

I suspect Dave Barry and Sam Venable aren't the only newspaper humorists who frequently type "I am not making this up." We have to. It's the only way we can assure readers that yes, by gosh, the wacky subject we're about to ridicule, expound upon, and milk for all it's worth is the truth, the whole truth, and nothing but the truth.

Barry's name for this artful selection of material is "booger journalism." I couldn't agree more—although, as a frustrated former sports editor of mine once noted, in a somewhat raised and strained voice, "If you didn't shoot so much (bovine scatology) all the time, you wouldn't have to specify what's real and what isn't!"

Had to admit he made a good point.

Anyway, I'm often asked, "Where do you come up with the crazy stuff you write about?" My answer is always the same: "Everywhere! It's low-hanging fruit! All you gotta do is reach up and grab it."

Or drive into it, as the case may be.

Such was the situation that occurred precisely seven hours and six minutes after the stroke of midnight on New Year's Eve 2009, welcoming in New Year's Day 2010. Most people were still in bed at that hour, or else fumbling through a medicine cabinet for antacids and headache relief. Not yours truly and cousin Frank. We were—I am not making this up—adrift in a sea of brown cow, and it was at that very moment I announced to Frank: "The way I see it, 2010 can't do anything but get better."

Frank agreed. We Venables prefer to remain positive, despite tremendous odds to the contrary.

What Frank and I were experiencing was our own little version of the infamous TVA coal ash spill in Kingston, Tennessee. Only decidedly more aromatic.

We were standing, thigh-deep, in a sea of liquid cow manure—and you don't know how desperately I want to use a more terse, realistic, and good ol' boy expression than "manure." We were holding onto the side of my pickup truck, which also was adrift in the aforementioned sea, trying to maintain our balance. And we were oh-so-thankful both of us were wearing chest waders and there was a cell phone in my pocket.

Frank and I got into this mess because we are lifelong duck hunters who made a New Year's Eve decision to go afield early on New Year's morning, if for no other reason than to wash away the bitter taste of Tennessee's 37-14 loss to Virginia Tech in the Chick-fil-A Bowl several hours earlier.

Little did we know the term "wash away" would soon take on a new and personal meaning.

We went to the same dairy farm where we have hunted for years. We let ourselves through the gate and entered the property through the same feed lot we have entered for years. We drove into the same pasture we have driven into for years. We started down the same hill we have gone down for years, pointing my truck toward the same flooded timber where we have decoyed ducks for years.

Ah, but there was one tiny detail that never had presented itself in all those years. Seems that one day earlier, farm crews had cleaned the feed lot with heavy equipment, pushing the aforementioned sea of brown cow into a depression in the pasture.

Which we managed to hit, dead-center.

There are two geophysical constants at all dairy farms: mud and liquid cow manure. In the headlights of a pickup truck, forty-five minutes before sunrise, both look the same. However, they do not support transportation the same. Mud can be traversed via four-wheel-drive. Liquid cow manure, with the consistency of exceedingly wet concrete, cannot.

It was over and done in less time than it takes to type this paragraph. One second we were rolling; the next second we were floating. Like a Chevy Colorado in a punch bowl, you might say. To the point that a tsunami was now flowing onto the floorboard.

Yes. Really. Not joking.

We were able to climb out of the cab and pull ourselves into the bed. That's where we put on our chest waders. And where I placed a cellular "Mayday!" to the kind farmer, who promised to bring a tractor and crew after dawn.

There being nothing else productive to do, Frank and I fetched shotguns and decoys out of the bed of the truck and slogged into the flooded timber, bagging four gadwalls (two drakes, two hens) and cleaning our waders at the same time.

Happily, tractor and log chain extraction worked. Even more happily, a Knoxville auto detailing company did a peachy job of stripping the truck to bare metal, setting off a chemical bomb to kill any hidden bacteria, steam-cleaning both the engine and the interior, and installing new pad and carpet. I drive that truck to this day, and—I am not making this up, either—there's not so much as a hint of an odoriferous reminder from that fateful day, even in the heat and humidity of summer.

See what I mean? There's no way even a team of Hollywood scriptwriters could come up with such a cockamamie plot!

Ah, but agricultural entomologists certainly could. And did. So help me.

Several months after my adventure adrift, I was invited to speak at an international agricultural-entomology conference in Knoxville. The sponsors of this event assumed I shared much in common with the highly trained delegates who—how do I put this politely?—specialize in bovine parasites. Vocational translation: They work in cow pies. Many cow pies. Lots of cow pies.

It didn't take long to realize I was way out of my league. Indeed, I was a rookie, a freshman, a rank amateur compared to these men and women. Not only were they postgraduate-degreed from their caps and gowns to their knee boots, they had more practical poop experience than a battalion of sanitation engineers.

One of them, Knoxville-native Dr. Brad Mullens (PhD from Cornell and now researcher at the University of California), laid a "9/11" story on me that evokes cold chills every time I recall it.

Please understand: On September 11, 2001, the worst places on Earth to be were the Twin Towers in New York City, the Pentagon, and a field outside Shanksville, Pennsylvania. Given the carnage of that day, Brad's experience was incredibly tame, timing notwithstanding.

On that horrible morning, oblivious to what was occurring elsewhere, he was at an Illinois dairy farm, accompanied by a research veterinarian and a graduate student from the University of Illinois.

"We were looking for the larvae of midges that transmit a disease called bluetongue," he said. "They live in manure-polluted mud, which, as you can imagine, is very common at dairy farms. We were in a barn, walking across a floor uniformly covered in liquid manure. Of course, we had our rubber boots on. Up ahead was a wall about two feet tall."

Mullens and the vet knew what was on the other side: a sloping concrete pit where manure can be stored until it is hauled out with a front-end loader. Unfortunately, the student wasn't privy to this information. Without warning, he hopped over the wall and into what Mullens describes as "manure-water slurry about six feet deep."

"He was up to his chin, flailing his arms and starting to panic," Mullens said. "The vet and I were trying to haul him back to our side when he spotted an 'island' that he thought would provide refuge."

Unfortunate choice. The "island" turned out to be the bloated carcass of an exceedingly dead cow.

"Yeah, it was pretty bad," Mullens told me. "We finally got him outside, hosed him off, and gave him some clean clothes. Then we took our larvae samples back to the university. I haven't heard from the student since, but I assume he stayed in the field of agricultural entomology."

Why not? Just as Frank and I concluded very early on that New Year's morning, things could only improve thereafter.

Before you panic, or reach for a barf bag, let me stress that not every entry in this chapter involves crude, unsavory, sophomoric subjects. Many of them are crude and unsavory at the junior and senior level, too. Just kidding.

Until I began compiling these columns, I didn't realize how often I write about criminal activity. Perhaps this is due to my formative years as a police reporter. It's just that whenever I read about a particularly bizarre whodunit, I immediately start having flights of fancy.

Like the time a guy—we'll call him "Mister George"—was nailed for bank robbery. Indeed, from the moment I became aware of Mister George and his exploits, that's exactly what I called him in print. It's part of my upbringing.

Mister George was many years my elder. Here in the South, we are taught to respect such rank by adding a "Mister" or "Miss" to older men's and women's first names. Like Mister Jim, Mister Herman, Mister Tom, Mister Randy. Oh, and the feminine "Miss" is applied despite a woman's marital status. Collectively, Miss Evelyn, Miss Betty, Miss Charlotte, and Miss Susan may have more than a century of enduring marriage, not to mention entire tribes of children and grandchildren. Doesn't matter. In the South, they're all "Miss Such-and-Such." You don't go back on your raising.

In any event, Mister George was arrested for robbing a branch of First Tennessee Bank—and if you think I'm making this up, I invite you to peruse the records of the Knoxville Police Department for December 2010. They're available for public inspection any time you choose.

According to these reports, Mister George came into the bank around five o'clock on a Friday afternoon, brandished a weapon and, after a minor stunt, "forcibly removed money from the teller drawers."

It's the minor stunt Mister George performed that caught my eye.

He jumped the counter. At age seventy-eight.

> **Pat Sisson was among a number of readers who called my attention to a recent headline in the *News Sentinel*: "Man competent enough to be declared insane."**
>
> **Said Pat: "Maybe that's the way we all ought to be."**

I am a mere pup compared to Mister George. In theory, I should be able to perform greater physical tasks than he, particularly given that I exercise (lap swimming and power walking) on a regular basis.

But jump the counter of a bank? Or any counter, for that matter? On the spur of the moment? Holy muscle spasm! My legs just cramped at the very notion!

There is only one way I could accomplish this maneuver. That would be by:

1. Hauling two lightweight, six-foot step ladders into the bank.
2. Setting up each one on opposite sides of the counter.
3. Climbing up the first ladder.

4. Stepping onto and over the counter. (This might require an assist by the nearest teller.)
5. Descending via the second ladder.
6. Taking the cash.
7. Repeating the process in reverse order.

All in all, a rather cumbersome operation and one that surely would attract the attention of the bank guard. Which, as it turns out, is precisely what Mister George did. As he was attempting to exit the joint, Mister George was grabbed by an on-duty security guard and held until the cops arrived.

That's why he deserves a kick in the buns for poor planning.

True, Mister George might have been out of breath after his leap-a-thon. Or maybe he had to nurse a charley horse. But he should have thought of that ahead of time and cooked up another ruse for evading the guard. As it is, he will have abundant opportunity for future planning on all levels.

Don't get me wrong. Robbery—armed or unarmed, of a bank or an individual—is serious business. Cops, courts, juries, and judges are not prone to take it lightly. But the least they could have done for Mister George was give him a Senior Olympic medal to hang in his cell.

Trust your Uncle Weirdness: You don't need to make stuff up. As long as there are crazy crooks and seas of cow poop, I'll never suffer from writer's block.

CARRYING EXCESS BAGGAGE

If you want to book a summer vacation flight that has a slim chance of being hijacked, I know just the ticket.

Not only ago, fifty-five passengers took off on a journey from Erfurt, Germany, to the Baltic Sea resort town of Usedom. The cost was about $735 American. Soon as the plane left the ground and stewards began dispensing drinks, I hope these travelers stuck with beer, wine, cola, or water. Surely they avoided coffee, tea, cocoa, or any other hot liquid. These flights tend to get bumpy, and a splash to the ol' nether regions under these conditions could prove to be excruciating.

That's because everyone's nether regions were on full display.

Yes, adventurers. Nekkid Airlines is ready when you are.

OK, so I made up the name of the company. But I'm not fibbing about the journey. It's a flight for nudists.

Reuters gets credit for unsheathing this story. Seems it's a package deal being sponsored by a German travel agency named OssiUrlaub. According to the news service, passengers had to remain clothed until they boarded the airplane. Plus, they had to re-dress before disembarking. Because of safety regulations, the crew remained clothed throughout.

But between Erfurt and Usedom, ticket holders flew together in their altogether.

This wasn't an orgy excursion. As travel agent Enrico Hess pointed out: "It's not that we're starting a swinger club in mid-air or something like that. We're a perfectly normal holiday company."

Just one that caters to folks who shuck their skivvies.

Count me out, thanks just the same—and not for reasons of modesty. Quite the contrary. It's a matter of comfort.

Skinny-dipping down at the ol' swimmin' hole is one thing. But squeezing my sweaty butt cheeks into the cramped quarters of an airplane, right next to someone else's sweaty butt cheeks, ain't my idea of fun. Not to mention chaffing from rough upholstery.

But my main objection can be credited to a tourism truism I learned years ago: most humans, and we know who we are, have bodies that ought to remain clothed.

This goes for men and women alike. Despite what you might see between the covers of "adult publications," the vast majority of us look like we were assembled by committees working miles apart and communicating with carrier pigeons.

You name the particular form of visual pollution on exhibit—pot guts to saggy chests, cellulite by the square yard to "very-close" veins, acres of back hair to legs like water tanks—yeeesh! Definitely not the sort of humanoid real estate I wish to view, on vacation or otherwise.

Nonetheless, this should prove to be a safe trip. It's difficult to commandeer when you're going commando.

Unless, of course, there are some serious caverns for weapons storage in someone's nether regions. Given the current epidemic of obesity, that could well be the case.

CURSE NOT THIS NEW PROJECT

Well, I'll just be *&$#!@!

Then again, #%& could be a more appropriate term. Or %$/@. Maybe even %&#*! Experts disagree on the fine points of language.

But there's no disagreement with a newspaper story I just read. Quite the contrary. I say, "It's about $%#&-ing time!"

The article was written by J. M. Berger of the *Boston Globe*. It reported an extensive, expensive study into the what-where-how-and-why of cussing.

The title of the project is "Expressive Content and the Semantics of Context." But when you peel off the fancy veneer and boil down the academic mumbo-jumbo, this is a look-see into coarse language.

Said Berger's story: "Christopher Potts, a linguist at the University of Massachusetts at Amherst, will catalog and analyze the use of obscenities, vulgarities, and racial epithets, as well as titles and honorifics." Potts's work is being funded in part by a $200,000 grant from the National Science Foundation.

Is he paying for volunteers? Sign me up, pronto!

Actually, I'm all for this research. As a lifelong student of spicy outbursts, I've always been fascinated by the reasons, origins, mechanisms, and dialect behind these blasts.

I'm too young to have experienced the social shockwave that reverberated across America the first time Clark Gable uttered his famous "Frankly, my dear—" line. But I do remember my mother talking about it whenever reruns of *Gone with the Wind* made the rounds—and chuckling how innocent his invective seems in comparison to the potty-mouthed cinema scripts of today.

Cussing is a lot like drinking. Some folks abstain completely. Some indulge on occasion. Some find abundant occasions. And some overdo it to the point of nauseous addiction.

I've always believed there's a time and place for everything, particularly in the application of crude words. (My &%#* wife will roll her #!/*& eyes at that &#% statement and tell you my idea of "moderation" in cussing means 90 &#$*-ing percent, but she's bad to exaggerate, %$#*&-it!) Teasing!

The truth of the matter is, incessant cursing assaults the ears the same way cigarette smoke burns the eyes. It's like too much seasoning in the stew. Ruins everything.

On the other hand, a well-turned vocal volley—light or heavy, as the situation dictates—can work wonders. Oh, and trust Mister Potty Mouth When It's Necessary: "Pootnanny," "fudge," or "ding-diddly-dang" need not apply.

> Shelby Feldman writes: "Whenever I walk our dogs, I always notice their habit of stopping and sniffing, stopping and sniffing, stopping and sniffing. It used to aggravate me. Then I realized they were simply reading their 'pmail.'"

FATHER, UH, MOTHER, KNOWS BEST

Listening in on a child-raising dilemma several years from now in the home of Thomas and Nancy Beatie—

"All right, you kids! This is the third time I've caught you writing on the wall! It must stop! Just wait till your father gets home! Uh, wait a minute. I *am* your father. No, that's not exactly right, either. I'm not actually your father; I'm more like your mother. In fact, I *am* your mother. Hmm, this is too confusing. Just go back to writing on the wall. Try blue crayons this time."

OK, so I'm being flippant, not to mention unfair. Like any couple, Thomas and Nancy Beatie will face enough hurdles as they raise their children. It's just that they're going to face far more hurdles than your average couple.

That's because the Beaties, who live in Bend, Oregon, aren't your standard Ward and June Cleaver.

Thomas was born female. He underwent a sex-change operation, but retained his female reproductive organs. When he and his wife decided to have a baby, he underwent artificial insemination. And got preggo. Three times, in fact.

I am not making this up. The Beatie family's weird situation has been all over the news. Thomas even wrote details of his experience for a gay magazine, *The Advocate.* What's more, he then appeared on Oprah Winfrey's and Barbara Walters's shows and displayed his distended belly. Then he delivered just like any other woman—er, I mean man; uh, hmmm, I'm not really sure what I mean, except that this ain't like anything I ever remember seeing on "The Adventures of Ozzie and Harriet."

Before you ask, the answer is no. This isn't the first time a man gave birth. According to the *London Guardian,* a female-to-male transsexual, Matt Rice, bore a son in 1999, and everyone is alive, well, and happy. All of which illustrates how interesting the times are in which we live.

Will the Beaties be successful at raising their children? Who knows? Nobody can answer that question any more than they can for the Smiths, the Johnsons, or the Whites down the street. Having a baby is forever a roll of the dice. You can only hope for the best, for parents and kids. That goes quadruple in this case because you know they will face persecution, stares, and derision.

I happen to have become a father, and later a grandfather, via the more conventional method. I cannot imagine my life being nearly as rich, as fulfilling, as loving, and as complete as it has been without my children and my grandchildren. I highly recommend both experiences to anyone interested, particularly if they earnestly want children.

Heaven only knows the number of unwanted babies who are aborted every year or born into a lifetime of neglect. If you've got two people—of any gender—who truly want a child and are dedicated to raising it in a loving home, more power to them.

Even if this particular situation is the strangest I could ever imagine.

DOC HAD IT RIGHT ALL ALONG

Too bad Doc Baird is no longer with us. Otherwise, he could finally get credit for the most ingenious phraseology in the annals of medicine, not to mention the English language.

Doc—some folks called him "Sonny," but he was known in highfalutin circles as Renfro Blackburn Baird Jr., MD—was one of East Tennessee's last old-time country doctors.

A Kentuckian by birth, he became an adopted son of Hawkins County. He practiced medicine for more than half a century until his death, at age eighty-one, in 2003.

Doc did it all: from lancing boils to delivering babies, setting broken bones to general surgery. He served as the county medical examiner as well as chief of surgery at the county hospital. Doc also was an associate professor of clinical surgery at East Tennessee State University and was instrumental in establishing the medical school there.

We got to know each other in the 1970s through the medium of bird dogs and bird hunting. Whether we were climbing ridges for grouse or wading broom sage after quail, Doc kept me in stitches—of the laughing variety—with a steady patter of tales and one-liners. The guy was a natural comedian.

But the joke was on him once. I still get tickled every time I think about it.

We were bouncing along a rutted lane in the outback near Mooresburg. A farmer who was burning brush in a nearby ditch recognized Doc's vehicle and flagged us down. The two of them chatted briefly. After being pointed in the likely direction of a couple of coveys, we pulled away.

"Who was that guy?" I asked nonchalantly.

"Hate to admit it, but I can't remember," Doc replied. "Reckon I'm havin' a senior moment. That fellow's been a patient of mine for years."

I thought nothing more about it. But the question tormented Doc like a hungry mosquito. He continued to chide himself as we drove. In frustration, he stopped, slapped the dashboard, and issued a jewel that will stick with me forever.

"Dammit, Sam! Why can't I think of that man's name? I distinctly remember doin' a hemorrhoid job on him once, and I never forget a face."

Immediately, I told Doc if I ever needed that operation, his services would not be required.

"Why?" he asked in surprise. "Don't you trust me?"

"It's not a matter of trust," I said. "It's a matter of direction. I think you start from the wrong end."

Doc and I laughed about that till the day he died. But recently, while reading news accounts of a new surgical procedure, I could just imagine the ol' coot hee-hawing even louder.

Seems physicians at the University of Pittsburgh Medical Center are experimenting with going through natural orifices of the body—nose, mouth, wherever—for certain surgeries. There's no scarring, quicker healing, less damage to other tissue, and reduced chance of infection compared to cuts through the skin.

I quote from the story: "Bowel surgery, for example, 'would be like going to the dentist and getting a root canal,' said Dr. David Rattner."

Big deal. Doc Baird could have told 'em that twenty-five years ago.

TAKING A BIG BITE OF CRIME

Is it just me, or is a distinct correlation between women, pastry, and crime developing south of Knoxville? This thought has been churning through my brain, not to mention my belly, ever since I read about the latest doughnut caper in Blount County.

Recently, the Richy Kreme Donut shop in Maryville was robbed by a woman brandishing a rifle. According to the Blount County Sheriff's Office, the thief was "a white female, approximately five-feet-eleven-inches to six-feet tall, wearing a hooded, long brown jacket and brown pants, with a black bandana covering her face." Furthermore, deputies said the suspect "fled in a newer-model Chevrolet Cobalt, traveling west on East Broadway."

The official report made no mention about the most important aspect of this crime, which I find incredibly incompetent.

No, I'm not talking about the type of rifle, its design and probable caliber, nor the license number of the getaway car. I'm talking about the suspect's doughnut preference.

If citizens knew whether this dastardly she-crook liked maple-glazed versus old-fashioned cake, or blueberry versus chocolate-covered, perhaps the crime could be solved posthaste. But then, what do I know about high-sugar sleuthing?

The Richy Kreme case came on the heels of another Blount County pastry-related incident involving a woman. Several months earlier, Alcoa police arrested a twenty-one-year-old female on drug charges. According to the cops, she had a white substance around her mouth, which she claimed was residue from a recently consumed powdered doughnut.

(On second thought, I *do* know a lot about high-sugar sleuthing, thank you very much. Please note Alcoa's constabulary obtained all the pertinent facts in this case. They didn't simply say the suspect claimed to have "doughnut residue" on her mouth. They specifically pointed out it allegedly came from a powdered doughnut, and the arrest was made shortly forthwith. I rest my case, Your Honor.)

Far be it from me to sound an all-points bulletin about this matter. Now is the time for calm, rational thinking, not some grease-crazed jump to illogical conclusions. The last thing lawmakers and law enforcement agents in Blount County need to do is treat this as an abrupt change in criminal nature and start shutting down doughnut shops willy-nilly. I'm just saying there appears to be a trend, and it bears watching.

What's doubly weird about this situation is the idea that someone with criminal intentions—male, female, in Blount County, or elsewhere—would attempt to carry them out in the vicinity of a doughnut shop.

Don't these people know this is a traditional gathering place for cops? Why, you couldn't swing a bag of crullers without hitting someone with a badge. It's like sticking your hand inside a den of snakes and wondering why you got bitten.

And speaking of biting, a freshly baked bear claw sure would hit the spot right now. Strictly for investigative purposes, you understand.

YOU'D BE NUTS TO BELIEVE IT

The first time Bill Dockery heard the question, he laughed it off as a telephone prank. Several months later another inquiry arrived. Then another. And another.

He started asking colleagues if they'd also gotten the request. Their collective reply was long the lines of "Duh! Where have you been?"

"That was five years ago," said Dockery, coordinator of research information for the University of Tennessee, "and I *still* hear the question. Matter of fact, I got a phone call about it just the other day."

The person wanted to know if UT is currently buying men's testicles.

I am not pulling your leg—or any other body parts. Neither is Bill.

"The reported price has gone up lately," Dockery said with a laugh. "When I first started getting the calls, the alleged going rate was ten thousand dollars. Now, it's fifty thousand."

Most inquiries follow a similar pattern. Such as: A trusted source of information (usually the friend-of-a-friend's first cousin on his uncle's sister-in-law's side who lives in Tulsa but travels through Tennessee every fourth summer on vacation) heard the story and checked it out, and it's true! UT is conducting research into human sexuality and is paying huge dollars for testicles! You—yes, YOU—could be rich! Yee-haw! Git me a knife, Gerty, and a stick to bite down on!

But it's also 100-percent false.

Repeat: It's an urban legend.

Repeat II: This is a myth.

Repeat III: There is no truth to it whatsoever. Put the knife back in the drawer.

"What's so funny is that by far, most of the calls come from women," said Dockery. "Maybe they have a soon-to-be-ex-husband and want to make some money off of him. At first, I thought this was limited to Tennessee. Then I started checking urban legend sites on the Internet and realized it happens at many universities."

Dockery directed me to snopes.com, which has compiled several reports of the rumor. In addition to UT, other institutions that are allegedly purchasing these research jewels are Vanderbilt and the universities of Virginia, Texas, and Florida. The prices I found ranged as high as $160,000. Per jewel!

"Unfortunately for men seeking quick windfalls, no university or other medical organization buys testicles," says snopes.com. "The National Organ Transplant Act of 1984 prohibits the sale of human organs and tissues, and that prohibition applies to testicles just the same as kidneys and other organs. Nonetheless, the rumor has run rampant in the last several years."

> **Two famous Americans— Harry Wesley Coover Jr., ninety-four, and Frank Neuhauser, ninety-seven— died in 2011. Coover was the inventor of Super Glue; Neuhauser won the first national spelling bee (1925). How do you suppose they sealed Coover's casket? And do you reckon someone triple-checked the spelling of Neuhauser's name on his tombstone? I wonder about these things.**

The site continues: "One interesting change in the form of this legend is that while 'body sale' rumors of years past specified a relatively modest fee (five-hundred to one-thousand dollars) for the sale of a whole corpse, modern rumors claim that a testicle donation will bring the seller anywhere from fifty-thousand dollars to one-hundred-sixty-thousand for a single organ."

Of course, this being a rumor shouldn't discourage anyone from creating cheap, crude jokes. If you want to say the Tennessee (insert your favorite sport here) team needs more of these organs, or that there should be a plethora of these things on campus already because everybody who works for UT has to hand 'em over the first day on the job—hey, don't let me stand in your way.

THE LATEST IN SELF-DEFENSE

I've been shopping for some self-defense weapons and had no idea there was such a variety. Too wide of a variety, in fact. I'm more confused now than at the start of my search.

Right off the bat, I thought how simple it would—huh? What's that you say? Was I looking for a pistol? Taser? Mace? Knives?

Heavens, no. Those are old-school, so twentieth-century. I wanted the very latest, the most innovative. That's why I went shopping in the furniture section of a local department store. This is headquarters for the finest merchandise to thwart the bad guys.

Don't take my word for it. Read for yourself. On November 15, 2010, the *News Sentinel* reported how the desk clerk at a Knoxville motel prevented a robbery in a most ingenious manner.

This would-be caper occurred in the wee hours. The night desk clerk was confronted by a knife-wielding man who demanded cash. Instead of forking over the money, however, the quick-thinking motel employee leaped off his butt and took matters into his own hands.

Literally.

He grabbed the four-legged bar stool he'd been sitting on and swung it at the thief.

The robber yelled, "Feets, get me outta here!" (or words to that effect) and hoofed out the door.

Upon reading this story, my first reaction was to recall the time at the Museum of Appalachia when a visitor demanded I stick out my hand so he could give me—his direct quote—a "stool sample." Just as I was about to punch him in the nose, he produced an itty-bitty, teeny-tiny, hand-carved wooden milking stool. It was a good five minutes before we quit laughing.

My second reaction was to hit the showroom and peruse the self-defense options available.

Since the clerk used a bar stool, that's where I started looking. I found two nifty ones from the Ace Bayou Corporation. Really stout. Appeared to be oak. The twenty-four-inch model sells for $15.96. The twenty-nine-incher is four bucks more.

Nice, but a wee bit heavy for emergency use, especially if the swing must be made one-handed.

No problem. Next to these was a display of Mainstay walnut veneer stools ($24.96 for twenty-four inch, $29.96 for twenty-nine.) Quite lightweight, with the added bonus of a large (nine-by-seventeen-inch) seat for the ol' tush during non-robbery moments.

Then there was the Whalen-Welgrove stool ($28.95) with metal legs and a sixteen-by-sixteen-inch beveled wooden top. I figured the beveled edge would prove handy for draining blood if you managed to clunk the crook over the noggin.

On and on I shopped: For the Kinfine parson's end table in cherry veneer (hmm, is it a sin to whack a robber with something associated with the ministry?); for the Canopy storage ottoman, a bargain at $78.95, but too hefty for overhead swinging; even a seventy-eight-inch-wide futon ($219.86) for long-distance fighting. Plus folding chairs, office chairs, computer carts, end tables, DVD shelves, and coffee tables galore.

Lordy, I had no idea this would prove so complicated! It may take weeks to pare my list. And then, of course, I'll have to navigate the paperwork required to register these weapons with the U.S. Bureau of Furniture and Fixtures and obtain a carry permit.

TURNING DOWN THE VOLUME

The news on the television front is so wonderful I'm tempted to shout hosannas. Except that would defeat the purpose, so perhaps polite applause will suffice.

The joy welling within me right now is due to a recent report from the Inside Science News Service, which is a real, honest-to-gosh news organization. It concerns sudden noise changes on TV commercials.

You're painfully aware of this problem, of course.

You're watching a movie or a documentary or a nature program or late-night talk show. Everything is moving along peacefully until the program cuts to a commercial message. Without warning, THE NOISE LEVEL INCREASES BY APPROXIMATELY TEN BEZILLION DECIBELS AS SOME JERKWAD TRIES TO SELL YOU A NEW CAR OR THE MOST CHEESE-LOADED, GREASE-DRIPPING PIZZA IN THE HISTORY OF JUNK FOOD!

Your only option is to grope for the remote and madly punch buttons until you either hit "mute" or find the volume control and run it down about twenty clicks on the "minus" scale.

Several minutes later, when the commercials end and the show resumes, no sound whatsoever comes from your TV until you strike "mute" all over again or punch twenty clicks on the volume control's "plus" scale. Not much fun either way.

But relief is on the horizon. A technical organization called the Advanced Television Systems Committee hopes to "provide a way to measure the loudness of television content based on current scientific understanding of how human hearing works," the news service recently reported. "Shows and commercials would be tagged with information about their loudness that TVs and audio receivers could use to counteract the audio tricks that make commercials jump out at us. It achieves results similar to a viewer using a remote control to set a comfortable volume between disparate TV programs, commercials, and channel-changing transitions."

In other words, no abrupt audio shock.

Excellent. This can't happen soon enough. But while they're at it, I hope these scientists eliminate some of the other annoying elements of TV commercials. Such as those fast-talking, horribly garbled messages at the end of an ad, spelling out every possible legal term and condition from the Magna Carta to the modern era:

"Allthewordsareruntogethermeaningthere'snowayinhellanormalhumanbe ingcanunderstandwhat'sgoingon."

I also wish they'd get rid of infomercials in general, especially those that mimic a legitimate news format:

"So please tell us, Doctor Jones, about what prompted you to discover and patent Colon Clamp, with its unique blend of all-natural ingredients, making it the most effective anti-diarrheal medication on the market today, especially since you're offering a thirty-day supply free to the first fifty viewers who call in and pay the nominal shipping and handling fee of $1,249.95, available in six low installments."

In memory of Walter Cronkite, an anxious nation begs for this relief.

LEGALLY REWRITING HISTORY

Forget what you learned in all those history classes. It doesn't seem to matter any longer.

That's the only deduction I can make after studying what the NCAA did a few years ago with the University of Alabama's football program.

The Tide wound up with three years of probation for a "major violation." This came in the aftermath of a textbook scandal. Seems certain Bama jocks were taking their free school books—the ones they got via their scholarships—and "obtaining" them, in exchange for money, to non-jocks.

In most areas of commerce, this type of transaction is called "selling." But why quibble over petty details?

According to the NCAA, the top four offenders "obtained" books worth more than three thousand dollars. The university insists none of the aforementioned "obtainings" resulted in a profit to any individual, which I will believe approximately seven seconds after the law of gravity is repealed.

But who knows? As a group, athletes aren't necessarily known for their business skills. Perhaps these young capitalists were, in fact, truly unable to show a profit after selling—I mean "obtaining"—free books to other students in exchange for a few Gs. Stranger things have happened.

The upshot was that Alabama had to "vacate" (another odd NCAA term) twenty-one football victories it posted between the 2005 and 2007 seasons. Meaning no matter what the final score said, the Tide didn't win. Thus, Tennessee's humiliating 6-3 loss to Alabama in 2005 was officially "vacated." Also a 41-17 shellacking in 2007.

Fine. I guess.

Even though those two losses were "vacated," Tennessee still got its butt kicked in both contests. At best, I would classify each of these "vacated" outcomes as a hollow victory.

In fact, this whole business of going back and legally rewriting history seems a bit odd, no matter what the mitigating circumstances. It's like discovering Ulysses S. Grant had his fingers crossed behind his back when he accepted Robert E. Lee's surrender in 1865; thus the Union's Civil War victory had to be "vacated."

But what the heck. Far be it from me to argue with an institution as all-knowing as the NCAA. I can only wonder what might happen if this trend is adopted in other venues of human endeavor. Any day now, I expect to see news stories on the order of:

Howard J. Turnipseed III of Axe Handle, Arkansas, was forced to vacate the apple-peeling championship he won at the 2002 Izzard County Fair when officials of the Arkansas Highway Patrol determined he had exceeded the speed limit by twenty-four miles per hour en route to the fairgrounds.

Frederick "Fuzzy" Fuztburger, the 2009 Copiah County, Mississippi, tobacco-spitting champion, has vacated his title after revelations he laced his Beechnut with molasses to add extra volume.

Billy Jones, eight, who beat the snot out of Bobby Eastridge, eleven, behind Moorehaven Elementary School last week, will vacate the victory. Even though Bobby suffered a black eye, a split lip, and the loss of one tooth, he has been declared the winner because Billy had secretly been learning the Warp Your Head Off Hold from his Uncle Ferd.

Don't wait another second, Americans! Order for your "vacate" application today! Operators are standing by!

HERE'S WHY OUR EYES ARE IN FRONT

I nearly broke my neck and wrenched my quarter-million-dollar back in the process, but I just disproved a hot new scientific theory.

This theory—which I swear on a stack of Bibles I'm not making up—recently was published in the journal *Psychological Science*. It was postulated by researchers from Radboud University Nijmegen in the Netherlands.

They claimed that people who walk backward think more clearly than those who take their steps in the traditional manner.

Repeat: This was a real test conducted by real scientists. It was a memory-cognitive thing in which participants were told to step four paces to the left, right, front, and back as their assignment became more difficult.

"Backward locomotion appears to be a very powerful trigger to mobilize cognitive resources," the team reported in the *Los Angeles Times*. "Thus, whenever you encounter a difficult situation, stepping backward may boost your capability to deal with it effectively."

So much for theory. Real life is different. Not to mention risky.

A few days ago, I was helping my wife with some yard work. ("Helping" should be construed in rather broad terms here, you understand. I have two black thumbs, not green ones, and when it comes to normal gardening tasks, I'm all thumbs.)

Anyhow, we were through for the afternoon. Mary Ann went inside to start supper, leaving me to put away the tools. I stored the shovels and rakes in the garage and shoved the other stuff under the front porch. All that was left was hauling a large, heavy tub of dirt to the woods.

Mary Ann has a long, U-shaped rope attached to this tub. Even so, it presented quite a chore. I grasped the rope and slowly leaned into it, avoiding any jerks and off-balance moves.

That's the way I do everything these days, from picking socks off the bedroom floor to

> **Mary Lou Benson of Tellico Village was telling me about her recent trip to South Africa: "One day our guide, a native Zulu, got out of the Land Rover, picked up some dried elephant dung, lit it, and said, 'Our people used to burn this and inhale the fumes to take away headache.' It sure made me glad I'd packed plenty of Tylenol for the trip!"**

lifting heavy objects into the bed of my pickup truck. Slow and easy does it. In 2007, my health insurance company shelled out more than $250,000 on my behalf for extensive back surgery. Neither I, nor the insurance company, wants to revisit that experience. Ever.

So there I was, slowly walking forward and pulling the tub across the lawn. Everything was progressing smoothly as I rounded the bend at the boat shed and reached the driveway.

Up on the concrete, there was less friction. The tub scooted along effortlessly. Since I had only fifteen or twenty more feet to go, I turned around and walked backwards, if only to break the monotony of the job.

Thank heavens that's the only thing that broke.

You see, I didn't know Mary Ann had left another tub at the other side of the driveway. Yes, of course, I dead-centered it.

Somehow, I managed to let go of the rope, execute a quadruple back flip, and land upright unscathed. I'd pay major bucks for a videotape of the performance. It would be hilarious to show at family gatherings.

Based on what came out of my mouth during the episode, however, I'd have to turn down the sound any time the grandchildren were watching.

Chapter **2**

STILL WAITING FOR Y2K

Roughly one month before his sixth birthday, my grandson shocked me with language he had picked up in kindergarten. I'm still having palpitations.

No, Max didn't utter a bathroom word. Or—be still my soul—something even more coarse. Nonetheless, I couldn't have been more stunned if he had unleashed a torrent of locker-room invective.

This occurred the afternoon he walked into my home office as I was hunting-and-pecking on a computer keyboard, leaned his elfin frame against my left knee, looked up at me through innocent brown eyes, and said, ever-so-sweetly, "Dipsey, will you find some Internet access for me?"

Frankly, I could have handled potty talk better. That part of grandparenting I understand. Kids come out of the womb knowing giggled expressions about "poop" and "pee" and "bottoms" will get an uncomfortable rise out of their elders every time. But the very notion that a five-year-old child would be so tech savvy that he would calmly request hookup to the World Wide Web?

Pour me another one, bartender—and make it a double.

Still numb, I hoisted Max onto my lap, tickled the necessary keys, and turned him loose. The tiny fingers I've grown used to watching as they snap Star Wars figures together seemed perfectly at ease on the mouse pad. He moved the cursor and double-clicked with no more conscious effort than sticking a spoon full of breakfast cereal into his mouth.

What Max wanted to show me was a spelling game he'd learned at school. Naturally—hey, he's a Venable!—the little varmint was an expert. Not only did he properly anticipate each successive word as it was about to appear on the screen, he also knew the correct arrangement of letters as well as the pronunciation.

Daa-yumn! At his age, I was yet to learn "See Spot run." Yet there he sat, reading complete sentences. I wanted to weep—in joy for Max embracing these exciting new horizons so eagerly and in sadness for my sorry techno-cretin state.

Oh well. What goes 'round comes 'round. I distinctly remember my paternal grandmother, Angie Anderson Venable, describing in infinite detail the day the first "motor carriage" sputtered into tiny Jonesborough, Tennessee, the Washington County town where her father worked as a blacksmith. (I also distinctively remember thinking to myself, "Good Lord! It was just a car, for Pete's sake! What's so special about that?" Except I knew better than to take in vain any biblical expression, however mild, in the presence of Grandmother Venable.)

I've tried to stay abreast of the times. Really, I have. The demands of my job mandate that I acquire at least a modicum of skills in modern communication. Unfortunately, my concept of "modern" communication peaked around, oh, 1992. Any time I'm in the presence of someone—young or old—when they whip out an iPhone and start fingering through photos and videos, or scrolling up and down their latest electronic messages, I resist the urge to (1) gawk in disbelief or (2) rapidly slobber an index finger between my lips—*"bbblllllllpppp!"*—like an ape at the zoo.

Things simply move too quickly for me in this modern era. About the time I make a change, I realize I'm already three changes out of date. (Saaaay? When is all that Y2K stuff supposed to come down? Isn't it going to mess up our microwaves or clocks or sundials or something? Note to self: Next time you're at the office, ask if anyone remembers the date when this is supposed to occur. Probably wouldn't hurt to be prepared.)

Whatever happened to that blissful, Norman Rockwell time in my life when everything seemed so orderly, so sensible, so uncluttered, and easy to remember? This notion occurred to me when I read news accounts of the bickering between Congress and the U.S. Postal Service over the issue of home mail delivery on Saturdays.

What?! No mail on Saturday? Whoever heard of such a preposterous idea?

It doesn't matter that my mail could stop being delivered this coming Saturday, and every Saturday thereafter for the next fifty years, and I'd probably never miss it. That's not the point. The point is, we've *always* had mail delivery on Saturdays—I think you can find a requirement for it mentioned in Leviticus. No sense in messing with tradition.

Then, just for the sake of argument, I thought, "Hmm. We don't have home delivery on Sunday, and never have, yet I don't recall ever missing that. So

I thought again, "Hmm" (I "hmm" to myself a lot; drives my colleagues nuts), "imagine how strange it might be some day trying to explain to young people that mail delivery didn't always cease on Friday and resume the following Monday."

All of which caused me to stop working altogether (this happens a lot, too) and start compiling a list of how the NOT—Natural Order of Things—has changed during my brief lifetime. Among them were:

Phone booths: Not necessarily pay phones, even though these devices also are going the way of the dinosaur. I'm talking about honest-to-gosh, stand-alone, folding-door phone booths. You know, those skinny buildings with the pointy roof.

There used to be one on virtually every street corner and in every parking lot. Besides housing telephone users, they provided merriment for college students vying to see how many bodies could be crammed inside, as well as a place for Clark Kent to change into his Superman outfit. Which may explain why college kids have turned to drugs for entertainment, not to mention the dearth of Superman sightings these days.

Milkmen: Residential ice deliveries largely had vanished by the time I was born, but I distinctly remember the metal box on our front porch that was magically loaded with iced-down bottles on milk day.

Come to think of it, would you have to explain the setup—or would anybody even understand—if you told a milkman joke these days?

Elevator operators: In the Pleistocene era of my childhood, Knoxville was far from a bustling metropolis. Still, nearly every multi-level public building employed a crew of workers, mostly female, who sat on itty-bitty stools, opened and closed the cage door and main door, and chanted, "Foundations, ladies' ready-to-wear, children's clothing" at the appropriate floor.

Hmm. (There I go hmming again.) How come there aren't cage doors on self-operated elevators? Did those elevator operators of long ago know something about safety that we don't know today?

Missing a TV program: Okay, so televisions themselves weren't all that common in households when I was a youngster. But once these beasts came into our lives, they ruled with an iron fist.

If you wanted to see "Bonanza," you had to be parked in front of the tube on Sunday night. And you *only* got that one-time shot until summer rerun season. These days, you can record every program offered on all 29,384,765 cable channels and watch them at your (insert laugh here) leisure. Even those goober reruns of "Bonanza" and "Adventures of Superman." I think this is called progress, but don't hold me to it.

Still, I don't want to give the impression I'm *totally* out of touch with what's going on. I'll have you to know I own one of those "—berry" systems to keep myself organized.

No, it's not a BlackBerry. It's a StrawBerry. I'm looking at it as we speak.

That's not its real name, of course. According to the manufacturer (MeadWestvaco Consumer and Office Products of Sidney, New York), my StrawBerry is an "At-a-Glance Standard Diary and Daily Reminder." It has a bright red cover and measures seven inches tall, five inches wide, and roughly one inch thick. True, the thickness swells appreciably throughout the year as I begin tucking reminders, notes, column ideas, and other information between the pages. So? That's why they make rubber bands.

If you haven't guessed by now, this is not an electronic gizmo. It's an everyday, run-of-the-mill date book. The *News Sentinel* has been buying me one of these things every year since I took employment in 1970. Back then, everybody on our staff used them. Then tragedy struck. The rest of the world either went modern or nuts, depending on your perspective. They quit using these red books, opting instead for all manner of wireless gadgetry.

> "People always complain about the high cost of gasoline," says Gene Rosenberg, "but they rarely say a word about the coffee they buy at the gas station. Think about it: At $1.09 for a sixteen-ounce cup, that figures out to $8.72 per gallon. It makes gasoline seem cheap by comparison."
>
> Maybe we oughta start sipping a cup of hot petrol for an early morning pick-me-up.

I am one of the few, the proud, the holdouts.

If my friends and colleagues chose to worship digitized devils via the BlackBerry, fine. I will stick to my StrawBerry, which is what I began calling my red book a few years ago when berries migrated from the briar patch to the office cubicle.

My StrawBerry stores all of the names, phone numbers, addresses, notes, and information I need. It offers simplicity in its purest form. It works at the touch of a page-flicking finger: A to Z in the name section, January 1 through December 31 on the appointment pages.

It never needs recharging. It works equally well in bright light or dim. It's never out of range. If I drop it, there is no crystal display screen to crack. Nor do I ever have to worry that someone will break into my vehicle to steal it.

What's that? You say your fancy BlackBerry comes with a GPS for finding locations? So does my StrawBerry. It's just a different kind of GPS: a Government Printed Sheet. Also known as a map.

I can't make photographs or place phone calls with my StrawBerry, but that's no problem. I already own several cameras; they take great pictures. If I want to call someone, I have a cell phone. It stays in my satchel alongside my StrawBerry. (Call me crazy, but not once have I ever picked up a camera and thought, "Man! I sure wish I could dial a phone number on this thing!")

Speaking of numbers, don't ask for mine. I don't know it—my cell phone number, I mean. I never can remember it. Home number—got it. Office number—got it. Cell number—duuh. The only way I'm able to give out my cell number is by turning the hateful thing on and waiting for the screen to light up.

Why don't I just leave it on all the time?

What?! And be bothered by all those annoying, unwanted incoming calls? I simply turn on my cell phone when I need to call someone, then promptly switch it back off. Extends the battery life and keeps my blood pressure low. As my wife and my editors learned long ago, if they really need to find me, check the nearest coffee pot.

See? Who needs all the complicated wizardry of modern life? It just leads to problems. One more example, and then I'll let you get on with this chapter:

While walking out one side of the double doors at the *News Sentinel* one afternoon, I abruptly hopped to my left and opened the opposite door for a young lady who was fast approaching. This was not altogether an act of manners on my part—although, as a proper southern man raised by proper southern parents, I've been known to open doors for women, whether they like it or not.

The real reason I did it was to keep the young lady from walking, *smack-dab-kerbash,* into the glass pane scant inches away.

Yes, of course; she was texting. Head down, thumbs stabbing furiously at the device in her hands, she appeared oblivious to her surroundings.

For all I know, she may have realized a door was looming directly in front. Maybe there's a radar app for people who walk and text at the same time. Soon as they stride within striking distance of a formidable object, a whistle blows.

Or maybe not.

Judging from the young lady's surprised reaction when the door suddenly flew open—not to mention the somewhat embarrassed-somewhat appreciative smile on her face—methinks I saved her from creasing her crown.

She said thank you (no doubt a proper southern woman herself), then resumed her relentless march. Head down, thumbs a blur of motion.

I went on my way, too. But not before saying a silent prayer of thanks for being an unrepentant, card-carrying, curmudgeonly, geezer-in-training with one less modern thing to worry about.

Happily, I can wear a baseball cap with the bill in front, not cocked to one side, so the sun stays out of my eyes.

Happily, I can cinch my jeans at the waist, with a belt, not hang them off my knees and tempt sartorial fate should I sneeze.

Happily, I don't have to decide which undeveloped and unblemished square footage of my hide will next be assigned the newest tattoo pattern.

And, happily, I don't have to fret about walking into things when I'm texting. Because I don't text.

Admitting in the twenty-first century that you don't text is socially akin to admitting in the twentieth century that you couldn't read.

Fine. No defense. Guilty as charged, Your Honor; apply whatever punishment you deem necessary.

For me, texting has a lot in common with golf: I tried 'em both a time or three and came to the swift conclusion my life is perfectly marvelous without either.

I will never suffer the same fate of that poor girl on YouTube who tumbles into the water fountain at a Pennsylvania mall while texting. Or the two North Carolina state troopers who got suspended for four days after sending profane texts about a suspect.

Don't need it, thank you. I already have enough ways to humiliate myself and get into trouble.

A LESSON IN DOLLARS AND SENSE

Even though I have a passing interest in football and the stock market, I'm not an expert in either. Not even remotely.

I was a running back on the Young High School varsity team during the seasons of 1962, '63, and '64. But my greatest contribution to the team was serving as cannon fodder during weekday practice sessions. The most serious injury I ever suffered on a Friday night was splinters in the butt.

Even more laughable is my stock portfolio. My net worth, if liquidated under the best of financial conditions, couldn't fund two nanoseconds of operations in the shakiest business in the poorest city of the most poverty-stricken nation under the sun.

All that notwithstanding, I can only scratch my head at the start of every football season, particularly during the economic downturn we're experiencing.

Pick up any publication—newspapers to magazines, books to pamphlets, media guides to betting tip sheets, not to mention chatter from radio and TV pundits—and you'll find thousands of predictions about the upcoming football campaigns. Kiddie leagues, high school, college, or professional. Doesn't matter. What does matter is the mishmash of rankings by all these experts.

Based on their vast years of studying the game, the coaches, the players, the weather, the equipment, the field conditions, the hot dog sales, and God only knows what else, these forecasters will tell you *precisely* who'll be the champion five months hence.

Hardly anyone gets it right, of course. There are too many variables in the equation. Somewhere along the line, an unbeatable stumbles and an eternal also-ran rises from the ashes. Never fails.

So what happens?

Nothing—at least not to the players on the field. Instead, it's the experts who feel the heat.

"Aw, what a goof (insert name of favorite pigskin prognosticator) is," everybody chides. "Haw-haw-haw! When it comes to football, he doesn't know his elbow from a jockstrap. Why doesn't he get a real job?"

Now, switch to the experts—aka "market analysts"—in the stock business. Check out their economic publications and radio-TV programs. Listen to their predictions about what's iron-clad, no-doubt-about-it *guaranteed* to succeed or fail.

Hardly any of these folks get it right, either. Again, there are too many variables. Somewhere along the line, old reliables falter, and itty-bitty startups morph into giants.

So what happens?

Nothing—at least not to the experts. They continue to reap millions of dollars for their advice. For Pete's sake, it's not their fault those predictions turned sour.

Instead, it's the fault of some business or industry that couldn't live up to wildly outlandish expectations. As a result, savage bloodletting takes place among workers up and down the line.

Nobody ever said life was supposed to be fair. I just wish it made more sense.

FLYING BY THE SEAT OF HIS PANTS

So summer has arrived and it's hotter than a depot stove and you're sweating like a racehorse and even the half-block stroll from your air-conditioned car to your air-conditioned office results in serious chafing Down There because your underwear is bound tighter than all the Boy Scout knots ever tied.

Count your blessings. At least you're able to change those unmentionables on a regular basis. That's an option Koichi Wakata didn't have.

Wakata, forty-six, was a member of the crew of the space shuttle Endeavour that spent four and one-half months in outer space before returning safely to Cape Canaveral. For the final month, he wore the same skivvies.

Let me repeat that. He wore them continuously. The same pair. Unwashed and unchanged. 'Round the clock.

This was not a matter of poor hygiene. It was done in the name of science. And you thought drinking Tang instead of real orange juice while orbiting the Earth was a sacrifice.

This was a test of "J-Wear," a line of clothing designed by Jaxa, the Japanese space agency. They are billed as "anti-static, flame-resistant, odor-eating, bacteria-killing, and water-absorbent."

Wakata's wardrobe also consisted of J-Wear shirts, pants, and socks. Presumably he changed them routinely.

Upon landing, Wakata confirmed that his underwear passed with flying colors—which, now that think about it, may not be the best choice of words in this context.

"My station crew members never complained for about a month," he told reporters, "so I think the experiment went fine."

Yeah, right.

Far be it from me to question official NASA information, but I'll bet you a six-pack of Hanes all-cotton huggers everyone else in the crew called this guy names like His Royal Flatulence, Dr. Foulwind, Sir Stinkification, and Mister Moisture behind his back.

In a related matter, which I swear on a stack of BVDs I'm not making up, NASA said the air-purifying system on the U.S. side of the space station continued to fail during this mission. Coincidence? You tell me.

According to Jaxa, these undies are a cross between boxers and briefs. They are seamless, silver-coated "comfortable everyday clothes for life in a spaceship."

Say *what?* In terms of underdrawers, the terms "silver-coated" and "comfortable" are mutually exclusive.

As one who breaks out in a rash even at the thought of polyester blends, I cannot imagine anything more grating on the nether regions than a layer of silver. I bet poor ol' astronaut Wakata would have given a month's pay for a tube of Gold Bond powder during his ordeal.

Amazingly, things could be worse than wearing the same undies for a month or working alongside someone who has worn the same undies for a month. I quote directly from the London Times: "His clothing has been placed in special bags ready to be taken to a laboratory, where experts will examine how well it held up to the challenge."

Surely these people will get hazardous duty pay.

USE IT, PITCH IT, BUY ANOTHER

Every generation has "throwaway" hurdles to overcome.

For my dad, it was the idea of disposable razors. In Big Sam's mind (which was geared to the concept of reusing and recycling back when "green living" meant you had lots of money or had eaten spoiled food), it was an abomination to toss a perfectly good shaver into the trash simply because the blade was dull.

He figured you oughta be able to open the unit, insert a replacement—Big Sam would even have re-sharpened his old Gillette Blue Blades if possible—and keep shaving. Throwaways were gaining popularity by the time Big Sam passed away, but he refused to convert.

> Tippi Lamson says a branch of the Smart Bank is about to open near her neck of the woods. Naturally, she wanted to know, "Is there a Dumb Bank somewhere?"
>
> Given the mega-billions in bailouts to certain financial institutions, I suggest the answer is a resounding yes.

I'm having the same trouble cottoning to the notion of disposable lawn care equipment. I am learning, however.

True, I'm still using a couple of vintage Lawn Boy mowers. But that's because they received decades of TLC from my ol' Mister Fixit friend, Foster Piciacchia. Now that Foss resides at 777 Big Yard in the Sky, I fear their days are numbered.

When it comes to trimmers and leaf blowers, however, I've slowly come to the realization that use it / pitch it / buy another makes economic sense.

There's no telling how many of these infernal machines I've purchased in the past two decades. I've owned top-of-the-line and bottom-of-the-barrel. During that time I've learned two important lessons:

1. Whether expensive or cheap, when they're shot, they're shot.
2. Having them fixed will cost dang-near as much as buying a new one.

Which is why I am pulling the starter cord on my umpteenth new El Cheapo blower. It matches the umpteenth new El Cheapo trimmer in my shed, the one I bought this past summer.

I dislike this endless cycle of consumerism. But I'm left with little choice. Why spend fifty bucks (which I've done) to breathe a couple more brief puffs of life into a trimmer or blower when you can buy a spankin' new one for twenty or thirty dollars more?

Doubly amazing about this process is that each new model is accompanied by an ever-expanding tome of safety instructions written in English, Spanish, and French.

Here are three startling admonitions that came with my latest El Cheapo:

1. "Do not smoke when handling fuel." (I found this listed three times; perhaps there are more.)
2. "Never attempt to burn off spilled fuel under any circumstances." (I assume this is a mistake you don't make repeatedly—unless you are an exceedingly slow learner with a sky-high tolerance for pain.)
3. "Keep all bystanders, children, and pets at least fifty feet away." (What? And have them miss the exploding fuel show?)

What lunacy. I just wish manufacturers would spend more time building longer-lasting equipment than writing multi-language legal encyclopedias.

BLOWING THE BUDGET FOR BOWSER

Over a career spanning more than forty years, I've tried to spend the *News Sentinel*'s money wisely. But a few days ago, I shot our fiscal policies to smithereens.

(Nonetheless, I expect full reimbursement of this largesse when I file my expenses. Yes, I have the receipt.)

My outlay was made while conducting research on some of the more idiotic goods and services Americans continue to buy, even as our nation wilts under a hellish economy. For $4.88, tax included, I purchased three one-liter, plastic bottles filled with water.

For dogs.

It was my original intention to get by for nothing. That's because an anonymous reader had sent me a Food City store coupon for a free gallon of "Paws" brand drinking water. According to the coupon, this normally retails for seventy-nine cents. But apparently many other customers had the same idea.

I visited three Food City locations—Western Avenue, Cedar Bluff, and Farragut—and found bare shelves. As the assistant manager at the Western Avenue store explained with a grin, "Lots of people are bringing those coupons in."

The shelf was not completely barren in Farragut, however. Next to the empty space for "Paws," I found "FortiFido" water in three vintages:

Parsley flavor, fortified with zinc "to help maintain healthy skin."

Peanut butter flavor, fortified with calcium "to help maintain healthy bones."

Spearmint flavor "to freshen breath."

At $1.49 per liter, plus tax, these puppies were far more expensive than an equal amount of high-test gasoline.

It is nutty enough that otherwise sane humans will plunk down more than a dollar on a bottle filled with less than one cent's worth of tap water for themselves. But to do so for Bowser defies logic.

Not so, according to the label.

"You love your dog and want to keep him happy and healthy—after all, he's part of the family. FortiFido fortified water can help," it said.

The label continued with a list of ingredients, starting with "Moisture 99.9%" It's been many years since I took math and chemistry, but I think that means the vast majority of these pricey molecules are plain ol' $H20$.

Nowhere on the label do the words "Not for Human Consumption" appear. Then again, those words don't appear on the labels of canned dog food. Leading me to conclude that if you and Bowser want to literally share a meal, have at it.

But it begs the question: "Why?"

That same thought crossed my mind in 1997 when dog toothpaste hit the market. Here's what I wrote then and still believe now: "Please tell me how an animal that rolls in dead fish, greets other dogs with The Sniff, drinks from the toilet, and spends hours at a time licking its privates could possibly tell—much less care about—how something tastes?"

IF THE SHOE FITS, FLING IT

I am not an authority on men's shoe fashions, let alone women's. When it comes to footwear, my expertise pretty much ends with tennis shoes, hip boots, chest waders, and flip-flops.

But that doesn't mean I can't poke around the Internet and see what's hot.

By "hot," I mean what's all the rage among beautiful people, not what I'd just as soon toss into the fireplace. There's a distinct difference. Besides, I wouldn't desecrate prime, aged, hand-split oak and hickory by smothering it with ugly, high-dollar clodhoppers.

At first, I was delighted to read these words of encouragement about men's shoes on Forbes.com: "The question, of course, is why a man should choose to wear anything other than Rockports or sneakers."

I was about to pump a fist into the air and shout, "Yesss!" when I read a few more sentences and realized the folks at Forbes.com were poking fun at Neanderthals like me. Then I discovered "a good pair of high-end men's dress shoes usually starts around three-hundred, fifty dollars" and nearly soiled my jeans.

Three-fifty? For shoes? I'm thinking that's more like a monthly bass-boat payment.

Nonetheless, I flipped through several pages of fancy new offerings by designers like Crockett & Jones, Edward Green, Jeffery-West, J. M. Weston, and John Lobb—who, by the way, had a custom-made black slip-on for $3,600. Or a full ten bass boat payments.

After that I moved to women's wares via the website Millionlooks.com and perused the latest from the houses of Dior, Gucci, Rodarte, Louis Vuitton, Jimmy Choo, and others. Some of these styles were so utterly hideous, I'd be tempted to approach any woman clad in them and sigh pitifully, "Oh, you poor girl! How long did the doctor say you have to wear those things before your crippled feet are healed?"

But I pressed on, flipping through digital page after digital page of orange shoes, pink shoes, buckled shoes, and zippered shoes. Not to mention shoes covered with floral patterns, leather fringe, and gladiator straps that wrapped to the knee.

But nowhere, in either the men's or women's selections, did I see a shoe that would be ideal for throwing.

Hel-looo! Do designers not follow the news? Don't they know shoe-throwing, a long-established practice in Arab cultures, is spreading throughout the world?

The most famous incident occurred in Baghdad, when then-U.S. President George W. Bush ducked not one, but two, shoes hurled by an irate Iraqi journalist. Not to be out-flung, a protester later threw his athletic shoe at Chinese prime minister Wen Jiabao during a speech in Cambridge, England.

Clearly, these incidents illustrate the need for airborne footwear. But best I can tell, the shoe industry is way behind the curve. Nowhere in the new designs are features to assist grip, modify aerodynamics, or improve marksmanship.

At $350 and up, you'd think shoe throwers would expect a lot more bang from their brogans.

JUST COLOR ME BEET-RED

I've never had much of a need for hair-care products. Certainly not a bunch of expensive, fru-fru ones.

The basics will suffice, thank you just the same: store-brand shampoo, store-brand conditioner, and a decent hair brush. My hair may be thinning—even AWOL in spots—but it is decidedly low-maintenance.

I have no intention of buying some of the newer, more radical hair care products on the market, such as "Go Away Gray." I learned about this stuff in an advertisement that wound up in my email. This is a pill you take twice a day. In six to eight weeks, the promo claims, gray hair goes back to its original color.

I quote directly: "The secret ingredient is an enzyme called Catalase."

Wait a minute. How can this be a secret ingredient if they immediately tell what it is? With logic like that, these people must work for the government.

In any event, it says that after beginning the regimen, "Dad can get his youthful looks back!"

Not in my case. It would take a lot more than a brown mane to restore my youth. Or a lot less, in matters of tonnage.

Gray hair is fine. So is white, which is what mine is rapidly turning. I earned every salt-and-pepper strand, every crease, every bald patch—including the naked hole on the back of my noggin that expands by the year.

Besides, I take enough pills already. Between prescriptions for blood pressure and cholesterol, plus some over-the-counter stuff my doc recommended, my swallow pipe is filled to capacity.

There's yet another hair care product being touted these days. But it's not for use on top. Or the chest area. Not the chinny-chin-chin, either.

Instead, it's for "down yonder," if you catch my drift.

I hold a press release from Betty Beauty, Incorporated. It describes a product for coloring hair in the nether regions. I am serious as a heart attack.

Curious, I did an Internet search and discovered this apparently is quite the rage. And not just for women.

At the website hairdye-info.com, I learned celebrities like Sean Combs (Diddy), Ben Stiller, and Jack Black all use "revolutionary hair dye to groom those areas that the general public really should not see."

And—I swear I'm not making this up—the most popular hue is bright pink.

Call me old-fashioned. Call me a goober. Call me a codger. Call me laughing hysterically. But if I have no desire to change the color of hair that shows, why would I dye anything else?

And to think Momma used to lecture me on the importance of clean clothes in case I had a wreck and people at the hospital saw my skivvies.

THESE FISH SURE ARE BITING

As Marie Antoinette once said, "If the people are too poor to eat fish, let the fish eat them!"

Oh, wait. I think Miz Marie's exact quote had something to do with bread, not fish. Or was it cake? Hmm. I distinctly remember she said something about eating. But she was nearly out of her head at the time, so forget I brought it up.

What we do need to consider, though, is why are Americans shelling out good money to have fish gnaw on their feet? Which is what an estimated five thousand have done—at a rate of thirty-five dollars for a fifteen-minute session—in the waters of the Yvonne Hair and Nails salon in Alexandria, Virginia.

Yes, children. One hundred tiny carp will chew the dead skin off your tootsies.

> **Homer Marcum of Greeneville was traveling through southwest Virginia, just north of Kingsport, when he noticed a hand-painted sign advertising "Flee Market" down the road.**
>
> **Homer says he sure wishes he'd gotten that message before the recession hit. No doubt, so do millions of other investors.**

According to a recent Associated Press dispatch, fish pedicures have become quite popular in the D.C. suburb. The process originated in Turkey and has spread to some countries in Asia.

The little beasties doing the work are garra rufa, or "doctor fish." They are toothless, so there's no way they can attack living flesh. Nonetheless, they apparently have quite an appetite for dead, flaky skin—and if you're into a bowl of dead, flaky Wheaties right now, please accept my deepest apologies. After the fish have dined and loosened the landscape, customers then undergo a standard pedicure.

The AP story quoted several happy customers including KaNin Reese, thirty-two, of Washington, who said, "It kind of feels like your foot's asleep." And Patsy Fisher (who, by the way, has a great last name for a story of this nature), of Crofton, Maryland, who said, "It's a little ticklish, actually."

Also quoted was podiatrist Dennis Arnold, who had never heard of the procedure and doubted it would achieve widespread acclaim. "I think most people would be afraid of it," he said.

Afraid? No, I wouldn't say that.

We're talking about a container filled with tiny fish, not black widow spiders, rattlesnakes, snapping turtles or—*bleech!*—garden slugs. But it does seem incredibly weird to pay to feed fish with your own skin.

Crazier things have happened, of course. If this fad catches on, I'm sure the fishing tackle industry will take note—and maybe bring the idea to full economic and piscatorial circle. Don't be surprised to see lures featuring human skin on dealer shelves near you.

But speaking as one who has turned many a finny critter into supper, I thought we were the ones who skinned the fish. Not the other way around.

WOES OF AN MCDI SUFFERER

I've been perusing Cabela's "fall preview" clothing catalog, but it's highly doubtful I'll make a purchase.

First, I'm hesitant to buy clothes through the mail because I can't try anything on. Just because shirts, sweaters, and pants look sharp on a tall, slim-waisted model doesn't mean they'll produce the same result on a short, beer-gutted typist.

What's more, I learned long ago that "S-M-L-XL" are more subject to interpretation than political speeches.

In my closet are some shirts marked "M" that hang off me like a mu-mu. Conversely, I own other shirts marked "XL" that fit tighter than snakeskin.

This isn't a problem in stores. A quick visit to the dressing room reveals if "M" means "medium" or "magnum" and "XL" means "extra large" or "exceedingly little." With mail order, the same process takes weeks, and you gotta pay postage for the privilege.

Oh, and don't get me started on the inch calibrations of waist size. It doesn't matter if a pair of slacks is officially a thirty-four, thirty-six, thirty-eight, or forty. What matters is whether you can perform the hitch-and-zip trick without turning blue.

The second reason I'm going to pass is because I'm too cheap to spend much money on new clothes. As long as my old jeans and tennis shoes hold together, I consider myself well dressed.

But reason number three is the clincher. I can't figure out what color is which.

I'm not color-blind. Instead, I suffer from acute MCDI: Modern Color Description Impairment.

In the innocent age I grew up in, colors were simple. Red was red. Yellow was yellow. Brown was brown. With maybe a "light" or "dark" tossed in for hue-splitting.

Not anymore. These days, red can be anything from "sangria" to "berry" to "merlot" to "henna" to "currant." And please understand those are Cabela's descriptions for shirts, not wine or fruit.

Same with yellow. The yellow shirts I saw in the catalog were called everything from "monarch" to "maize" to "sunrise."

But brown is still brown, right?

Nope. It could be "dark khaki" or "grouse" or "desert clay" or "tobacco" or "dark mushroom" or "buckskin" or "earth" or "espresso" or "rust" or "timber."

Indeed, I encountered visual alchemy on nearly every page.

Black is now "ink." (No mention whether it's black ink, blue ink, blue-black ink or, heaven forbid, red ink—which, I suppose, could be sangria ink, berry ink, merlot ink, henna ink, or currant ink.)

Green is now "sagebrush," "ivy/sand," "foliage," and "forest."

(Huh? Depending on season, forests and foliages can be green, brown, red, yellow, or orange. Or bare. Transparent clothes, maybe?)

Orange is now "desert fire." (Not to be confused with "desert clay," which, if you've been following closely, is a new name for brown.)

I would say the experience left me blue. Except I can't decide if I feel "blue horizon," "mallard," "slate blue," or "river/sand."

Maybe none of the above. We sufferers of acute MCDI alternate between "blue fog" and "blue haze" all the time.

THE OTHER INK-STAINED WRETCHES

The desire to get tattooed certainly has changed since I was young. Every time I gaze at the vast, multicolored bodily road maps on public display these days, I remember the four simple requirements for acquiring a tattoo Way Back When.

1. Drop out of high school.
2. Join the military.
3. Go on leave for the first time since basic training.
4. Get drunk out of your mind.

Not today. Men, women, boys, and girls—theoretically sane and sober, but the jury's still out—have gone under the needle. By the millions. No doubt some day they will sober up, look in the mirror, recoil in horror, and gasp, "Arrrgh! What th'hell was I thinking?!"

Please understand. Even though I am decades removed from my collegiate experience, I vividly remember the pleasures of rebellion, the primal urge to lash out against tradition—whatever, whenever, and wherever tradition is encountered—and the burning desire to express your own, special, and unique individualism by dressing and looking *exactly* like five hundred of your closest and dearest friends.

Somewhere in the dark recesses of a file cabinet at my house is photographic proof from that period. It shows me in long, flowing, curly locks. Plus a beard Wolfman would sell his soul for.

Fortunately, I came of age in a pre-Pleistocene era when the remedy for personal-appearance rebellion was available at the snip of scissors or the stroke of a razor. Getting a "tat" removed is much more complicated, as legions of soon-to-be middle-aged and codgerly hellions will discover.

Besides not having to ever worry about tattoo removal, I know I'll never be harmed by a body-piercing procedure gone awry.

An intentional body-piercing procedure, I mean. Fish hooks, steak knives, finishing nails, staples, and other metal shards that accidentally penetrate the skin don't count. I'm talking about tongue studs, belly button rings, and similar "ornaments" inserted into a person's hide on purpose!—like what's happening with many of the Under-Thirty crowd.

Our newspaper recently published a story, written by Sandra Boodman of the *Washington Post,* conveying stern cautions from medical authorities about the dangers of amateur piercing. Case studies described in the article read like the script from a sci-fi movie: everything from flesh-eating bacteria on nipple rings to major organ damage from botched belly-button insertions.

(We pause here long enough for all doddering geezers to say a prayer of grateful thanksgiving that they aren't compelled by peer pressure to be cool. Amen and amen.)

To reiterate: We of the Metamucil set understand all about keeping up with the Teds, Janes, Williams, and Sallys in homeroom. Anytime we forget, a quick flip through the family photo album will reveal proof of our with-it insanity in the form of leisure suits, frilly shirts, and stack-heeled shoes.

To reiterate furthermore: Our nuttiness was a lot easier, cheaper, and less painful to reverse.

True story: A few weeks ago, I was being waited on by a young man in a Knoxville restaurant. Anytime the guy asked a question about my selection, I had to reply, "Huh? I can't understand what you're saying."

At first I thought my hearing had abruptly ratcheted down one notch. Comes with being a baby boomer. So I turned an ear closer and listened intently.

Nope. Everything was working just fine in my audio department. Whether I was relaxed or straining, his slurred gobbledygook came in loud and clear.

Then I thought, "Oh, this poor soul has a speech impediment!"

But about that time, the goof opened his mouth to speak even louder, and I spied the problem: He couldn't enunciate properly because a huge metal stud was protruding from his tongue. It looked like a nickel-sized barbell. Or a dumbbell, as the case may be.

Why someone would endure pain and expense for such "beauty" is mystery enough. But there's an even more baffling question: What sort of outrageous fashion statement will the next generation of cool-seeking cretins be making?

MONEY BY THE POUND

Joe Green has two words of advice for cash-strapped officials at the University of Tennessee: tape measures.

Go buy a few hundred of these dandy devices immediately, he says. It'll be money well spent.

Green came up with this brilliant idea after considering two sobering facts of life.

First, we are a state filled with tubbos.

In a recent survey by the federal Centers for Disease Control and Prevention, the South was declared the fattest region of the United States, and Tennessee placed third among individual states. A full 30 percent of citizens in the Volunteer State are obese, says the CDC. Only residents of Mississippi (32 percent) and Alabama (.01 percent higher than Tennessee) were fatter.

Second, but just as important, is lipid-laden Tennesseans who wish to see UT football in the flesh (eeeeww!) are being required to park their ample butts in the narrow confines of seats at Neyland Stadium.

As I have noted in this space several times before, the average width of seats at Neyland Stadium is eighteen inches. Meaning the only posteriors that fit comfortably in them belong to Twiggy, Pee-wee Herman, and a Q-tip.

Neyland veterans are well aware of this constriction. They are the ones who, if forced to stand for the national anthem or The Wave, plunk themselves down the instant: (1) the verse hits "land of the free" and (2) adjacent Wavers stand. That way, blood flow to their buns is restored for a precious few seconds.

Green proposes UT capitalize on this situation by imposing a levy on the most egregiously obese. Hence the need for tape measure at every gate.

"Violators would be charged an 'excess' fee," he explained to me. "The amount could be a flat rate or a proportional one based on a per-inch system."

This guy may really be onto something. Think about it: The official seating capacity at Neyland Stadium is 102,038. Assuming Volunteer football fans mirror the same average of obesity as other Tennesseans, that means 30,713 on any given Saturday are chubolas.

At an excess fee of fifteen dollars per body, that amounts to nearly half a million bucks. Over the course of seven home games, we're talking more than three million dollars—or roughly what it costs to educate several hundred students for a semester or employ one football coach, but that's not the point.

Bob Luttrell's most recent telephone bill was for $30.51. Inadvertently he wrote a check for $30.50 and mailed it in. The phone company immediately sent him a notice stating "Past Due! Please Pay Immediately!"—along with a separate sheet of paper showing his outstanding balance of one cent. Bob hopes his phone service won't be stopped before he can arrange terms for settling this massive debt. These skinflint days, you never know.

The point is that UT has yet another way to bleed the faithful and help alleviate its budget shortfall in one fell swoop!

Green also proposed that each person's excess tonnage be broadcast over the public address system as an incentive to lose weight—"although having lived here a long time, I know it's impossible to shame anyone."

I say we all meet at the concession stand and discuss this concept further. You buy the hot dogs. I'll get the nachos and cheese.

HURRY UP AND WAIT

I was waiting in line at the post office a few days ago—which is as redundant as saying I was flying in an airplane or swimming in water. Waiting in line is what everybody does at the post office. It's our sacred duty as red-blooded Americans.

The U.S. Constitution decrees that no citizen shall enter any branch of the U.S. Postal Service and proceed directly to a clerk. If, on the 1-in-150,000 chance nobody else is in line, the clerk is required to go on break, leaving the lone patron to languish at least fifteen minutes before being served.

Forgive me. The post office is an easy target. I could just as easily have said Walmart, McDonald's, or Kroger. Seems everywhere you turn these days, the lines grow longer and the prices escalate.

But I brought up this matter after reading an article in the current edition of *Japan Close-Up* magazine. It was a report on one of the twenty-first century's main pastimes.

Waiting.

Four hundred business people in Tokyo were quizzed about their patience, or lack thereof, in a variety of situations. Waiting in an office, for an ATM, for a train, elevator, traffic lights, whatever.

The stats are too complex for complete review here, but it struck me that the Japanese are more patient than your average Joe and Jane from Jacksonville. Whether it's a fast-food meal or a book of postage stamps, we want to be served—NOW!

It would take a team of psychologists and efficiency experts to quantify this phenomenon for the record, but my guess is that the faster paced our society becomes, the quicker we expect things to happen. And that's a false expectation.

Never mind that the hassled McClerk is juggling six burger-fry orders, four fish-sandwich requests (hold the tartar sauce on one), and a special toy for the Happy Meal—while earning minimum wage in the process. What matters is that we didn't get the extra ketchup we asked for!

Similarly, I don't ever recall being vexed with waiting when a long-distance telephone call required the assistance of an operator, not even for a person-to-person message. But these days, if a phone in California doesn't ring two seconds after being speed-dialed in Tennessee, we find ourselves finger-tapping in frustration.

Nonetheless, if I have a fault with waiting on service these days, it's with employers who either won't or don't hire enough help. Apparently it's far more important that the CEO earn an extra million bucks than a couple more underlings be assigned to the front desk.

WHAT SHADE OF YELLOW DO YOU PREFER?

Every January, I'm reminded of Navin Johnson and his literary "discovery."

Navin, of course, was the central character in the hilarious 1979 movie *The Jerk*. His role was played by an equally hilarious actor, Steve Martin. The scene I'm talking about occurs when Navin runs in, clutching a telephone directory.

"The new phone book's here!" he shouts. "The new phone book's here!"

When another character questions how somebody could get so excited over nothing, Navin isn't fazed: "Nothing? Are you kidding? Page seventy-three— 'Johnson, Navin R.' I'm somebody now! This is the kind of spontaneous publicity that makes people! I'm in print! Things are going to start happening to me now!"

If I published phone books, I'd try to buy the rights to this piece of movie script and use it in my advertising. That way, I could show customers how important it is to be seen in print. Maybe I could sell 'em super-sized type for their listing, or even a personalized photo.

Another thing I'd do is change colors in the business section.

Right now, these things come in one hue—yellow, duh—and it has led to a commercial tug-of-war for our affections. My latest inventory includes *The Real Yellow Pages,* along with its smaller cousin, *The Real Yellow Pages Companion,* plus the *Yellow Book.*

Why doesn't someone get innovative and issue the *Lime Green Pages* for a change? Or the *Chartreuse Pages*? Maybe the *Pink Pages*. For Pete's sake, the *Big Orange Pages* oughta go like proverbial hotcakes in this region.

Nope. Just as Henry Ford only offered his Model T in black, we're stuck in commercial-page monotone. Yellow.

Color aside, these books stack up quite differently against each other. Literally.

Compressed, my copy of *The Real Yellow Pages* measures an inch and three-quarters in thickness. The diminutive *Companion* is a mere half-inch. Hefty ol' *Yellow Book* is two and a quarter.

At this point, I'm keeping all three—even though I don't have room for them in my phone-book drawer. Perhaps I'll pit them against each other over the next few weeks, like basketball playoffs, and see which stays and which winds up in the recycle pile.

Then again, maybe not. Both *The Real Yellow Pages* and *The Real Yellow Pages Companion* have a dire warning on the cover: "Do Not Discard Before December."

Huh? Is there a law against getting rid of a phone book ahead of schedule? Will the phone police come calling? Or—gasp!—will an angry Ma Bell show up at my door, hickory switch in hand?

But at least there's one cover warning I don't have to worry about violating. It's on the front of *The Real Yellow Pages Companion*. And I quote: "Caution: Please do not use this directory while operating a moving vehicle."

Good grief! What do these people think I am, stupid or somethin'? I'd never try to read a phone book while driving.

I'm always too busy running my electric razor or dialing the cell phone.

CONFESSIONS OF A SURE-NUFF GOOBER

Oh, the shame! Oh, the embarrassment! Oh, the barbs from family and friends!

If there ever was any doubt I am a drooling, fossilized geezer, it was put to rest a few days ago. Let me set the scene:

Daughter Megan and son-in-law Tommy were hosting a Low Country boil— one of those gastronomical binges involving shrimp, corn, taters, spices, and other of Gawd's most heavenly delectables simmered in a gumbo pot over an open fire. I'm about to break into a caloric sweat just thinking about it.

Anyhow, as a dozen or so of us gathered in the backyard to drink beer and nibble from a veggie tray, the conversation rolled around to something I remembered from a recent email. I excused myself from the crowd, asking Tommy if I could use his computer to access my account.

Normally, this is an easy task because the only keyboards I type on are at home or the *News Sentinel*; thus, my links are automatically built in. Not so with Tommy's keyboard, of course, and—are you surprised?—I couldn't remember the exact sequence of commands. So I went upstairs to call the *News Sentinel* for technical help.

On an end table in Tommy and Megan's living room sat a pile of equipment: BlackBerries, cell phones, and other gizmos. A few Thirty-Somethings were sitting around, and I made an all-inclusive request: "Anybody mind if I use a phone?"

Go right ahead, voices said. I grabbed the one on top of the heap, pressed the "On" button, and held it to my ear.

Nothing.

"Hmm," I thought to myself. "Just as stubborn as my own cell phone. Takes a minute to get its revs up and running."

So I turned it back over and pushed the "On" button again. Harder.

Ah-ha! A red light illuminated. Now, we're making progress!

I put it to my ear for another second. About that time, Jen Mowrer snickered from across the room.

I looked again at the device in my hand. Especially the "On" button. Also the word printed after it: "Demand."

Arrrgh! Double-*arrrgh!* This wasn't a cell phone at all. It was the $#%& remote for Megan and Tommy's TV.

Since that night, I have been pilloried by everyone under the age of forty who hears the story. Also a good many over forty, not the least of which is Tony, my lowlife brother-in-law, who has labeled me "Dunce of the Decade."

Just thinking about Tony's crude, cruel, insensitive remarks has made me so mad, I'd like to call him right now and give him a piece of my mind. But since there's no TV in this room, I'll just have to wait until we see each other and cuss him out in person.

Chapter

A STRONG REGIONAL BIAS

As a native son of Knoxville, a lifelong resident of Tennessee, and a graduate of the University of Tennessee, it gives me tremendous pleasure to join my fellow citizens in a rousing chant of, "We're Number One! We're Number One! We're Number One!"

Uh, no, sadly; this exuberance rarely has an association with team sports over on the UT campus—especially the two biggies, football and basketball. The Volunteers' fortunes on the gridiron and in roundball seem to rise and fall across the seasons like the stock market on a volatile day: up for a while, down for a while, back up, back down, steady, climbing, falling. Investors and Tennessee fans share many of the same emotions. Gnawed fingernails too.

 Nonetheless, Knoxville is consistently at the top of the heap when it comes to sneezing, hacking, coughing, nose blowing, and eye wiping. Indeed, there are tears in my baby blues as I type these words. I'm not certain if it's from pride or pollen; trust me, we have both.

In 2010, 2011, and 2012, Knoxville was named El Numero Uno in the United States by the Asthma and Allergy Foundation of America. Among all cities coast-to-coast, California to Carolina, Seattle to Sarasota, we whupped every last one of 'em, by golly!

Meaning—*haaackk!*—we are the worst place in America when it comes to spring allergies. Makes you want to grab a tissue and weep, doesn't it?

This may not be a proud talking point for the Chamber of Commerce, but facts are facts. Just ask anybody in this region—and we know who we are—suffering from what is commonly called "hay fever." On second thought, don't ask. Listen instead. Between the wheezing and sneezing, K-town's allergy victims create their own brand of music.

This is a true story, so help me: One day in April 2010, I emerged from the men's restroom at the *News Sentinel* and was nearly deaf from the noise. I'm talking a symphonic collection of wall rattlers and shingle shakers. This was not your typical restroom music, however, which is unusual because the Editorial Department's men's room has a proud audio history. Especially on Chili Dog Fridays.

On the contrary. These were of nasal origin.

One performer, his head buried in a mound of tissues, ripped off an aria that ranged into the upper limits of the musical scale. Quite impressive.

Not to be outdone, the baritone standing alongside him at the sink yanked a sheet from the automatic paper-towel dispenser and plumbed the opposite end of the scale. Never has there been such deep, sonorous blasting, with the possible exception of foghorn factories in the Great Lakes region.

I added my patented "scared goose" solo into a handkerchief but readily admit this weak performance paled in comparison to the others. I did not lose by a mere nose. I was trounced by sagacious sinuses and schnozzles. No doubt similar concerts were being played in office restrooms all over town. Not to mention living rooms, kitchens, bedrooms, and hallways.

This misery is all due to a weird blend of geography, botany, and meteorology.

In the first place, Knoxville is located in a valley.

In the second place, we are lush with grasses, trees, flowers, and fungi that crank out pollen and spores like a trillion nasal-irritant factories.

And in—*brooonk!*—the third place, our spring weather patterns run the gamut from moist to arid, sunny to cloudy, hot to cold, windy to calm. And everything in-between.

"For the last eight years, the Top Ten list has fluctuated," said the AAFA's Angel Waldron. "But every year Southeastern cities dominate. Oak, pine, poplar, maple, and elm trees are the primary spring pollen contributors."

I don't require a guide for official notification, thank you. All I have to do is look at my truck, my bass boat, my shoes, or anything else exposed to the elements. During spring, they retain a permanent pollen patina. And as any Knoxville homeowner knows, pollen is only one portion of this equation. After the yellow cloud lifts or is washed away, it is followed by the pitter-patter of little seeds.

I live in a log house atop a wooded ridge. There are trees galore. Around my place, many of them—red maples, in particular—often take to heart that biblical be-fruitful-and-multiply command. They produce veritable tsunamis of seeds. One morning, I stood at my kitchen window and marveled how it literally was snowing red maple seeds. They were falling and swirling like a Boston blizzard.

They accumulated like snowflakes, too. I swear there were times the piles on my driveway were so tall and full, I could have gathered them with a snow shovel.

Naturally, I then had approximately 500 quadrillion-trillion-bazillion red maple seedlings sprouting from every orifice on my property. Wherever there was so much as a thimble of exposed dirt, I had "maplettes."

And then—oh, joy!—the oak catkins began falling. By the multiplied blue billion. My driveway was mounded with these little squiggly lines of vegetative material. So was the parking lot at the *News Sentinel* building. When the wind blew on dry days, balled-up oak catkins could be seen rolling across the pavement. This is our version of tumbleweed.

But what the heck. It's a small price to pay for living in God's country. All those trees, grasses, and flowers may be loaded with pollen, but they also produce April bloomathons and October foliage extravaganzas rivaling any landscape on this continent. Verily, our natural beauty is nothing to sneeze at. Even if—*ah-choo!*—we occasionally do.

Knoxville is highly ranked in another category, as well. In 2008, we were named by Amazon as one of the Top Twenty cities for sales of romance books. (Pardon me for a moment while I gasp for breath and wipe my moistened brow. It's just that Cassandra, resting her head on the satin pillow next to me, just closed her eyes in satisfied bliss. But her moment of calm was fleeting. Abruptly, almost savagely, she pulled herself closer. Her hot bare skin, adrip with sweat, touched mine and—Oops! Sorry! I digress!)

According to the online retailer, which charted sales of romance novels, relationship books, and sex texts for cities around the United States, Knoxville ranked twentieth out of 236 on a per-capita basis.

Mike Powell was hiking in the Great Smoky Mountains National Park when he encountered a peahen near the shelter at Ice Water Springs.

"Peafowl are tropical, do not migrate, and at an altitude of nearly six thousand feet on the Appalachian Trail, it's not likely that she wondered off of somebody's farm in the neighborhood," he said. "One of the guys in our group said he would not have been more surprised if we had seen a flamingo."

Actually, Mike, flamingoes are rather common in the East Tennessee mountains. Just check the tourist shops in Gatlinburg.

Who says we don't know fine reading material when we see it? Knoxville was the only city in Tennessee to receive this prestigious honor, proving readers around here are interested in something besides a steady diet of sports. Indeed, we were among only a handful of cities in the entire South to be mentioned. I know I speak for teachers of English literature throughout Our Fair City when I say to all the readers who made this honor possible: "Hold me, you beast! Kiss me! Caress me! Make me read Keats!"

Ah, but there is even more regional pride, this time on a statewide basis: Tennesseans have been named the "most friendly" people in the United States. This comes to no surprise to natives, of course. Yet it took researchers in England six years and nearly 620,000 test subjects to discover what we've known all along.

The conclusion was announced by the University of Cambridge. It came from a massive study—"the first analysis of its kind"—and was led by Dr. Jason Rentfrow, a lecturer in social and political sciences at the esteemed British institution.

In a press release, a copy of which is clutched in my mitts as we speak, the university stated, "Tennesseans overall exhibited a high level of 'agreeableness,' a personality trait usually associated with people who are warm, compassionate, cooperative, and friendly."

Researchers wanted to see if there was a link between "prevalent personality types" and the "social and cultural life" in each of the fifty states. To find out, they invited Americans to participate in an online survey involving forty-four questions. A total of 619,397 people participated.

"Obviously, it's not as simple as saying that a person is guaranteed to be more anxious if they come from West Virginia or more religious because they happen to live in New Mexico," the university said. "But we did find pretty clear signs that there are meaningful differences in the personalities of people living in different areas of the United States."

Forgive us for grinning from Memphis to Mountain City, but Tennesseans have understood this truism all our lives. Being friendly is something we do by second nature.

For instance: I don't know if anyone—in England or the United States or anywhere else—has ever quantified it, but I bet more Tennesseans use the generic term "honey" in casual conversation than any other group on this orb. Doesn't matter if the "honeyee" is old or young, either.

When I was a kid, store sales clerks routinely referred to me as "honey." At sixty-five, I often hear myself exchanging that very expression with friends, male and female alike. They do the same with me. Then or now, this has nothing to do with sexual overtones or overtures. Nobody worries about gender boundaries. This simply is a term longtime Tennesseans tend to use with one another, just as the British are wont to call their chums "old darling."

Unfortunately, this practice may be on the wane, thanks to the Politically Correct Speech Police. I can't imagine any college professor uttering the term "honey" to a student. And speaking of colleges, it just dawned on me that there are certain other exceptions to the friendliness rule.

Which brings us back around to the business of football fortunes at the University of Tennessee. Drive to Neyland Stadium on the day partisans from the University of Florida come calling for a "friendly" game, and see for yourself. The only application of honey in this regard would be direct, as in straight from the jug. Preferably when the recipient is tied to a stake in close proximity to a mound teeming with hungry ants.

Yes, we can, and do, occasionally get peeved. It tends to happen most often when someone NFAH (Not From Around Here) takes us to ridiculous task. Newspaper columnists love getting into word fights over defense of their turf, and I never fail to seize the opportunity. One of the more recent occurred when Wayne Greene, who writes for the *Tulsa (OK) World,* elicited some NFAH nonsense.

Wayne considers himself an authority on K-town because his mother lives here. Like any good son, he visits from time to time. But he always gets his undies in a wad because our streets aren't laid out in a precise north-south-east-west pattern like they are in his moonscape.

Thus, he returned to Flatland, USA, after one trip here and lamely sniped,

> There are two kinds of people in Knoxville: Those who were born there and those who are lost. The two groups are not mutually exclusive because some of the people who were born there are still lost most of the time.
>
> The streets in Knoxville were organized about two-hundred years ago. It was a much smaller city then. The traffic jam on Interstate 40 was only one mile long at the time. One theory is that the city's founders set loose a herd of particularly wandery [sic] cattle in the town square and tracked where they went. Any route a cow followed was declared a road. If the cow stopped for a few minutes to eat grass or swish flies, that was chosen as the spot where the street's name would change. The other theory is that they plotted

every homestead, outpost, and still in greater Knoxville on a map in 1800 and then connected all the dots.

What a moron.

For the record, our streets were not laid out by "wandery" cows. We used hogs. Furthermore, our stills were not plotted in 1800 any more than our pot patches and meth labs are today. Now as then, these are closely guarded secrets.

But to answer his question: There are two reasons why our roadways are not uniform. First, duh, we are a region surrounded by ridges, hills, valleys, and other undulating landforms. It's impossible to walk a straight line around here, let alone drive. Even if you're sober.

The second reason our roads seem foreign to furriners is because we designed them that way—to weed out inferior, incompetent, and unimaginative drivers. Like the Marines, we're looking for a few good motorists. Not every Tom, Dick, and Wayne who simply know how to turn an ignition key need apply.

Good grief! Any three-year-old could navigate a strip of Oklahoma asphalt running straight as a plank for fifty miles! We expect to be challenged, lest we drift off to sleep from sheer monotony. That's why we also like to sprinkle in a few interesting road names.

In his column, Wayne made a big deal out of how the more complex routes in his city have "east" and "west" added for clarification.

Ho-hum. Yes, we can do that, too—as witness East Beaver Creek Drive and West Beaver Creek Drive. But how utterly boring. We like to add *real* spice!

That's why Knoxville is blessed with roads on the order of Beaver Creek Lane, Beaver Dam Lane, Beaver Ridge Road, Beaverbrook Drive, Beavers Bend Lane, Beaverton Road, and Beaverwood Drive. If

Charlie Gavin swears this is true: "There was a fillin' station just up the road from me that was goin' out of business, and they were sellin' all their inventory real cheap. One ol' boy bought an entire gross of condoms. Somebody asked him what he intended to do with all those rubbers, especially at his advanced age.

"He said, 'The old lady can use 'em to freeze roastin' ears'."

(Translation for Yankees and other unwashed: That's what we call sweet corn. Roastin' ears, I mean. Not the other thing.)

Wayne wants to drive with the big boys on these thoroughfares, we might consent to give him a lesson next time he comes to visit mama. But he needs to leave his tricycle in Tulsa.

In all fairness, I must point out that Knoxville did fall woefully short in one national survey: We do not have a single funeral home that uses its parlors for wedding as well as funerals. Such isn't the case in at least two forward-thinking burgs—Lanham, Maryland, and Indianapolis, Indiana. There, you can hear "I do" right along with "Why, don't he look natural!"

This idea certainly makes business sense. Funeral homes already have the space, chairs, chapels, parking lots, flower pots, and other accoutrements found in conventional marrying establishments. As the *Indianapolis Star* noted in a recent story about this new custom, "There are plenty of similarities between weddings and funerals. Both have organ music and flowers. Friends sign guest books, people cry, and families come together."

Just don't look for it around here. At least not yet. I did a spot check of Knoxville undertakers, and none said they were branching into the field of matrimony. Can't say that I blame them, either.

If I enter a funeral home for the traditional purpose and whisper "Herb Jones" to the guy at the front door, I want to be sure he knows I mean Herb Jones, dearly departed, not Herb Jones who's about to marry Ila Sue Cranberry down the hall.

What's more, if this wedding chapel–funeral parlor business catches on, grooms and groomsmen will need to pay close attention when they're renting a tux. If they sign on the wrong dotted line, they could be in for an exceedingly long period of payments.

But who knows? Maybe funeral homes will start offering combo packages. That way, if some papa angrily declares his daughter "will marry that good-for-nothing bum over my dead body!" he can literally, and handily, be a man of his word.

HOW TO "TAWLK GOOD"

A longtime buddy was telling me why he and his college sweetheart broke up.

"It was mostly a matter of cultural differences," he began, launching into a litany of religious, social, economic, and political chasms they would have to bridge if there was any hope of a future together. Then he summed up the situation succinctly: "She said 'frankfurtah' and I said 'hot dawg.' No way we could ever have made it work."

Ah, yes. The spoken word, Southern Appalachian style. Of all the local idiosyncratic problems facing newcomers to this region, this can be the most irksome.

"Why do you people mispronounce so many words?" they always want to know.

Hate to disappoint, but we aren't the ones mispronouncing. We know how to speak the King's English, thank you very much; Queen's too, for that matter. If the imports would simply train their ears and tongues, they could speak properly with us.

Consider the Powell community in northwest Knox County—along with its Powell High School, Powell Chevron Service Center, Powell Scale Company, Powell Florist and Gifts, Powell Chiropractic Center, Powell Power Equipment, and dozens more proud Powell places.

If you telephone any of them, the person answering the phone will not say the name of the establishment in two syllables: "POW-well." Instead, he or she will correctly say, "Pal." (Unless, of course, he or she ain't from around here and haven't been learnt how to tawlk good.)

I don't care how "Powell" is spelled. I don't care what some highfalutin dictionary declares to the contrary. Nor do I care how they say the word in Boston, Omaha, or Salt Lake City. Here, it's "Pal." Period.

A somewhat similar situation exists with a village to the south of Knoxville: Maryville, in Blount County.

A phonetics teacher from elsewhere might tell you this is a three-syllable word with the emphasis on the first: "MARE-ee-ville." Which proves the phonetics teacher doesn't know phosgene from phooey because the word has only two, equally emphasized syllables: "murr-vul."

Want more? Then take a gander at the Corryton community in Northeast Knox County.

"CORRIE-ton" may seem like the correct way to say this word. But "CORRIE-ton" does not roll off the tongue fluidly. That's why locals refer to it as "Carton."

But without a doubt, the Number One mispronunciation, the King Daddy, the separator of Us versus Them is the name of this region itself: Southern Appalachia.

The Appalachian mountains run roughly from northern Georgia to New England. The landscape is much the same up and down the range. So, in many respects, are the people.

But if you happen to be from Up There and want folks to know it in one word, say "apple-LAYSHA." Down Here, it's "apple-ATCHA." Has always been. Will always be. Get used to it.

One of the funniest stories I ever heard about this pronunciation was passed on to me by Doug Midkiff, a transportation specialist who spent the bulk of his career with Eastman Kodak in Kingsport. A native Virginian, Midkiff was always incensed when foreigners came into his homeland and called it "apple-LAYSHA."

Midkiff says the sin once was committed by none other than NBC reporter Douglas Kyker in a broadcast from Appalachia, Virginia. Midkiff called NBC News, got Kyker on the phone, and set him straight.

"He apologized, saying he was going by the NBC style book, but promised to correct it," Midkiff remembered. "A few months later, I was flying to Saint Louis on business and transferred to another airline in Louisville. Who would sit down beside me but Douglas Kyker, whom I recognized immediately. I waited until we were airborne and served our coffee, then leaned over and asked him, 'Are you still calling it 'apple-LAYSHA?'

"He looked startled, then asked, 'Are you the $#@% who called me?' It was an interesting moment, but we parted in peace."

Go thee and speak likewise.

OTHERWISE, NOT MUCH HAPPENED

One sleepy day in the 1860s, Knoxville made a big splash in the Big Apple. I know for a fact because I hold a full-sized photocopy of the front page of the *New York Times.*

It is dated Friday, November 20, 1863. The lead story comes from none other than Our Fair City. It is datelined Thursday, November 17. (Hmm, Thursday would've been the nineteenth, not the seventeenth. Oh, well; this merely proves factual errors aren't a modern newspaper phenomenon.)

The main headline proclaims, in capital letters, "IMPORTANT FROM EAST TENNESSEE."

Stacked heads were de rigueur in those days. So it's not surprising that the main banner is followed by five others. Some are capitalized, some caps-and-lower-case, some light face, some bold. To wit:

"The Rebels Advancing upon Knoxville."

"THE PLACE COMPLETELY INVESTED."

"HEAVY SKIRMISHING YESTERDAY."

"The Position Very Strongly Fortified."

"THE REBEL FORCES UNDER LONGSTREET."

Actually, these headlines got more than the usual bang for their repetitious buck that day, because the main story was followed by another Page One dispatch, simply labeled, "A MORE DETAILED ACCOUNT." It, too, is datelined from little ol' Knoxville—although this story correctly lists November seventeenth as Tuesday.

The gray matter flows most of the way down the left side of the page. It describes—in the flowery newspaper narrative of the era—military activities that would culminate on November 29 in the Battle of Fort Sanders. Here's how the opening paragraph begins:

"The enemy began skirmishing from their position on Kingston Road, at ten this morning. Our advance alone, composed wholly of mounted infantry and cavalry, occupied the position, under command of General Sanders, and each man fought like a veteran. At noon the enemy opened with artillery at short range, their battery protected by a large house. Benjamin's battery was the only one which replied, occupying the chief fortification, half a mile in front and to the right of the town."

Why do I bring up this nugget of historical information? Because of Knoxville's amazing timing and coincidence. On the very day Knoxville led the news in one of the nation's most heralded papers, there was another story out front. But it was, as we say in this trade, "down the page." Indeed, it was buried closer to the center.

This is not surprising, since it covered a ho-hum political speech. Seems President Abraham Lincoln had made an appearance the day before, spoken briefly, and the *Times* felt obliged to note the occasion. The president's words apparently were so insignificant, they even took second fiddle to the event's opening prayer and the list of distinguished guests.

Finally, his short speech was chronicled. It began, "Fourscore and seven years ago . . ."

Yes, children. K-town received higher play than one of the most famous speeches in U.S. history, the Gettysburg Address. Proving that misjudging the importance of an event isn't a modern newspaper phenomenon, either.

TRICKS KNOW NO BOUNDS

Soon as I read about a government scandal brewing in Japan, I said to myself, "Well, I'll be! That's got Southern Appalachia written all over it!"

"You'll be what?" myself answered.

"Huh?" I replied. "Oh, that's just a local expression—you know, like, 'theyyyyy.'"

"They who?" myself persisted. "Sometimes you sure don't make much sense."

Arrgh! This is what happens whenever I try to converse with an idiot, so I quit the conversation altogether. Nonetheless, I do want to pass along news of the Japanese brouhaha and its good-old-boy connections.

According to news reports out of Tokyo, the government has launched an investigation into fraud regarding old-age claims. It all started when authorities started searching for a 111-year-old man, who was thought to be Tokyo's oldest male. Indeed, the government had been paying benefits to the ol' coot and his family all this time.

When they got to his house, though, all they found were mummified remains. He had croaked thirty years earlier, but the kids kept Pa's corpse around so his guv'mit check would keep rolling in.

On the heels of that case, officials then launched a search for the oldest woman, presumed to be 113. They couldn't find her, either—and were starting to smell a similar rat, if not a very old and moldy body.

Monetary trickery knows no geographic bounds, of course. But the hills and hollows of this region breed some of the best practitioners. And it doesn't matter who gets hoo-doo'ed: the feds or the fellow down the road.

John Rice Irwin agrees. I caught J.R. in his office at the Museum of Appalachia and read him the Japanese story.

"Reminds me of the Hendrickson brothers and their goose," he said with a laugh. "This was, oh, back in the late 1930s, best I remember. These two brothers, Roscoe and Allen, had a feed store in Clinton. They also bought and sold hides, fur, beeswax, and freshwater pearls from the Clinch River. Anyhow, a fellow came in one day, carrying a goose he had for sale. The brothers had been wanting a pair, but they settled for this one, which was a male.

"They kept feeding it and feeding it, hoping somebody would come in with a female. After several weeks went by, they got concerned that the dadburn goose was going to eat up more corn than they could sell him for.

"One day, while Roscoe was away, a customer came in and inquired about buying the goose. Allen was more than happy to sell him, at whatever price the customer offered. They closed the deal, and the customer led the goose out of the store with a string around its neck.

"Well, he got about half-way down the street, when he ran into Roscoe—who was delighted, finally, to see someone with 'another' goose. Roscoe got to dickering with the guy and wound up buying the same goose Allen had just sold. At twice the price! And that's a true story."

See? When money's on the line, the thrill of the chase takes on a brilliant luster. That goes for Tokyo, Tennessee, or Timbuktu.

THIEVES HAVE THEIR STANDARDS

High crime has invaded the heartland. Innocence lost indeed. I feel personally violated, even though it's not my property that was attacked.

Instead, it was Piedmont General Store, the century-old headquarters of hardware, farm news, local gossip, bull sessions, and fine dining in Jefferson County.

For the first time in anyone's memory, the building got burgled. Happened a few nights ago. What was stolen may provide a clue to whodunit, but more on that in a minute.

Piedmont General Store sits just off West Dumplin Valley Road near Highway 25W-70. I love this old place. It's my home away from home.

No offense to Cracker Barrel, Buddy's, and other citified establishments attempting to camouflage polished urban roots with country-kitsch décor, but what we have here is the real deal. You know as soon as you pull into the gravel lot, park between tall-tired pickups and log haulers, and remove the worst of your mud with boot scrapers mounted near the front porch.

The spring-hooked door swings open to reveal a ramshackle, low-ceiling, wood-floored, squeaky-jointed, living history museum—the likes of which, alas, have all but disappeared from Americana. In some remote corner of this ancient collection sits the ghost of Norman Rockwell, contentedly puffing his pipe and painting.

Where else can you paw through dusty shelves for high-topped brogans, canning wax, floral arrangements, nails, and seeds, while munching a fried baloney sandwich and minding the sign that requests, "Please Do Not Spit on Floor"?

Trust your Uncle Cholesterol: I have consumed more post-hunting-trip breakfasts (two over medium, fresh tenderloin, sliced tomatoes, biscuits, gravy, toast, jelly, and coffee enough to float a johnboat) at this location than all other rural East Tennessee eateries combined.

For more than two decades, Jan Reagon has been Piedmont's proprietor, chef, dishwasher, inventory clerk, and head cashier. She worked at the store a couple of years before buying it. But back to the break-in.

Someone(s) busted through the front door. Among the items stolen were two watches and three knives from a display case, a couple of car batteries, a pistol, approximately two hundred dollars from the cash register, plus some drinks and cigarettes.

"Some" is the definitive word in this regard.

"They took thirty twenty-ounce Mountain Dews, two gallons of milk, and all my Winstons, Marlboros, and Camels," Jan told me. "They didn't touch anything else. No Pepsis, Cokes, or Sprites. No Dorals, Salems, or Newports. They didn't bother with the eggs, cheese, or meat, either. And they left one gallon of milk—I reckon so I could start makin' biscuits the next morning. One of the deliverymen said this has to be the weirdest break-in in the history of crime."

Either that or the crooks were quite brand-loyal with their smokes and liquid refreshments.

SHALL WE GATHER WITH A REPTILE?

Ed Carter swears this tale is true. Frankly, I don't care if it is or isn't. As a person who rarely lets facts, figures, and other pesky details ruin a good story, I rank this one in the Top Ten best I've ever heard.

Ed, who grew up in Blount County, now lives in Nashville. If you venture into the outdoors, you probably recognize his name, for he is the executive director of the Tennessee Wildlife Resources Agency.

Ed and I were hiking together a few weeks ago. During that time, he shared a number of hilarious experiences from his years in wildlife law enforcement. Among them was the time two of his officers were conducting a deer season roadblock in Clay County, way up yonder on the Tennessee-Kentucky border. If you've never been there, this is the very heartland of rural America.

Anyhow, it was early on a Sunday morning, and the wardens were spot-checking vehicles on a lonely country road. About that time, a battered pickup truck came roaring around the bend. Dang-near ran 'em over—and kept going.

> Sage advice from wood-carver Robert Mahon: "Anytime you pick up a knife and start to carve, always count your fingers. When you finish carving, count them again. If you've still got the same number, you've done good."
>
> I suspect this wisdom also applies to chain sawing, apple peeling, watermelon cutting, and a variety of other endeavors that require sharp instruments.

The wardens figured a drunk driver had to be behind the wheel. Or maybe someone who'd just killed a deer illegally and was trying to escape. They leaped into their state truck, turned on the blue lights, and gave chase.

Amazingly, the speeding pickup pulled to the shoulder of the road as soon as the driver realized he was being pursued by the law. He sat calmly behind the wheel, no inclination to hot-foot into the woods.

"The two officers looked inside the truck," Ed said, "but instead of finding drunks or deer hunters, there was a man and a woman with a whole brood of young'ins. Everybody was scrubbed clean. The woman was wearing a nice dress. The man had on his best starched overalls and a white shirt."

One of the officers said to him, "Where you folks headed?"

"To church," said the driver.

Startled by the reply, the warden continued: "You nearly ran us off the road back there. How come you were in such a hurry?"

The driver apologized profusely, then offered: "Mister, if you don't git to our church early, all the good snakes are taken."

See what I mean? Doesn't matter if that's 100 percent fact or fiction; it makes for a knee-slapper. And it brings to mind a similar tale Rutledge pharmacist Doug Smith passed along to me at the Grainger County Tomato Festival.

"The preacher at one of the most remote churches in our county came into the drugstore the other day," Doug said. "While I was working up his order, he looked awfully worried. So I asked what was on his mind."

"My flock says they want to take up the handling of serpents," the minister announced.

"Wow! That's pretty serious!" Doug exclaimed. "What kind are you going to handle? Copperheads? Rattlesnakes?"

"Oh, nothing that drastic," the preacher answered with a smile. "I'm gonna recommend we start with red worms and see if we can slowly build our faith."

POUR ME ANOTHER

Recently I was seated behind a long banquet table inside the Alcoa Service Center, saying a silent prayer of thanks that I was among five people on the left of the dais, not five on the right.

The ten of us had been assembled for a water-judging contest. We fortunates on the left would be testing liquids from various public taps: aka "drankin' water." Those on the right—each had been issued blue plastic gloves and a large bottle of hand sanitizer—would be testing liquids from the, uh, "other end" of municipal water operations.

Yes. The stinky stuff that flows from the discharge pipe.

"But don't worry," John Hall of the Tennessee Association of Utility Districts was telling members of the Poop Patrol. "We've never lost a judge yet. Besides, you folks won't actually be tasting any water. You will be judging clarity, bouquet, turbidity, and pH."

(At that point, my sophomoric mind was having a field day with the likes of "bouquet" and "turbidity" in terms of effluent. But for once I held my tongue. My side of the table had already been charged with assessing clarity, bouquet, and taste of the Good Stuff, and I didn't want to ruin our sweet deal.)

This was the fourth annual "water-off" among the cities, towns, and utility districts that slake the thirst—and sanitize the you-know-what—of folks throughout East Tennessee. And even though I was grateful to make the short list of taste testers, one question burned in my brain.

How do you cleanse your palate between samples?

I have judged wine contests. Twice, in fact—which is amazing because I boorishly insisted on swallowing the samples instead of spitting them out, an act I consider bad manners, not to mention a waste of good hooch. In wine competition, judges are encouraged to sip water between slugs to wipe the oral slate clean.

Thus, you can imagine my unbridled joy at the thought of swilling wine, or maybe even likker, between shots of water. Unfortunately, that's not how it works.

The officials did offer crackers for this purpose, but I nixed the idea after my first bite because the next water I tasted had a distinctive aura of salt. Knowing East Tennessee is hundreds of miles removed from saline conditions, I went back for a second gulp, then third, of the sample and tried to judge fairly.

In the end, we (public relations maven Susan Richardson Williams; David Leverton, field rep for U.S. Senator Bob Corker; Marisol Torres, of the U.S. Agriculture Department; Michael Atchley, Tennessee Department of Environment and Conservation; and your obedient servant) rated Knox-Chapman Utility District's entry as best of the Good Stuff.

Verily, there is something in the water at Knox-Chapman. And it's fabulous. This was the district's third victory in four years.

Over on the Poop Patrol, Brian Boyd of the National Weather Service; Steve Roberts, TDEC; Mary Short, USDA; Tracy Tramel, SRW and Associates; and Nathan Babelay, McGill and Associates, awarded Number One discharge honors to the Webb Creek Utility District of Gatlinburg.

From the look on their faces, they were flush with success.

TAKEN TO THE CLEANERS

South Knoxvillians Jake and Betty Huffaker aren't sure whether this should be filed under the category of "Don't Try This at Home" or "It Seemed Like Such a Good Idea at the Time." Then again, it might make a great story line for Opal and Earl, central characters in the syndicated "Pickles" cartoon strip.

Whatever the case, the Huffakers learned a valuable lesson in Maintenance 101.

Officially, it was Jake's idea. But Betty is quick to admit she seconded the motion and urged immediate action. So they both share equal blame for the catastrophe that ensued. Perhaps this sense of spousal equality, leavened with mutual good humor, is one of the reasons the Huffakers have stayed married so long. They have celebrated sixty years and counting together. But back to their grand scheme that went awry.

"It all started when we thought the refrigerator sounded like it wasn't running right," Jake said. "We both noticed it."

Best they could tell, the odd noise was coming from beneath the appliance. They suspected a lint buildup. But precise diagnosis presented a logistical problem.

"I'm eighty-one and Betty's seventy-nine," the retired grocer told me with a laugh. "Neither of us could get down on the kitchen floor and look underneath the thing."

He paused and laughed louder. "Well, I guess we could get down there—but it would have taken A. J. Metler (the old Knoxville crane and erection service) to get us back on our feet!"

Couldn't they move the fridge?

"No," he answered, "it's hooked up to a water line for the ice maker."

They pondered awhile and decided this was a job for the vacuum cleaner. But that option was short-lived. The nozzle was too large to slide under.

So they thought a bit longer—and that's when the light bulb went off in Jake's head. If the lint couldn't be sucked out one side with the vacuum cleaner, then maybe it could be blasted out the other.

By their leaf blower.

"Those things are really stout," Jake noted. "Why, they can lift leaves ten or fifteen feet right in front of you. Soon as I mentioned it, Betty said that was a great idea. So I went out to the shed and brought it in, along with the extension cord. We got it all plugged up. Betty went to one side of the fridge, and I went to the other."

You know where this is going, don't you? Of course you do. When Jake hit the switch, Betty disappeared in a cloud of fluff.

"She was hollerin', 'Turn that thing off! Turn that thing off!' I finally got it turned off, and when I walked around to her side, she was spitting lint and blowing lint out of her face and wiping lint out of her hair. It was everywhere."

"I had to clean the whole kitchen," Betty said when I got her on the phone. "It took me two days."

But as Jake was quick to point out: "Well, at least she didn't have to worry about the bottom of the refrigerator. It was clean as a whistle! And the sound went away, too."

HOLLYWOOD, EAT YOUR HEART OUT

All you ladies are going to be *soooo* jealous when you hear what Charles Pless bought his wife for their fiftieth wedding anniversary. Here, let Doris Pless tell you in her own proud words:

"A big stone."

Except "big" really doesn't do justice to this rock. Neither does "huge." Not "gigantic" or "humongous," either. This stone is so incredibly massive, it can't be measured in traditional karats. Pounds is more like it. Then again, since this baby checks in at four-hundred-plus, you might even go so far as to describe it in portions of a ton.

Never heard of a diamond that size? Of course you haven't. Neither has any movie star in Hollywood. Or Doris Pless. That's because this golden anniversary stone isn't a diamond.

It's granite. As in a tombstone, five feet in length.

"It's beautiful!" Doris said. "It won't be finished for a couple of weeks, but it will have our names, our birth dates, and our wedding date—July 16, 1960. Oh, and some dogwood blossoms."

Once the final polishing and installation is complete, you can drive to the cemetery at Spring Hill Baptist Church in Canton, North Carolina, and see for yourself. No, Charles and Doris don't have immediate plans to put the tombstone to use. But it'll be there when the appropriate time comes. And therein lies a humorous, yet touching, tale.

First some background: Although Charles and Doris are North Carolinians by birth, they've lived in Knoxville for most of their adult lives. They first arrived in 1961 so Charles could work on his master's (entomology) at the University of Tennessee. Later, they moved to South Carolina, where he finished his Ph.D. at Clemson. Then he was hired on the UT faculty, so they returned for keeps, raising a family in the Rocky Hill community.

During those years of intensive study, Doris also earned an advanced degree. "I got my PhT," she laughed. "Putting Husband Through."

Charles retired from the university in 2001. A few years later, Doris also retired after a long career as receptionist for dentist C. L. Greenblatt Jr. All along,

> **According to news reports out of Florida, a piano mysteriously showed up one day on a sandbar in Biscayne Bay. The puzzle was solved shortly thereafter when a Miami high-school student said he had done it as an "art project" in hopes of padding his résumé for college.**
>
> **Gosh. I had no idea we had so many artisans here in East Tennessee. Based on the number of car bodies, mattresses, and refrigerators I've seen in our waterways, this area must be a hotbed of artistic expression.**

they've been active in their church, Rocky Hill Baptist, and have served as community volunteers.

So how does this explain such a bizarre gift?

Said Doris: "We'd been thinking for some time about taking care of funeral arrangements now, while we're still in good health. That way, it will spare the survivor any additional turmoil and grief. Our fiftieth was approaching, so we just thought, 'Why not buy it for an anniversary present?'"

They chose plots at Spring Hill Baptist in Canton because that's where they went to church as teenagers and later were married.

"It's a beautiful place—way out in the country," she said, "and it's near some mountain property that has been in Charles's family for years."

You gotta admire a couple so secure in their faith and their relationship that they could make a decision like this in the context of an anniversary celebration. Maybe it runs in the family.

"Recently, my mother took my aunt to a mortuary to pre-plan her own funeral," said Doris. "She picked out a casket—and then asked the funeral director if it was OK if she tried it on for size."

Perfect fit! And it'll be ready when she is.

A RECORD RIGHT OVER BERT'S NOSE

If Bert Vincent could sit up in his grave, he'd see one heck of a story.

Bert—the *News Sentinel*'s beloved "Strolling" columnist who died in 1969—is buried alongside his wife, Ellen Hynds Vincent, in Hopewell Cemetery, Dandridge, Tennessee. Just to the east of their graves is the story I'm talking about.

It's a magnificent sugar maple sixty-nine feet tall, with a crown that spreads seventy-seven feet to its widest tip. The trunk of this behemoth measures 56.2 inches in diameter and 14.7 feet in circumference.

But hold on a minute. I'm getting ahead of myself.

I had come to Dandridge with Jim Cortese, a Knoxville tree specialist, to check on a potential candidate for Tennessee's record-tree list. It's a giant white oak growing in a thicket, roughly three hundred yards west of the cemetery. A friend had pointed it out to me, and I contacted Jim, who keeps tabs on these things.

As soon as we walked to the site, Jim whistled and remarked, "That's a humdinger!"

He set about the task of measuring. Here's his tally: trunk 16.37 feet in circumference, 62.5 inches in diameter; height 102 feet; crown spread 108 feet. Without elaborate testing, the exact age of this tree can't be determined. But Jim is certain it dates to the Revolutionary War era.

Think about that for a moment. Smack in the middle of Jefferson County is a link to history—a tree that was fully mature long before Union and Confederate forces met in combat, long before the birth of aviation. And it's alive and prospering.

We left the thicket and were nearly back to Jim's car when I said, "Let me show you Bert Vincent's grave."

We stepped across the ditch and were standing at the Vincent headstone when Jim whistled again. Said "humdinger" again. And reached for his tree-measuring tools again.

He marched over to the aforementioned sugar maple and recorded its statistics.

"That's a mighty big sugar maple," he said, estimating it as Civil War era. "I'll see how it stacks up against the record holders, too."

Back home, Jim consulted the Tennessee Division of Forestry's official list. Lo and behold, he did have a new entry. Just not the one he had come to see.

Turns out that the white oak, monstrous as it may be, is smaller than one growing in Union County. But the sugar maple near Bert's and Miss Ellen's graves blew the existing record (from Sullivan County) off the charts. And a new champ was crowned.

It's interesting enough that a record sugar maple casts a shadow across the grave of one of East Tennessee's journalism icons. As Jim noted with a chuckle, "Bert's been fertilizing that tree for quite a while."

And now get this: While browsing through Bert's file at the *News Sentinel,* I came across a story from September 29, 1969. Written by the late Willard Yarbrough, it described Bert's funeral service.

"The maple's green was turning crimson," Willard reported. "Soon the red and golden leaves would fall and swirl atop his grave."

And four decades later generate a brand new story. No doubt Bert would have loved it.

HOW DOES HER GARDEN "GROW"?

For gardeners throughout East Tennessee, spring is the best of times and the worst of times. Best because you can almost smell the lilacs, worst because every flower in your garden can turn to ice on three hours' notice.

But there is one flower lover in our midst who doesn't worry about temperature or precipitation. Whether relentless sunshine bakes the land or snow is piling up in drifts, the specimens in her beds stay drop-dead gorgeous.

Mainly because that's what they are: dead.

"The only thing I have to be careful about is putting out the right flowers at the right time," she told me. "You don't want daffodils blooming in the middle of summer. And you don't want to set out your mums too early in the fall."

Meet Martha Holt—longtime resident of the Powell community, coordinator of events for the Bearden Banquet Hall of Buddy's Bar-b-q, and my hands-down candidate for Princess of Plastic Plants.

In Martha's world of bizarre botany, "prepping the soil" means arranging dirt around fake stems, "preparing for emergent foliage" means shaking a can of green spray paint, and "extensive floral arrangement" means everything you can cram into a buggy at Hobby Lobby.

"I oughta own stock in that place," she said with a laugh. "I hit Michael's and Walmart, too. But Hobby Lobby is closest to our home, and I make regular trips to check out their flowers. Just the other day, I saw a big selection of hydrangeas and thought, 'Hey, I've never had those before! This could be their year to bloom in my yard.'"

True, these hydrangeas also were blooming on the shelf. They were blooming in her car on the way home. And they currently are blooming inside a large bin in her garage. But why fret over details?

Martha comes by her skills honestly. "I was born with a black thumb," she lamented. "I inherited it from my mother. She was a serial killer of plants."

Martha tried to break the curse. Every summer she sowed, fertilized, watered, pruned. And every summer, the result was the same. Dead on arrival.

"Finally, I realized I could save myself a lot of time and effort by just sticking with artificial. It takes a bit of effort to get everything arranged and placed appropriately—we've got a two-level flower garden in the back—but after that, it's no work at all!"

What beauties "grow" at the Holt homestead? A plethora of plastic! A field of faux! Pansies, daffodils, hyacinths, forsythia, azaleas, daylilies, even monkey grass—each in its bed of rubberized mulch. Mmm! I can almost catch the sweet scent of petrochemicals now.

"Sun can be tough on the dark colors," she advised. "Reds and oranges are real bad to fade, so I keep plenty of spray paint on hand for touchups."

Oh, there is the occasional example of Mother Nature's finest in her yard. Thus far, Martha has managed not to kill her Bradford pears.

"I even raked real leaves last fall!" she boasted.

Speaking of trees, I just had to ask: Do the Holts put up an artificial one at Christmas?

She recoiled in shock: "What?! Is there any other kind?"

THE GOOD, THE BAD, THE KUDZU

Is kudzu a "good" plant or a "bad" one? Frankly, I've lost track of the score as kudzu bounces from one side of this botanic tennis court to the other. Methinks the scientific community has too.

When it was introduced to America from the Orient in the late 1800s, kudzu was "good." The government touted it as the ideal solution to soil erosion and encouraged its planting throughout the South.

Then kudzu turned "bad." It covered eroded ground, all right—also everything else in its path: barns, trees, utility poles, slow-moving cars, lethargic children, sleeping dogs, and lost Yankees. (Well, yes; technically, kudzu's tendency to conceal lost Yankees should put it back in the "good" category. But because barns, trees, dogs, and children also fell prey, it remained "bad.")

But nothing, even kudzu, stays "bad" forever.

Two different studies—one at the Harvard Medical School, the other at McLean's Hospital in Boston—cited a substance found in kudzu roots that, when administered to humans, curbed their appetite for alcohol. Both studies gave great hope that this substance could one day be used in the treatment of alcoholism.

Again, technically, kudzu owed this to Dixie because it turned as many Southerners to drink during the twentieth century as Reconstruction did during the nineteenth. In any event, it was back to the "good" side of the equation.

But not for long.

Recently, researchers bounced kudzu back to "bad." Manuel Lerdau of the University of Virginia and Jonathan Hickman of the State University of New

York believe kudzu is releasing ground-level ozone and contributing significantly to smog, breathing difficulties, and global climate change.

According to an Associated Press dispatch about their study, kudzu emits "a volatile organic compound called isoprene into the air, and its roots convert atmospheric nitrogen into ammonium, some of which can leak into the soil where it is converted by bacteria into nitric oxide. In the presence of sunlight, isoprene and nitric oxide mix together to make ozone."

Yet there's another argument for "good." Seems there's a big patch of kudzu near Cocke County's Hartford community that arsonists ignite every year when the leaves die back from frost. A spokesman for the Tennessee Division of Forestry said the blaze grew to two hundred acres before being contained.

How is this "good"? Authorities say it keeps arsonists from torching much more valuable woodlands, that's how.

Excellent! If a bunch of good old boys are determined to set fire to the boonies and sit back to watch it burn, I'd much prefer they do it to kudzu than oaks, pines, beeches, poplars, and maples.

In fact, whether these Jethroes and Bubbas know it, they're conducting a variety of research projects of their own—not the least of which is quantifying how hard it is to flick a Bic and light a Molotov cocktail while under the influence of a Tennessee cocktail.

Here in Southern Appalachia, this is known as multi-tasking.

LET'S HEAR ONE FOR KNOXVILLE

If there's a song in your heart, Knoxville sure could use it. By my calculations, K-town is way behind in the music business—and I'm talking rock, rap, blues, country, jazz, classical, and every other genre.

The musical *name* business, I should specify.

This deficiency came to my attention via a recent announcement from the Rock 'n' Soul Museum in Memphis. According to museum officials, Memphis is the most popular city name in the history of recorded music. The museum boasts a list of 899 ditties in which the word "Memphis" appears in the title or lyrics.

You're familiar with many of these numbers, of course. Such as "Walking in Memphis" by both Mark Cohn, who wrote the song, and Lonestar; "Memphis," a Chuck Berry tune whose best-known version is by Johnny Rivers; "Back Seat of a Greyhound Bus" by Sara Evans; as well as Alannah Myles's "Black Velvet," which, by the way, never fails to break me into a honky-tonkin', beer-drinkin' sweat.

Some of the others are not so widely known. Try as I may, I can't recall "Whiskey-faced, Radioactive, Blow-dryin' Lady" by Beck.

The list of performers who have recorded M-word songs runs the gamut from megastars Jimmy Buffett, Johnny Cash, Hank Snow, Alan Jackson, Tim McGraw, and Dinah Shore all the way to groups like Asphalt Ballet, Five Iron Frenzy, and Wet, Wet, Wet.

(If you're a dedicated fan of Asphalt Ballet, Five Iron Frenzy, or Wet, Wet, Wet and are astounded the dim-witted geezer writing these words isn't privy to your vast storehouse of musical knowledge, there's no sense calling to raise hell because I'll be guzzling my daily dose of Metamucil or filling out the latest AARP survey. Just accept my apology and save your time.)

In any event, Knoxville is behind. Our local minstrels need to pick up their pens and put more native names to paper.

Sure, we've had a few moments in the limelight. What would "Thunder Road" be without "blazin' right through Knoxville, out on Kingston Pike"? Or "Smoky Mountain Rain" without "I thumbed my way from LA back to Knoxville"? Or "Copperhead Road" without Steve Earle's gut-ripping "he was headed down to Knoxville with the weekly load"?

We also get mentioned in "Knoxville Courthouse Blues" by Hank Williams Jr., "Daddy's Gone to Knoxville" by Mark Knopfler, and Todd Steed's "North Knoxville"—"where this town still looks like itself."

But of all local lyrics, "The Knoxville Girl" is surely the most famous. Also the most dreadful. It's been recorded by a host of performers, most notably the Louvin Brothers. Based on an Old World tale, this tune describes, in gruesome detail, the bludgeon murder of a fair-haired maiden.

I'm certain I read some time back in the 1960s that "The Knoxville Girl" had been declared Knoxville's official song—probably by politicians who never had listened to it. Apparently I was mistaken. City officials did an in-depth search into the matter at my request, but couldn't find any such declaration, official or otherwise.

Oh, well. It must have come to me in a foggy vision out on Copperhead Road.

THE TALE OF A MIGHTY COLD BEER

Thirty years after the fact, Knoxvillians still love their World's Fair. That's because the 1982 version was "our" fair, and the world sure came to see it. Even now, there is a brisk trade in memorabilia from the big event.

I've never been much of a collector of anything, but the phenomenon itself amazes me. Whether we're talking stamps, baskets, cars, coins, hats, decoys, bottles, cans—or World's Fair pickle pins—I am forever impressed by people who hone in on one particular item and, over time, become an expert on its manufacture and history.

Then, ahem, there are the folks who randomly select "something," lay it tenderly aside for years, and then cannot explain what-in-the-name-of-commonsense possessed them to acquire it in the first place!

Such as the acquisitions made by Knoxvillian Patricia Keene.

In 1982, Patricia was living in Pikeville, Kentucky. But that did not stop her from visiting Knoxville and its famous fling.

"I came at least once a week," she told me. "I loved it. Oh, especially the train and its music! I wish I'd bought a recording of it."

Despite her many visits to the fair, Patricia acquired only three souvenirs.

One was an "I Was There on Closing Day" button.

The second was an official 1982 World's Fair cigarette lighter.

The third was a can of World's Fair beer, perhaps the most ghastly purgative ever brewed.

Please check the previous sentence carefully. Note I did not say Patricia has a six-pack of World's Fair beer. Or, perish the thought, a full case. No, indeed. She bought one—as in uno, singleton—can of the stuff.

She still has it. In her refrigerator.

"I've moved four times since then," she said with a laugh. "Every time, I've brought that silly can of beer with me. I've gotten a cooler full of ice and stored the beer inside so it will stay cold. Then I put it back into the refrigerator."

OK, so the lady handles her sudsy souvenir with figurative kid gloves. Nothing wrong with that. She's grown attached to it over the years. It has special meaning for her.

Except for one itty-bitty detail.

"I'm a teetotaler," Patricia told me, laughing even harder. "I've never taken a drink in my life."

There's more: "I've never smoked a cigarette, either."

So why did she collect World's Fair mementoes linked to these vices?

"That's the beauty of it!" she exclaimed. "I have no idea at all!"

Yowza! Like I said, Knoxvillians dearly love their long-ago party. Wouldn't trade the memories for anything. Even if they are still scratching their heads and asking themselves, "Why?"

THE AWFUL PUN-ISHMENT CONTINUES

NORRIS—During the joint meeting of the Brotherhood of Unruly, Lowdown, Lying Hillbillies Observing Creative Knowledge Every Year (BULLHOCKEY) and the Society of Appalachian Saintly Sisters (SASS) at the Museum of Appalachia's annual Tennessee Fall Homecoming, the following business was transacted:

Melissa Anderson, Chairwoman of the Committee on Distant Travels, reported on her recent vacation to Alaska.

"While there, I thought I saw my eye doctor," she began, "but it turned out to be an optical Aleutian."

Dr. Bill Alexander, Chairman Emeritus of the British History and Math Committee, reported that a heretofore unknown member of King Arthur's round table recently had been discovered.

"His name was Sir Cumference, a beast of a man who weighed nearly five hundred pounds," Doc said. "Apparently he acquired this size from too much pi."

Several members noticed that traffic appeared to be backing up on nearby Highway 61, so Sergeant-at-Arms Allen Longmire was dispatched to determine the cause.

"It was an old hound dog giving birth to puppies," Longmire announced upon his return. "I gave her a citation for littering."

Curtis Blanton, Editor of the BULLHOCKEY-SASS *Weakly Times,* said he hopes to win a Pulitzer Prize for the headline he wrote on the story about a dwarf fortune teller who successfully escaped from prison: "Small Medium at Large."

Several members asked for an explanation. None was forthcoming.

Andrea Fritts, Chairwoman of the Bovine Production Committee, reported that all the cows in the county had been artificially inseminated.

"Yes, it's true!" she exclaimed. "No bull!"

Several members noticed that Carolyn Cornelius was limping and inquired about the cause.

"I went to a seafood dance hall in Florida last week," she said, "and dang if I didn't pull a mussel."

Which prompted Charles Sherwood to ask if anyone had heard the one about the dyslexic who walked into a bra.

Three members said, "dah," meaning they had.

Bonnie Peters announced she had started working on a new book but abandoned the effort.

"It was about an invisible man who married an invisible woman. Sounded like a good idea, but then I realized their children would be nothing to look at, either."

Long-standing member Doug Fritts was absent, recuperating from recent appendix surgery, but sent in a written inquiry: "What was the best thing before sliced bread?"

By voice vote, all agreed Doug's half-baked notion was due to delirium caused by pain medication.

Megan Smith, Diva of Definitions, had scheduled an elaborate presentation on the meaning of common words and expressions. She started well enough by describing shin as "a device used for locating heavy furniture in the dark." But when abruptly questioned from the floor why "fat chance" and "slim chance" mean the same thing, while "wise man" and "wise guy" are opposites, Megan broke down hysterically and revealed she was hooked on phonics.

A resolution was hastily approved asking Megan to research the questions "Do windbreakers really break wind?" and "Why is 'bra' singular and 'panties' plural?" during treatment for her cruel affliction.

Speaking of medicine, Dr. Anthony Deaton, Curator of Historical Archives, noted that emergency room procedures in ancient Rome often were stymied when the physician called for an IV and someone handed him a four.

Gene Horner, Chairman of the Fiscal-Physical Fitness Committee, said he joined an expensive exercise club but was initiating legal proceedings to get his money refunded.

"Those idiots told me to wear loose clothing," he complained. "If I wore loose clothing, I wouldn't need to join in the first place!"

The Rev. Dr. Billy Ray Joe Bob "Slick" Fitzhugh III, Chaplain of the Committee on Overseas Evangelism, reported the sad news that a missionary friend of his had been eaten by cannibals. Said the sorrowful cleric: "At least they got a taste of religion."

Earnest Payne, Viscount of Vintage Videos, said Forrest Gump had it all wrong.

"Life is not like a box of chocolates," he said. "It's like a jar of jalapeños: what you do today can burn your butt tomorrow."

Several attendees stirred nervously in their seats.

Randy Underwood reported on his spring vacation to witness the Kentucky Derby: "My best horse came in at twenty-to-one. Unfortunately, the race started at 12:15."

A love offering was taken to help defray Randy's expenses.

Speaking of vacations, Blaine Anderson revealed that his whitewater trip turned into a disaster when the temperature plummeted abruptly.

"I lit a fire, but it went out when the dadgum boat sunk," he sighed. "This proves you can't have your kayak and heat it, too."

A motion was made to take another love offering to help with Blaine's expenses, but Sergeant-at-Arms Longmire pointed out that any boat operator this stupid needed a good paddling. All agreed, and the motion failed for lack of a second.

Ben Adams, Chairman of the Agricultural Production Committee, advised that strawberries can be vastly improved by the addition of either cow or sheep manure. Whereupon someone whispered aloud, "Sheeew! Has he never heard of sugar and cream?"

Larry Mathis apologized for arriving late but offered a plausible excuse: "Drivin' up the interstate, I saw a sign that said, 'Stop at Next Exit, Clean Restrooms.' That's what I did—and wow, countin' the men's and women's sides, I bet there was at least a dozen dirty stalls. I never worked so hard in my life."

Elaine Meyer said she looked in the mirror several days ago, sighed mournfully, and cried to her husband: "Just look at me! I feel awful! I'm old, I'm fat, and I'm ugly! I really wish you'd pay me a nice compliment." He thought for a minute and responded, "Well, honey, even at your age, your eyesight's still 20/20."

Funeral services for Ed Meyer are pending.

Gene Purcell, Chairman of the Medical Needs Committee, announced there has been one minor change since last year.

"Doc Jones, our community dentist, has given up his practice and is studying to become a proctologist," he said.

When asked why, Gene replied, "He was tired of people coughing in his face all day."

An empty bean can was passed and a love offering taken to help defray Doc's new educational expenses.

> **Was the Gospel of Luke written by an East Tennessean?**
>
> **That notion crossed my mind when our priest read a portion of the text—specifically the part where John the Baptist says, "Every valley shall be filled, and every mountain and hill shall be laid low."**
>
> **I couldn't help but marvel what a true visionary the guy was. Fully two thousand years ago, he was a voice crying in the wilderness about the practice of mountaintop removal by coal companies.**

In a related matter, Matt Mowrer implored the sergeant-at-arms to speed up the proceedings. Said Matt: "This meetin' is movin' along so slow, my butt's goin' to sleep."

Tommy Smith concurred, noting he was being bothered by the snoring.

Terry Morrow, Chairman of the Committee on Aging, reported that despite the relentless march of Father Time, he still feels like a newborn baby—"no hair, no teeth, and I think I just wet my pants."

Sergeant-at-Arms Longmire ordered Matt and Terry to sit on the same bench.

Mike Snider, Associate Conductor of the Music Committee, apologized for the introduction of rap on the band's latest CD of bluegrass music: "It's called cellophane, but it comes off real easy with a sharp pocketknife."

Jacob Williams, Chairman of the Student Scholastic Society, reported that on the first day of school, his teacher asked what he had done over the summer.

Jacob said: "Well, we traveled a lot. First, we visited my grandmother in Natchitoches, Louisiana. Then we visited my aunt in Pascagoula, Mississippi. Then we visited my uncle in Saskatoon, Saskatchewan. Then we visited my cousin in Sheboygan, Wisconsin."

"Wow! What a summer!" exclaimed the teacher. "Would you please go to the chalkboard and write all those places for the class?"

"Aw, I lied," said Jacob. "We just went to Ohio."

Coach Earl Sherwood, Chairman of the Physical Fitness Committee, reported that the region's population is decidedly stronger than ever before.

"Twenty-five years ago, it took at least three people to carry seventy-five dollars' worth of groceries," he said. "Now, a single person can perform the same feat, often using only one hand."

Mark Payne, Chairman of the Hire Eddukashun Cumitee, announced that a .270 Winchester Model 70 rifle, equipped with a 3x9 Leupold scope; a Remington Model 870, 12-gauge shotgun featuring a three-inch chamber and Real Tree camouflage; plus a Gerber fixed-blade knife with Softgrip handle, had been confiscated from members of his algebra class because they were weapons of math disruption.

The news prompted Patricia Outland to shout from the audience, "My gosh! What do we intend to do about this situation?"

Sergeant-at-Arms Longmire volunteered to take bids and immediately was swamped with offers.

Floyd Anderson, Chairman of the Standing Committee on Hygiene, reported he finally had found a way to quit arguing with his wife about the position of their toilet seat: "I just started using the sink."

A love offering was taken to help defray Floyd's legal bills.

Mention of judicial matters prompted Steve Colburn to admit he had been arrested for shoplifting at the Hootin' Holler General Store.

In court, the judge asked, "What did you steal?"

"A can of peaches," he replied.

"How many peaches were in the can?" His Honor queried.

"Six," Steve responded.

"In that case, I sentence you to six days in jail."

Whereupon Steve's wife, Donna, leaned over to the judge and whispered, "Psst! He also stole a can of peas."

John Rice Irwin, President of the BULLHOCKEY-SASS Ornithological Literary Club, asked if a chicken crossing the road should be classified as poultry in motion.

No one offered a contradictory opinion, so the matter was approved by cluck count.

Hoss Wyatt revealed the sad news that his grandson would not be in attendance because the lad had been hospitalized. When asked why, Hoss replied, "It was a freak accident. He had crammed some M&Ms in the pocket of his jeans, and when he grabbed a handful and wolfed them down, two pennies and three dimes also got swallowed by accident."

Upon request from the membership, sergeant-at-arms Longmire phoned the hospital to get an update on the boy's condition.

"No change yet," he reported.

Mary Etta Sherwood asked if anyone had heard about the two silk worms that set off on a foot race and ended up in a tie.

No one had.

There being no further business, the meeting was adjourned. Refreshments were served well into the night. No arrests had been reported by press time.

Chapter 4

A TWO-RING CIRCUS WITH ELEPHANTS AND DONKEYS

From Baja to Bangor, a predictable cry rises from the hoi polloi any time high-level officials of the government travel into their midst.

If that official is a member of the Republican Party, nearly everyone associated with the Democrats—from the lowliest ward heeler to chairman of the state committee—will object to this "ridiculous, outrageous, dare-we-say-criminal waste of the public's money!" Conversely, if that official is a Democrat, the moaning, groaning, and hand-wringing from GOP circles will be just as loud, just as visceral, just as emotional.

When George W. Bush was president and came to Knoxville for a speech, the Dems reacted as if Air Force One was burning gold ingots instead of jet fuel. Not surprisingly, in September 2009, several days after Ken Salazar, secretary of the interior under President Barack Obama, visited East Tennessee as part of re-dedication ceremonies for the Great Smoky Mountains National Park, I received a number of phone calls and emails from hardcore Repubs, demanding our newspaper investigate "how many millions were wasted!" on this partisan fluff.

(Just for fun, I scrolled through microfilm and checked on the aftermath of President Franklin D. Roosevelt's 1940 trip to Gatlinburg to mark the original dedication of the park. Sure enough, there was a story from Washington, quoting Joseph W. Martin Jr., chairman of the Republican National Committee, who excoriated Hizzoner's trip as nothing but political pandering funded by taxpayers.)

You can cuss this phenomenon, or laugh about it, but it should be filed under the heading of "'Twas Ever Thus and Ain't Likely to Change."

Same thing with spending at virtually any level of government.

Doesn't matter if you're Joe Blow from Plowhandle, Idaho, or U.S. Senator Big Cheese, fattest cat in the Beltway: If it's "your" party that's writing the check, or it's "your" state that's receiving the benefits, this is a brilliant example of prudent expenditure of taxpayer dollars; indeed, a great investment in the future of America. Just as predictably, if "they're" writing the check, and the cash is flowing "out there" instead of "over here," this is pork-barrel waste at its lowest, grossest level, an economic holocaust for which our great-grandchildren will still be suffering long after we have been crated to the boneyard.

Forgive me for taking such a flippant look at government and politics, but that's the way things operate. Unless you're a radio talk-show host who rants incessantly about how the United States is going to hell in a handbasket because of "them," you might as well worry about the weather or the stock market for all the difference it'll make.

Yet please understand: Voting for the clowns who occupy our public offices is not something to be taken lightly. This is a sacred privilege, and I always do my part to encourage participation. Nonetheless, things can go horribly wrong—and I don't mean with chads, pregnant, hanging, or otherwise—before the final tally.

On Election Day 2008, in the borough of Clemmons, North Carolina, a young man named Nathan Wood was about to cast his first ballot. Nathan, then a senior at West Forsyth High School, had just turned eighteen, making him eligible to vote for president. He took his role seriously. Unfortunately, events quickly went downhill shortly after Nathan showed up.

I learned about it from Janette Amos, a retired school teacher who lives in Etowah, Tennessee. Janette is Nathan's grandmother. She was delighted to share her grandson's travails—which neither she, nor I, am making up.

"He went to the polling place, a church in Clemmons, and noticed he was the only person under ninety years of age," Janette began. "Nathan was on his way to football practice and was dressed in shorts, a muscle shirt, black knee socks, and flip-flops. To make matters worse, he had a gaping hole in his mouth because a front tooth had gotten broken off in a game the week before."

OK, so he wasn't exactly your stereotypic Victor V. Voter. Big deal. The kid was still ready to perform his civic obligation.

"There were six voting booths, all in a row," Janette continued. "Nathan went in, marked his ballot, then turned around and said, 'I'm done!' very proudly."

That's when the poop hit the propellers.

Nathan's not sure what part of his clothing caught on the booth. But when he pulled away, the booth toppled onto the one beside it. Which caused it to crash into the next. And on and on until all six were on the floor.

Said Janette: "They were using paper ballots, and they went flying everywhere. Other voters were trying to pick up their ballots, but nobody was supposed to touch anything. They had to call an election official."

It grew worse.

"Finally, Nathan was given his ballot and stuck it into the box. But he put it in the wrong way, and the box froze up. The official had to unlock the box and fix that, too.

"The next day, my daughter called to say she had heard North Carolina hadn't declared a winner because there were problems at three precincts. She was worried one of them might be Clemmons. It wasn't, so Nathan didn't mess up any results. But he sure did cause some excitement!"

There was one casualty, however. In the melee, Nathan didn't get his "I Voted for President!" sticker, so he wasn't able to redeem it for a free doughnut offered by a sweet shop in nearby Winston-Salem.

What the heck. Nobody said life in a democracy was a piece of cake.

Do I occasionally get pure-T steamed about the political/bureaucratic antics in Nashville and Washington? Sure. I've even been known to craft a serious column about hot-button issues every now and then. But mostly I have fun because this circus is too good to miss.

Like the many times our hard-working men and women of the Tennessee General Assembly wrestle with one of the toughest issues to plop into their legislative laps. On cue, they begin debating—again—whether we need another official state song.

Most states are content with one official tune to rally the troops and swell bosoms with pride. According to the website 50states.com, such is the case in the majority of southeastern states—Alabama, Georgia, Kentucky, Mississippi, North Carolina, South Carolina, and Virginia.

Louisiana, Florida, and Arkansas have two. West Virginia stretches the list out to three. But nowhere, from Maine to California and all points in between, is there an entity to match Big T.

We have so many, I've lost count. Our impressive repertoire includes "My Homeland Tennessee" (adopted in 1925); "When It's Iris Time in Tennessee" (1935); "My Tennessee" (1955); "The Tennessee Waltz" (1965); "Rocky Top" (1982); "Tennessee" (1992); and "The Pride of Tennessee" (1996).

Don't take a breath yet. We also have four official state bicentennial songs, adopted in 1996. One of them is a gangsta number (I swear on a stack of flat-billed caps) called "A Tennessee Bicentennial Rap." It contains this toe-tapping verse: "Whisky, whisky, sipping smooth / Moon, Moon Pies and Goo Goo Goos!"

As they are fond of saying on Capitol Hill, "Who's counting numbers, unless you're talking about lobbyist money?"

Of course, you are familiar with only two of these songs. Those would be "The Tennessee Waltz" and "Rocky Top," which deal, respectively, with the linchpins of Tennessee culture: stolen love and corn liquor.

Far be it from me to heap ridicule upon members of the state legislature for this lunacy. They don't need the likes of me; they heap more than enough themselves. Wouldn't bother me if they came up with something like:

"O, Tennessee, land of my birth; the home of bellies round;

Where teeth are green and football reigns and six-guns loudly sound."

In the meantime, I'm thinking about having a bumper sticker printed up. It oughta sell all across Tennessee—at truck stops, restaurants, hardware stores, beer joints, beauty parlors, shoe shops, service stations, anywhere people gather. That's because the message resonates throughout Volunteer country. To wit: "Honk if you've ever written an official Tennessee state song."

Why? Allow me to clear my throat, take a deep breath, and collect my thoughts . . .

Because with all the other serious issues threatening Tennessee, the General Assembly actually got down to really, really, really serious business—*by approving yet another official ditty!* I kid you not.

This one is called "Tennessee." It was penned by the late John Bean of Knoxville.

What's that? What about the other "Tennessee," the one from 1992? No problem. Apparently we have so many official state songs, we've run out of official titles and are now lapping the field. But why fret over details?

The truly sad thing about this nuttiness is that John Bean should be honored by the legislature for a lot more than a catchy tune. He should be recognized as the redneck icon he was. You see, Bean, who died in 1984, was the genius behind "Leroy Mercer" and the gut-splitting audio tapes that were created as he placed prank phone calls to area stores.

If you're under the age of thirty, you've likely never heard of these tapes. But I'll guarantee your older friends and relatives have. If you want to watch them melt in laughter, ask if they've ever heard this line: "It ain't nothin' for me to whup a man's ass."

That was the common thread in Bean's tapes. His most famous was a call to Eddie's Auto Parts in Knoxville. In it, Bean speaks to the owner, Ed Harvey, and claims a defective oil filter caused his engine to tear up. One hillbilly threat leads to another as the audio rolls. And before you can reach for a tire tool, both Bean and Harvey are calling each other vile names and threatening fisticuffs—"'cause it ain't nothin' for me to come down there and whup a man's ass!"

Alas, Bean didn't live to profit from these tapes. After his death, several envious copycats pulled off similar ruses, recorded them, and reaped financial rewards—although I understand the real McCoy is now available through a website called asswhupper.com.

Too bad John Bean isn't still around to accept his well-deserved glory and put the polish on a rock-'em-sock-'em number. Trust your Uncle Metronome: If the lines in the chorus of our newest state song rhymed with "ain't nothin' for me to whup a man's ass," it would leave "Rocky Top" in the dust.

So much for Nashville nonsense. What about craziness on the federal bureaucratic level? I thought you'd never ask.

As anyone who ever visited D.C. can attest, there's never enough time to see everything—especially at the Smithsonian Institution. But the next time I'm up there, I simply *must* inspect the National Museum of American History and focus my peepers on President George "Zeus Bob" Washington.

No, that's not the real name of this statue. Officially, it is the "George Washington sculpture by Horatio Greenough." But by whatever handle, this monumental artwork is proof that governmental nuttiness is not a recent phenomenon. As evidence, I present research materials from the Smithsonian, plus an ancient newspaper story by the late syndicated columnist Frederick Othman.

Greenough was a famous Massachusetts sculptor of the mid-nineteenth century. In 1832, he was commissioned by Congress to create a heroic statue of Washington for the U.S. Capitol. Greenough took his five-thousand-dollar fee up front and immediately set sail for Florence, Italy. For six years he labored on the ten-ton marble masterpiece.

Getting it to America, however, proved problematic.

On the first leg of the trip, workers had to cut down olive trees along one side of the road, just to make room for the crate. The bill came to $8,311.50. It was an omen.

As the piece was being loaded onto a ship, the rope broke. Mister Prez busted through the hull and was buried in mud. The ship sank atop him. Only after the U.S. Navy dispatched a battleship to Italy was His Georgeness resurrected and forwarded to New York.

Tunnels between New York and D.C. back then weren't wide enough to handle the statue. So it was redirected to Washington via New Orleans. By now, associated costs had billowed to nearly thirty thousand dollars.

Ah, but Mister President finally was home! A great unveiling was scheduled on the anniversary of his birthday in 1841. After many speeches and excessive amounts of pomp and circumstance, the shroud was removed.

To gasps of horror.

Seems Greenough had taken his patterns from the Greek god Zeus. As Othman wrote, the president was "clad as a Roman senator on his way to the bath. His chest muscles rippled in the cold sunlight. A wreath held down his curls. A marble sheet, loosely draped around his middle, barely saved the proprieties. His king-sized toes were encircled with thongs to keep his Roman sandals from falling off."

Revulsion, inside Congress and out, was so strong that plans were drafted to blow the hideous thing to kingdom come. Then—oops!—someone discovered a federal law preventing the government from destroying its own artwork.

The statue remained at the Capitol for sixty-five years, hidden in a wooden shed. In 1908, it was hauled to the Smithsonian and stayed in a cellar of the main building. It reached its present location in 1964.

"It's right by the escalator on the second floor," museum spokeswoman Raphael Sikorra told me when I telephoned for details. "You can't miss it."

I don't intend to.

Yet as much as I raise good-natured hell with "the guv'mit," I only wish East Tennessee's homespun ability to approach conflict in a common-sense manner would spread to all chambers. Back in the middle of 2011, when the debt-ceiling crisis loomed dangerously, I offered a true story from more than thirty years earlier:

Allen Longmire owned two oak logs, each ten to twelve feet in length, and had no immediate use for them. John Rice Irwin, on the other hand, wanted those logs for lumber at his Museum of Appalachia. Thus ensued a spirited session of backwoods bargaining.

"I can't remember the exact price John Rice and I settled on," said Longmire, who lives in rural Anderson County. "I just remember how we worked out the details."

The problem revolved around a single piece of paper money. Allen thinks it was a ten-spot. It had to be broken to consummate the deal, but neither man had the correct number of ones to square the account.

Both of these characters are longtime friends, so the principle of their negotiations demanded that neither be taken advantage of—or "slicked" in local parlance. But with innovative thinking, they arrived at an equitable solution.

"I gave John Rice three 'possum hides," Longmire said with a laugh. "He needed 'em for a trapping display at the museum, and the amount of difference on the logs was about the same as I could get at the fur market." Handshakes all around.

I brought up that snippet of East Tennessee history for two reasons.

First, it showed how differing parties could achieve consensus if both were willing to consider all options. At that moment, the Republicans had their plan for addressing the debt ceiling, the Democrats had theirs, and ne'er the twain would meet. Enough hot air billowed from Washington to supply us with energy well into the next decade. Everybody was talking, but nobody was listening—except to their own ideological screed.

Both sides had valid arguments. Yes, too much money was going out. Yes, more money needed to come in. It reminded me of the early years of my own marriage, when Mary Ann and I were a young couple with one salary and two kids. We scrimped, did without, cut corners. But at the same time, we also found new sources of revenue: she through private tutoring, I through writing articles for magazines. A single solution would not work for us. We needed both. Same with Washington.

The second reason I cited Allen's and John Rice's deal was more ominous. I figured if the United States defaulted on its loans, we would topple into a cataclysmic economic cavern, the likes of which this country has never seen. I'm still not sure we won't.

Just to be on the safe side, hold onto your 'possum hides. You may need 'em.

> Here's an old saw that gets reworked at every political twist and turn. Still, each rendition is funny. Frank Jones is the latest to send it my way: "The Ruger Company is coming out with a new pistol in honor of our senators and representatives in Washington. It's called 'The Congressman.' It doesn't work, and you can't fire it."
>
> Even if it could be touched off, the only result would be a plume of smoke and hot air.

ANOTHER LAW WE DON'T NEED

Let us hope Tennessee's lawmakers continue to stay away from late-night talk-show history by refusing to weigh in on truck testicles.

No, trucks don't come from the factory with these things. Instead, they are purchased online or at specialty shops and attached to the trailer hitch. They have entered the accessory scene as part of the vehicle "pimping" fad sweeping the nation. You may have seen them dangling below a passing pickup. They come in pairs and resemble the south end of a northbound bull.

Let the record show that they are crude and sophomoric. Anybody who buys a pair and hangs them off his truck—I assume only young males would follow this trend, but these days you never know—might as well also purchase a bumper sticker proclaiming "I Am a Redneck Goober." But for Pete's sake, there's no sense trying to outlaw them.

Nonetheless, legislators in Florida, Maryland, and Virginia have proposed to do just that, with the resulting effect of generating riotous laughter and giving the manufacturers of these hideous things thousands of dollars in free advertising.

The Florida bill was introduced by Senator Carey Baker, a Republican from Eustis. Under his proposal, the public display of truck testicles would result in a sixty-dollar fine. Senator Steve Geller, a Democrat from Hallandale, responded with extraordinary common sense when he told reporters, "There's got to be better things for us to spend time debating."

As the old saying goes, there's no accounting for bad taste. Trying to legislate stupidity is a waste of time. The dolts won't understand, and the only people who'll benefit are smart-assed newspaper columnists in search of cheap material.

Same song, umpteenth verse. Back in the 1990s, the Georgia state legislature outlawed bumper stickers, T-shirts, and other media carrying the then-popular expression "(S-word) Happens."

The only result, besides giving jokesters a warehouse of ammunition, was to set the stage for a First Amendment showdown. Which, naturally, was won by the "S-word" crowd. Once the law was struck down, the bumper stickers and T-shirts largely disappeared.

That's what'll happen here if lawmakers will simply butt out. Let the buck-toothed goofs drive around for a while with their truck testicles on display. When they realize nobody is shocked, they'll find something else to waste their money on.

Who knows? Perhaps legislators and smart-assed newspaper columnists will even find real issues to discuss.

CASTING A SPELL ON THE IRS

If you're starting to come down with a bad case of ITDF (Income Tax Deadline Fever), here's a suggestion that might help alleviate your suffering: Put a hex on the Internal Revenue Service.

You know, an old-fashioned witch's curse—"double, double, toil and trouble" and all that. Just thinking about it makes me want to perfect my cackle and boil a cauldron of water.

This idea isn't original with me. I learned about it in a news report from Romania, where curses, spells, and hexes are a part of daily life. So much a part, in fact, that the government has begun taxing them. I swear on a stack of tarot cards.

Everyone in Romania practicing the arts of witchcraft or fortune-telling must now pay a 16 percent income tax, plus contribute toward health and pension plans.

Predictably, the irate witches are striking back. No, not by dressing in three-cornered hats or writing heated letters to the editor. That's the wimpy American way. In Romania, they're taking the time-honored direct route. They're casting evil spells on President Traian Băsescu and members of his administration.

And it's working. The prez and cabinet have begun wearing purple clothes at least one day a week in hopes of warding off these attacks.

(Far be it from me to tell the Romanians, who are steeped in ancient folklore customs, how to counter the effects of a curse. But since some of the spells I read about involved cat excrement and dead dogs, I wouldn't worry about color. Purple-smurple. My choice in protective attire would lean heavily toward Gore-Tex and vulcanized rubber. But I digress.)

OK, let's get down to business.

First thing we need to do is identify our target. I suggest standing on a street corner, waving a fist in the air, and shouting, "Curse you, IRS!"

Not only will this convey your ill will in the appropriate direction, it separates you from street preachers, hookers, politicians, and other regulars vying for valuable sidewalk space.

Next, we gotta come up with an evil concoction, a potent brew. Something smelly, bubbly, noxious—which, oddly enough, reminds me of the *News Sentinel*'s men's room late in the afternoon on Chili Contest Day.

Probably best to avoid eye of newt, wing of bat, toe of toad, and other conventional ingredients. Our goal is to irritate the IRS, not alert the Interior Department's endangered species police.

Oh, I know! Let's get a bunch of tax forms and fill out the rows, pages, and columns with incomplete and out-of-sequence numbers. That drives bean counters totally bonkers.

Every Social Security number is three-digit, two-digit, four-digit, right? So on the curse form, write yours out as two-digit, one-digit, three-digit.

Next, start entering data willy-nilly. Such as: Put info for Line Five on Line Eight. Info for Line Nine on Line Two. Info for Page Six on Page Three. And so on.

Continue this course on the entire form, and I'll guarantee you'll get someone's attention.

True, subsequent responses might have to be prefaced with "Your Honor"—but, by gum, the IRS will know it's been hexed something fierce!

LOOK! UP IN THE SKY! AIIIEEE!

The federal government is about to embark on the world's largest skeet shoot.

According to a recent Associated Press dispatch, the Pentagon is drawing a bead on a broken spy satellite that is on track to strike Earth. Officials have settled on a plan to launch a missile from a Navy cruiser and "intercept" (translation: ka-blooey!) the satellite before it enters Earth's atmosphere.

The intent is to reduce the satellite to crinkly smithereens, thus saving our planet from ruination or, at the very least, the untimely elimination of a large chunk of prime real estate, populated or otherwise.

Well, yes, now that you mention it, there could be complications.

In the first place, the Pentagon's marksmanship record is not without blemish. You may recall that in 2000, military experts conducted three tests to shoot down an incoming projectile like this. Only one worked. The others were big-time goofs costing taxpayers one hundred million dollars. But, hey, who's counting?

In one of the snafus, a "bad guy" dummy missile was launched from Vandenberg Air Force Base in California. Twenty-one minutes later and four thousand miles away, a fully armed "good guy" missile came hurtling off Kwajalein Atoll in the Marshall Islands. Less than three minutes into the test, a mechanism in the "good guy's" booster rocket failed to deploy. And the entire affair was chalked up, officially, as Oops 101.

In the other screw-up, water in a heat-seeking component of the "good guy" missile caused it to veer drastically off target. This, I assume, prompted authorities to insist our enemies attack only in hot, dry weather.

I don't point out these high-dollar misses to make fun of the Pentagon. For Pete's

Do-As-I-Say-and-Not-As-I-Do Department: In February 2007, U.S. Representative Jack Kingston of Georgia complained bitterly about the new House rules mandating a five-day legislative work week instead of the three-day week to which he had grown accustomed under former leadership. About one month later, in a House speech arguing against an increase in the minimum wage, Kingston said poor people simply need to work longer hours.

sake, as a rifle and shotgun shooter myself, I know aiming and hitting quite often are mutually exclusive endeavors.

What I do want to point out, however, is that if you gaze into the night sky sometime soon and see a large chunk gouged from the moon, or one of Jupiter's rings dangling to the side, or a giant hole in Uranus, please know your government is genuinely sorry and promises to do better on the next shot.

What if there's a direct hit, on first volley or two-hundredth? Uh, that brings up another itty-bitty problem: Falling debris.

You see, the satellite hurtling toward us weighs roughly five thousand pounds. This debris—some of it potentially hazardous—could scatter over several hundred miles.

"The satellite is outfitted with thrusters: small engines used to position it in space," the feds say. "They contain the toxic rocket fuel hydrazine, which can cause harm to anyone who contacts it."

But don't worry. Remain calm. Resist the urge to panic. This mission will probably come off without a hitch, and no one will suffer so much as a scratch.

Signing off now. See you in the cave.

NO HOPE FOR THE RED OF NECK

It sure is tough to be a redneck these days.

Legislators in Texas have just approved a measure that makes it a felony to tell fishing lies. And in Coral Gables, Florida, officials are issuing tickets to the owners of pickup trucks.

Well, OK; both situations are a bit more complex than that. Still, they're enough to make a fellow choke on his Beechnut.

In Texas, they haven't outlawed barbershop and general-store stories of the big one that got away. Or the time you and Uncle Herb hooked Ol' Mossback and it towed your boat all over the lake. What they've done is outlaw lying in tournaments where big money is on the line along with fish.

Under the new rule, anyone caught cheating in a fishing contest offering a payout of more than ten thousand dollars faces a prison term of two to ten years and fines up to ten grand. In smaller tournaments, the violation is listed as a Class A misdemeanor.

The anti-truck ordinance in Florida dates to the early 1960s. It hasn't been enforced in some time because a Coral Gables resident fought it through the courts. And ultimately lost.

This is a property codes regulation. It forbids the parking of pickups in driveways and on city streets at night. Instead, they gotta be garaged. Fines start at one hundred bucks and can run as high as five hundred.

The fishing law does make some sense—although high-dollar tournaments these days are light years removed from the cheat factories of old. Between blind drawing for partners, on-board media observers, lie-detector testing, and an overall improvement in the professionalism of this sport, the fraud factor has been greatly reduced.

As for the anti-truck law? Have mercy.

Sure seems strange to me that a fifty-thousand-dollar pickup truck would be considered trashy while a dinged-up, oil-dripping sedan makes the social registry.

Oh, well. Yet another reason to live Up Here with the real people rather than Down There among the snoots.

What do you bet they've also gotta a law that says you can't pee, or shoot deer, off your back porch?

PLACE YOUR OWN AD HERE

Tennessee's highways, byways, and waterways are about to take on a new look.

Legislation approved by the General Assembly and signed into law by Governor Bill Haslam permits advertising in places where it's never been before. In the coming months, expect to see commercial messages to show up on: vehicles, including boats, operated by the Tennessee Wildlife Resources Agency; those yellowish Tennessee Department of Transportation "HELP" trucks assisting disabled motorists up and down the interstates; the 511 highway traffic information telephone system.

I'm not fibbing. Tennessee's official space is now officially for sale to the officially highest bidder. Check the official websites of TWRA, TDOT, or the legislature itself for all the official fine print.

There are some restrictions about what cannot be advertised—at least for now. Alcohol and tobacco products, for instance. Also "adult-oriented establishments," political campaigns and candidates, as well as "any unlawful conduct or activities." But beyond that, show Uncle Bill the color of your money, and feel free to post your pitch.

This is going to take some getting used to—despite the fact that advertising has become so pervasive in modern society. You can't swing a dead cat anywhere in America these days without hitting an ad for feline food, kitty litter, or pet burial services. So why shouldn't the "guvmit" get in on this lucrative action?

TWRA already accepts paid advertising in its hunting and fishing guides. Thus, it's not going to be that strange seeing the likes of "Gander Mountain" or "Bass Pro Shops" on the side of the boat as a TWRA creel clerk inspects your catch. Reckon these clerks will also dole out free samples of the hottest new lures?

And since beggars can't be choosers, it wouldn't bother me one iota to see "Shell" or "Texaco" or, harrumph, even "Pilot–Flying J" on a HELP truck if I'm out of gas and stranded along the shoulder of Interstate 40.

The 511 option, however, does have the potential for ire.

If I'm headed to Bristol on Interstate 81 or U.S. Highway 11W and dial 5-1-1 to see if there's a wreck or road construction project somewhere along the way, it's going to peeve my parts royally to have to listen to a commercial for "Floyd's Fabulous Flea Market, home of two-dollar duct tape and a complete selection of imported screwdrivers" before getting the low-down.

Even worse is the dread of knowing this is merely the tip of a huge iceberg. What, pray tell, is next?

Texas already allows commercial advertising on license plates for private vehicles, and Illinois is testing the water. We're not talking about vanity plates like "IMAVOL," "GRANNY" or "RAYSRIDE." We're talking about full-bore, high-dollar ads on the order of "EAT AT JOE'S BBQ" as an official state plate.

It gets worse. What they're doing in California is downright freaky: They're feeding advertisements onto the state's seven-hundred-plus electronic interstate message boards. Typically, these signs are used to broadcast Amber Alerts, weather advisories, traffic updates, lane closures, and safety tips regarding seatbelt use and the danger of driving impaired. Those would still have top priority. But how long will it be before they begin combining both functions?

Just think: Tennessee also has a network of these signs. One hundred are posted statewide; seventeen are in the Knoxville metro area alone. Thanks to the wonders of electronics, information on these boards can be changed at the flick of a finger. So why not sign up a bunch of advertisers in advance, quote them a rate, and have their commercials ready to go at a moment's notice?

Such as: "Amber Alert! Be on the lookout for a red Ford pickup, license No. 127 DVS—just like the F-150s now on sale at Fred Ferd's Ford Farm on the Airport Motor Mile. New models arriving daily! No money down!"

Or perhaps: "Two lanes closed twelve miles ahead—so why not pull off at Exit 397 and enjoy a hearty breakfast at Waffle House? Half off on all orders of smothered-and-covered hash browns, today only."

Then there's: "Four-car wreck at Mile Marker 236. If this happens to you, call Tommy's Towing Service, 555-1846."

And we can't forget: "Booze It and Lose It. Brought to you by the Governor's Highway Safety Council and Billy Bob's Bail Bonds, operators on call 24/7."

Actually, the anti-drinking message could even be further refined: "Want to booze but not lose? Stay at Fairview Lounge and Motel, Exit 413-A. Two-dollar pitchers and great room rates."

After that, the names of public properties surely would be next on the auction block. Such as "Big Ridge–Sprint Wireless State Park" or "House Mountain–UPS State Natural Area."

All in all, I fear we are opening a giant can of worms. (Brought to you by Bubba's Bait and Bobbers, your one-stop nightcrawler headquarters.)

REGULATING THE GAMES KIDS PLAY

You'll be happy to know Tennessee isn't the only state where time and money are wasted on official nuttiness.

True, we do manage to stay well ahead of the pack in most of these matters. Witness this bold action our legislators just took: They declared macaroni and cheese a vegetable.

Not that it's any consolation, but at least this was fomented by elected officials, who—in theory, hahaha—are held accountable for their folly at the ballot box. It's much more difficult to undo official foolishness when it comes at the hands of bureaucrats.

Consider a measure that almost became an ironclad regulation in New York. Almost, I reiterate, proving that common sense is alive and well Up There. Not long ago, the New York State Health Department issued guidelines governing certain children's activities that pose a "significant risk of injury."

Chainsaw juggling, perhaps? Bed sheet parachuting? Meth manufacture with chemistry sets?

Uh, no. We're talking more placid childhood endeavors like tag, dodgeball, horseshoes, and capture the flag—and I swear on a case of Wiffle balls I'm not making this up. Oops. Speaking of Wiffle ball, add that game to the list of dangerous activities, too.

According to the proposed rules, any summer recreational program offering these games would have needed a medical professional on staff. Plus a director with a bachelor's degree and at least twenty-six weeks of summer camp experience. Not to mention detailed recordkeeping to track the number of, and treatment for, skinned knees, bloody noses, and other "significant" injuries.

Sanity ultimately prevailed. Under pressure from State Senator Patty Ritchie—who apparently swings a mean ball bat along with her briefcase—the department announced its "re-evaluation" of the proposal. (Hillbilly translation: "Git that %$#@! thang outta here!")

In a news release from her office, Ritchie said: "At a time when our nation's number one health concern is childhood obesity, I am very happy to see that someone in state government saw that we should not be adding new burdensome regulations by classifying tag, red rover, and Wiffle ball as dangerous activities. I'm glad New York's children can continue to steal the bacon, play flag football, and enjoy other traditional rites of summer."

I call your attention to this Yankee brouhaha because our own schools have just now let out for the summer. All over K-town, kids will be playing kick the can, skipping rope, and swatting softballs. Well, at least the .00002 percent who aren't holed up on the sofa, playing video games and texting their friends will be. But that's not the point.

The point is, there's a distinct possibility that some chillen will gather to recreate in the lazy, hazy, crazy days of summer. We can only hope certain homophobic Tennessee lawmakers will monitor this dangerous activity to make sure nobody has a gay ol' time.

SINKING A TOOTH INTO CRIME

Hey, I've been ripped off! I just finished a scrumptious Rice Krispies Treat, and all it contained was rice cereal, corn syrup, and marshmallows!

Well, yes, plus a bunch of minor ingredients listed on the label, like "vegetable oil with TBHQ and mixed tocopherols for freshness, corn syrup solids, water, two percent or less of dextrose, glycerin, natural and artificial butter flavor, niacinamide, BHT preservative, pyridoxine hydrochloride, thiamin hydrochloride, riboflavin, vitamin A palmitate, vitamin D, soy lecithin, and less than half a gram of trans fat per serving."

But not so much as a smidgen of marijuana. I couldn't even get the foil wrapper to light, no matter how many times I flicked my Bic.

How's this for a fish-fowl-follicle conundrum: In 2010, the Tennessee General rescinded an ancient law prohibiting live birds and fish tanks in barber shops.

Does this mean we can now walk into a pet store and expect to get a haircut?

Should have known something was fishy from the start. All I had to fork over for my treat was fifty-nine cents, plus another nickel for the governor. That's a rather substantial saving over the going rate of $11,506.

According to the Tennessee Department of Revenue, 11.5 Gs is the value of a "rice creeper treat" confiscated at the Bonnaroo music festival. And that pricey sweet sits at the center of a lawsuit filed a few days ago in Nashville.

Seems a Bonnaroo attendee named William J. Hoak possessed a batch of these goodies for concert munching. Since they allegedly contained a few dashes of whacky weed, enforcement agents deemed they fell under the "crack tax" law, which calls for revenue stamps to be affixed to any product containing illegal substances. The value of these stamps is based on weight. And therein lies the heart of Hoak's lawsuit.

Does the weight apply only to the pot itself? Or does it include the whole shebang—rice, marshmallows, butter, BHT preservative, pyridoxine hydrochloride, et al.?

(Of course, this assumes Hoak folded BHT preservative, pyridoxine hydrochloride, et al., into his Bonnaroo mixing bowl. For all I know, he merely sprinkled weed onto commercially manufactured Rice Krispies Treats. The news stories I read about the incident didn't specify and, frankly, I was lusting so breathlessly for a delicious Rice Krispies Treat by that time, I threw my newspapers aside, dashed to the nearest concession stand, and plunked down fifty-nine cents, plus tax. But I hungrily digress.)

At any other time or place in Tennessee history, we'd write off this legal lunacy to the record-setting heat. Three straight weeks at or near one hundred degrees will fry anyone's brains, dope or no dope. But ever since Hoak raised the issue, I've been scratching my head in deep thought, not to mention dry skin. You see, depending on the outcome of this case, the value of unstamped contraband could rise or fall appreciably.

Consider moonshine, which traditionally is delivered via quart-sized Mason jars. Does this mean its "crack tax stamp value" is based on the weight of the likker itself? Or the likker plus jar and lid, not to mention any peppermint candy that was stirred into the potion to file off the rough edges?

These questions are important. Current hot weather notwithstanding, it's getting toward winter. You never know when a touch of elixir might be necessary.

Strictly, harrumph, for medicinal purposes.

MAJOR MONEY MATTERS

I've got some frustrating problems with money—and that doesn't mean what you may think.

I'm not broke. Not completely, anyway. What's more, classifying my money frustrations as a sure-nuff "problem" would be a lie. Let the record show I like money. Any kind of money. Any amount of money. If somebody wishes to increase these "problems" by adding them to my bank account, have at it. Throw me as far into this briar patch as you can heave.

It's just that all this "new" money floating around town—or clinking, as the case may be—sure does take some getting used to.

Consider the clinking category.

I recently picked up a new presidential gold dollar and noticed two problems right off the bat. First, it ain't gold; it's pale yellow. Second, George Washington looks like he's having a terrible day, like maybe he just got word the British won after all.

If you haven't seen one of these coins, get ready. The U.S. Mint has cranked out three hundred million of them. They're coming to a pocket near you.

This is the government's third attempt at weaning us from paper to metal. First was the Susan B. Anthony dollar, then the Sacagawea dollar—which, by the way, truly looks "gold," not pale yellow like these new Washingtons.

As you know, the first two fizzled. My guess is this one will, too.

That's because Americans—and I speak as a red-blooded, tax-paying, money-clip-carrying version of the species—prefer our lucre to be quiet, not noisy. For my money, there's nothing more annoying than a pocketful of jingle-bling. Anytime change builds up in my jeans, I pass it off as quickly as possible.

I know this doesn't make sense. I have read all the government's propaganda—uh, I mean "informative statistics" about the matter.

I know paper money wears out in as little as eighteen months, while coins can stay in circulation as long as forty years.

I know drink machines and snack machines are being retrofitted to accept dollar coins.

I know paper bills are more expensive to manufacture—who'da thunk the feds ever worried about financial waste?—and easier to counterfeit.

So? I still would rather slide my clip across layers of Washingtons, Lincolns, Hamiltons, Jacksons, even the rare Grant and Franklin, and tuck them into my pocket, thank you.

We've been down a similar road before. Do the words "metric system" ring a bell?

Do you remember how the feds tried to convert us from miles to kilometers back in the '70s? Do you remember all the arguments about how much more logical metric is compared with the stodgy English system?

Of course you do. And you also remember how the feds finally gave up in disgust as the rest of us blithely continued to "pound," "ounce," "quart," and "mile" our way along, just as we had grown accustomed to doing. Our habits refuse to change—especially when we're talking pocket change.

But you never know. If these coins do turn out to be successful, it'll probably be because of slick marketing—and I'm not talking about silly advertising campaigns teaching us how to spend money, like what happened when newly designed ten- and twenty-dollar bills premiered.

Instead, I'm talking about how the feds are pushing these things as collectibles, along the lines of the state quarter series.

In the latest effort, the face of the president will change regularly. Soon to be joining Washington will be John Adams, Thomas Jefferson, and James Madison. Abraham Lincoln and Franklin Roosevelt aren't far behind.

At least that's the schedule. My money says that before FDR hits the scene, these presidential coins will be cuddling up next to Susan B. Anthony and Sacagawea in government warehouses. No doubt Uncle Sam will find vast cubic meters of storage space for them, many kilometers away from Washington.

As frustrating as metal money is, however, I'm not so sure the stiff, silky-slick, new paper variety isn't even more of a royal pain in the, uh, budget. Give me the old, crinkled, musty stuff, thank you.

This new money is the worst social aggravation since polyester. Anybody who still deals in cash—yes, there are a few of us fossils remaining—knows what I'm talking about.

One-dollar bills are the worst offender. At least that's the denomination I'm having the most trouble with. In the small financial circles I travel, ones are the currency of choice; occasionally a five, maybe a ten, every now and then a twenty. But for day-in and day-out expenditures, we threadbare legions deal mostly in George Washingtons. Whatever the denomination, though, these stiff notes seem to be everywhere.

They show up in your change at restaurants, gas stations, bars, and grocery stores. They show up when you cash a check at the bank or credit union. For all I know, they show up when you extract money from an ATM. Since I rarely use ATMs, I can't speak authoritatively.

Wherever the source, you're left with a pocketful of green roofing shingles bound together with Gorilla Glue. You've got to lick your fingers half a dozen times and then scrunch these hateful things back and forth between thumb and fingertip to separate them. Unless you're careful, you'll pass on two or more as a single bill.

I know I'm not imagining this situation. I've heard too much complaining about it from sales clerks, cashiers, and readers. But when I consulted money managers in the federal government, they acted like it was no big deal.

A few days ago, I spoke with Claudia Dickens, a spokeswoman for the U.S. Bureau of Printing and Engraving in Washington. These are the folks who print paper money.

"There's been no change in the manufacturing process," she told me. "All the currency is being printed under the same standards as before."

Well then, is there more fresh currency in circulation than usual around Knoxville? Not according to the public affairs office at the Federal Reserve Board in Washington.

OK, so maybe it's merely coincidence that I'm handling so many of the hateful things—like when you hear the same song on three radio stations and then when you get to the office two other people are humming the exact tune.

Agreed, this isn't a problem in the larger scope of life. Anytime you're holding a fistful of lucre—filthy, pristine, or otherwise—it's hard to complain.

Nonetheless, what we need is a money-laundering service here in Knoxville. Not one of those shady operations used by gamblers and drug dealers to disguise their ill-gotten gains. I'm talking about a real laundry—with soap suds, hot water, rinse cycle, and fluff dry.

Sounds like the kind of business enterprise where a fellow could really clean up.

THE PRYING MIND OF UNCLE SAM

Oh, joy. The Venable household has been chosen by the U.S. Census Bureau to fill out an American Community Survey.

"Chosen" in this sense is about as ominous as "Greetings" was for young men of my generation during the Vietnam War. It means, "You now belong to Uncle Sam."

I first received notification about this "honor" by way of a postcard. A few days later, a twenty-eight-page questionnaire arrived. It says I have to fill everything out. By law. Meaning I get to spend the next thirty-eight minutes telling Big Brother's snoops what's going on at my place.

What's the significance of thirty-eight minutes? That's how long Uncle Sam estimates the task will take.

Baloney. I just perused the form, and I'm guessing thirty-eight days is more like it. That's because Uncle Sam intends to know more about me, my wife, and our personal lives than our doctors, priests, bankers, and bosses combined.

This reminded me of a similar "time estimate" on my 2010 Census form. Back then, the number-counters posed a little quiz: "Filling out your Census form takes the same amount of time as: (a) making a hard-boiled egg, (b) watching your favorite sitcom, (c) changing a flat tire or (d) none of the above."

According to the government, the correct answer was (d) "none of the above."

No way!

No matter what your political leanings happen to be, you gotta love this joke submitted by Joanna Kelly: "A cannibal was walking through the wilderness and came upon a restaurant operated by another cannibal. He sat down and looked over the menu. It offered broiled missionary for ten dollars, fried explorer for fifteen dollars, and baked politician for one hundred dollars. The customer called his waiter over and asked, 'Why such a high price for the politician?' To which the waiter replied, 'Oh, goodness! Have you ever tried to clean one?'"

Agreed, the boiled egg and TV options would take a while. You gotta dig a dozen eggs out of the back of the refrigerator, then clean up the milk that spilled when you tried to yank the %$#* eggs around the $*#@! milk carton. Plus you have to squat down to the bottom cabinet—why does your wife insist on storing utensils so far away?—and bang around until you locate a pot. Then you blow another twenty minutes since the water hasn't boiled because you forgot to turn on the eye.

As for watching TV? Hey, by the time you push those itty-bitty buttons on the remote and scroll through 6,473 channels searching for an "Andy Griffith Show" re-run, the episode will be over.

But I can change a flat quicker than filling out all that paperwork because I did it one morning several years ago in Newport. I was going deer hunting and was already running seriously late. Then a back tire went south. So help me, I pulled into a beer joint parking lot, jacked up my truck in the dark, changed the tire, peeled out, hoofed through the woods, and still climbed into my stand before the sun crept across the eastern skyline. It was a NASCAR-quality moment.

But back to my thirty-eight-minute American Community Survey sitting before me as we speak. I tried reading its introductory questions and immediately began scratching my noggin.

Uncle Sam wants to know how many people "are living or staying at this address for more than two months?"

Beats me. It's the holiday season, for Pete's sake. We've got family and friends scattered all over the map. This time of year, we don't know from one day to the next who's going to show up. Or how long they plan on staying.

Another question wants to know if I have "serious difficulty concentrating, remembering, or making decisions."

Amazingly, the only answers are "yes" and "no."

For complete accuracy, there should be several "depends" options. As in depends on (1) how much I've had to drink, (2) what's on TV, and (3) what type of decision is to be made: whether, say, to go fishing or fill out some stupid government form.

Indeed, the more I looked, the more nonsensical inquiries I spotted.

Such as how well do I speak English? The answer choices were: "Very well?" "Well?" "Not well?" "Not at all?"

Again, it depends. What kind of English are they talking about? Elizabethan English? California English? Cajun English? Hillbilly English? There's a world of difference, as any trained tongue will attest.

The final question was downright embarrassing: "When did this person last work, even for a few days?"

In my case, I'd say sometime around 1970.

TIME FOR MORE STATE CHANGES

"It's time we retired Tennessee's official state slogan!"

That thought sieved its way through the detritus of my pea brain a few years ago when Ron Ramsey replaced the venerable John Wilder as Speaker of the Senate and lieutenant governor. Wilder had been "Th' Speakah" since 1971—when Bill Battle was head football coach at the University of Tennessee, Richard Nixon occupied the White House, a gallon of gas cost thirty cents, Ma Bell ran the phone company, and blackberries went into pies instead of briefcases.

Thus the notion of giving the state slogan a gold watch and sending it to the old folks' home.

Geez Louise! "Tennessee—America at Its Best" has been on the books since 1965. After more than four decades on the job, it needs to be waltzed out to pasture.

There's nothing necessarily inaccurate about this slogan. As a proud Tennessee native, I agree wholeheartedly with the intent behind the words. But age takes a toll on the best of 'em, and here is no exception.

"Tennessee—America at Its Best" sounds like one of those cheesy public service announcements that used to be broadcast during the newsreel segment at the movies. Speaking of which, allow me to remind you James Bond was ducking Oddjob's flying hat in *Goldfinger* when this bromide was coined.

Surely we can think up something more trendy. Something that plays on our strengths. Something that reflects our redneck stereotype. Something along the lines of

Tennessee—
"Home of the Great Smoggy Mountains National Park."
"Not as Many Crooked Politicians as Your State."
"King Cotton May Be Dead, but Polyester Lives On in Style."
"Elvis Was Dam-Sho' Alive Last Time We Saw Him."
"Term Limits? We Don't Need No Stinkin' Term Limits!"
"Got Meth?"
"Come Watch the Sunsphere Rust."
"Edukashun Ain't Us'ins."
"Tattoo HQ, USA."
"Habla Espanowhut?"
"Our Teams Can Lose Better Than Your Teams."
"Your Next Lottery Ticket Is Bound to Win Big."
"Not Gonna Have No Evolution."
"Our Women Have the Perfect Figure: .44, .38, .357."
"Free Orange Highway Cone Every Hunnert-Thousand Miles."
"Still Barefoot, Pregnant, and Proud."
"10-4, Good Buddy."
"Huntin' Season and Football Six Months a Year, Yee-Haw!"
"Why Diet When Walmart Stocks XXL?"
"Far Enough Away from Michigan and Florida!"
"A Chicken in Every Pot and Two Dogs under Every Porch."
"All the Craziness of Cajun Country without the Hurricanes."
"Where Yore Cuzzin Can Be Yore Wife—and Probably Is."

"Chow, Baby!"

"No Income Tax, Low Cigarette Tax."

"You Ain't from Around Here, Are You?"

"No Shoes? No Shirt? No Diploma? No Problem!"

"At Least We're Ahead of Mississippi."

Makes your eyes tear up, don't it?

DRINK AND BE MERRY

The folks at Jack Daniel Distillery have been drinking too much of their own joy juice if they really think Congress is going to declare a federal holiday in honor of their founder.

But you never know how things will play out in D.C. As master distiller Jeff Arnett recently commented on the final leg of a ten-city tour promoting the cause: "When you make whiskey for a living, one of the things you have to learn is patience. It takes time."

True. And you could argue that getting the Republicans and Democrats to agree on *any*thing would be better than their normal gridlock. But between staggering unemployment, wars on two fronts, and other pesky details, we have more pressing matters than naming a holiday to celebrate an iconic whiskey maker—even if his product is really good stuff.

Maybe it's coincidence or maybe it's a sign of these frantic times, but strong drink is making a bit of news lately. In addition to the Daniel's blitz (which, no doubt, will be written off as a costly public relations-advertising ploy), there's new research indicating heavy drinkers outlive teetotalers.

To reiterate: People who slam likker big time have statistically longer lives than those whose idea of riotous partying is Diet Coke on the rocks with a twist of lime.

I'm serious. The results appeared in a technical journal called *Alcoholism: Clinical and Experimental Research,* and were reported by media outlets all over the country.

Indeed, *Time* magazine noted, "Even after controlling for nearly all imaginable variables—socioeconomic status, level of physical activity, number of close friends, quality of social support and so on—the researchers . . . found that over a twenty-year period, mortality rates were highest for those who had never been drinkers, second-highest for heavy drinkers, and lowest for moderate drinkers."

Time's story went on to say, "The authors of the new paper are careful to note that even if drinking is associated with longer life, it can be dangerous. It can impair your memory severely, and it can lead to non-lethal falls and other mishaps . . . that can screw up your life. There's also the dependency issue. If you become addicted to alcohol, you may spend a long time trying to get off the bottle."

I shall leave it to your (hopefully reasoned) judgment to know when it's OK to uncork the jug and when to leave it on the shelf. In the meantime, consider a nugget of alcohol trivia that cycles around every year.

On October 21, 1805, the British fleet commanded by Admiral Horatio Nelson defeated French-Spanish forces in the Battle of Trafalgar. This would have provided another boost to Nelson's illustrious military career, except for his getting killed in action.

According to the story told to me by a tour guide when I visited London in 2003, Nelson's body was preserved in a barrel of rum during the journey home for a proper burial. But when the ship arrived in port and the barrel was unsealed, its contents were dry, having been consumed on the sly by his sailors. This gave birth, the guide said, to the term "drinking the admiral dry."

Whether that story is 100 percent accurate is debatable. But I've never cared for rum ever since.

"UNCLE I.D." WAS NO FAN OF DST

If you happen to be driving through tiny Dixon Springs, Tennessee, during a certain day in the spring or fall and feel the ground trembling, have no fear. It's not an earthquake.

Instead, it's the grave of I. D. Beasley, a former—and formidable—state representative who almost single-handedly made it against the law for Tennesseans to observe Daylight Saving Time. All because he missed his bus.

Tom Jellicorse, a retired Knoxville insurance executive, knows the hilarious story well. It's part of his family's history, and he's happy to share it whenever this seasonal time adjustment rolls around.

"Uncle I.D. was my mother's brother," Jellicorse said. "He died in 1956, but served in the legislature for thirty-eight years before that. He was a bachelor. He never learned to drive.

"He lived at the Walton Hotel in Carthage. On days when the legislature was in session, he'd catch the bus to Nashville. Then he'd stay at the Andrew Jackson Hotel until it was time to come back to Carthage.

"One morning, Uncle I.D. walked down to the bus station in Carthage, just like always. But the bus was already gone. He'd forgotten about the switch to Daylight Saving Time. Made him mad as a hornet."

For Hizzoner Beasley, this was a call to arms.

A carryover from World War II during that era, DST was never popular with farmers. Beasley controlled the rural bloc in his part of the state, so it was a simple matter for him to draw up a bill abolishing the practice and guide it along to final approval.

Eddie Weeks, librarian for the Tennessee General Assembly, did some archival digging for me—and sure enough, he found Beasley's bill, which was signed into law on February 4, 1949, by Governor Gordon Browning.

Tennessee hasn't been alone wrangling in and out of the DST maze through the years. In fact, there has been such a hodgepodge of local and state laws, this exercise became the time-keeping equivalent of "Who's on First?"

Weeks directed me to the website webexhibits.org/daylightsaving that details this regulatory mess. It's a fascinating read. Consider: "One year, twenty-three different pairs of DST start and end dates were used in Iowa alone. And on one Ohio-to-West-Virginia bus route, passengers had to change their watches seven times in thirty-five miles!"

Everything changed with the federal Uniform Time Act of 1966. There's been some tweaking along the line, of course, and a couple of states and U.S. territories still are holdouts. But by and large, the entire country "springs forward" in March and "falls back" in November.

Even if the ghost of I. D. Beasley howls every time it happens.

Oops!
We're experiencing
difficulties in humor.

PLEASE STAND BY...

T SMITH

WE INTERRUPT THIS PROGRAM . . .

Whoa! Wait a minute! What's a bunch of serious material doing in a nutty book like this, especially when announced like some cheesy radio broadcaster from the 1940s?

Good question. I hope to provide a satisfactory answer.

In 1996, the *News Sentinel* published a collection of my humor columns under the title of *I'd Rather Be Ugly than Stuppid*. Susan Alexander and the late Jacquelyn Brown, editors of that book, inserted a chapter called "Seriously Speaking" smack-dab in the middle. It featured some of my essays on child abuse, war, illness, death, and other somber elements of the human experience.

This was a risk; customers don't expect to go from chuckling to getting dope-slapped. But it proved to be a smart decision by Susan and Jackie, and I understood the point they were trying to get across: If your business is human emotions, transitioning from light-hearted to heavier fare is just a matter of switching gears and changing pace.

"I've never been accused of being a pulpit-pounding preacher," I wrote in the introduction to that chapter. "Don't ever expect to be one, either. When I feel a serious thought coming on, my first reaction is to take a cold shower and hope the mood passes. But not always. As the title suggests, these entries are presented without any hint of tongue in cheek. Even though humor is the medium I use most often to treat the ills of society, there are times when laughter is not the best medicine."

Same situation here. When you crank our four columns every week, they can't always be funny—intentionally or otherwise. And yet the ability to laugh and satirize can often be a bridge between sadness and happiness.

This was never truer than in the aftermath of September 11, 2001. Given the dedication, determination, and ultimate measure of human sacrifice displayed by police, firefighters, rescue workers, and ordinary—make that extraordinary—citizens on and after that horrible day, what I'm about to propose may seem callous. Perhaps even trite. But in my mind, an unsung hero of that awful era was a most unlikely person: comedian and talk-show host David Letterman.

He told us and showed us it was OK to remember we could laugh. Some day. Even as tears streamed down our faces and rage boiled in our veins.

As you surely remember, regular television programming was bumped off the air during, and seemingly forever after, the attacks on New York, Washington, and Shanksville, Pennsylvania. As a nation and as individuals, we were numb with shock and grief. Our world had been turned upside down, oh so painfully.

Twenty-four hours a day, seven days a week, the airwaves reported this tragedy and its aftermath. We cried rivers of tears. How could something so violent, so off the scale of depravity, be visited upon any country, let alone the United States of America?

Then on September 17, Letterman went back on the air. He was the first major talk show host to do so. The seven-minute, fifty-one-second soliloquy he delivered that night should be bronzed and placed on the Washington Mall along with other national treasures.

I'm not going to regurgitate Letterman's entire sermon here. Look it up for yourself on Google or a variety of search engines. There are scads of YouTube renditions.

As you view, listen for the hoarseness in his voice.

Watch for the pain in his eyes, the nervousness in his hands.

Indeed, look at the blank stare on his face as he tells America in as many words: We gotta get through this thing, people. And we will.

Here's a man who had made a twenty-year career out of mocking public officials. Yet he praised then–New York Mayor Rudy Giuliani as "the personification of courage."

In one particularly poignant segment, Letterman talked about the perpetrators and their mission. He noted that these heinous acts were done in religious fervor. "Even in a thousand years," he said, all but tearfully, "will that make any goddamn sense?"

We all know how difficult it was to crack wise—in print or in person—after 9/11. I felt a great sense of relief when Letterman told us it's OK to laugh. Some way, somehow, we'll get through this together.

That being said, I'd much rather write knee-slappers than tear-jerkers. If you were born a class clown—and we know who were are—that's the easiest work in the world to do. I have to pinch myself every time a paycheck goes into my bank account. But there are situations where humor simply isn't applicable when you're spinning a yarn.

I'll never forget a bizarre set of circumstances that occurred in the lives of my sister and brother-in-law, Suzy and Tony Deaton of Cleveland, Tennessee. This couple met two new friends, and then lost them forever, inside the space of a single day.

It happened in June 2007, when Suzy and Tony were spending a couple of days visiting the Shaker Village near Harrodsburg, Kentucky. They stayed at the historic Beaumont Inn. By chance—or maybe fate—they ran into another Tennessee couple, Eddy and Linda Childers of Maryville.

Tony and Eddy met first. Amateur photographers, both men were wandering the inn's grounds, snapping pictures. They nodded howdy and shared casual comments about their mutual hobby. This convivial chatter continued some time later as the two, waiting to meet their wives for dinner, happened to be rocking alongside each other on the inn's spacious front porch. Suzy arrived shortly, then Linda, and the foursome exchanged more friendly banter.

It wasn't until then that the two couples took time for formal introductions. After that, their warm, comfortable conversation picked right back up. That's how folks are in the South. They spoke of careers, families, travels—plus the fact that the Childerses had come to the Beaumont Inn to celebrate Linda's sixtieth birthday.

"That was pretty much it," Tony told me later. "Each couple went separately to dinner at the inn. The next morning, we ran into them again at breakfast. Linda was so excited about a diamond necklace Eddy had given her for her birthday. By pure chance, we saw them once more, about an hour later. They were checking out, and we were leaving for the day. We admired Linda's necklace a final time and wished them a safe journey back to Maryville."

End of encounter.

The next morning, Suzy and Tony finished breakfast at the inn and were relaxing with a copy of the *Lexington Herald-Leader*. Abruptly, Suzy shouted, "Oh, my God!" and went tearfully silent.

"What?!" Tony exclaimed.

Suzy couldn't reply on her own. Instead she read, numbly, the words of a traffic accident story from the newspaper in her lap:

A Tennessee couple was killed yesterday morning when their car collided with a pickup truck pulling a horse trailer. James Eddy Childers, sixty-one, and his wife, Linda R. Childers, sixty, both of Maryville, Tennessee, died from their injuries after the wreck at the U.S. 150 bypass and Old Stanford Road on Danville's east side, said Boyle County Deputy Coroner Mike Wilder. The accident happened shortly before 10 A.M.

If there's a credit crisis in America, you sure can't tell it by the junk that piles up daily in my mailbox. In one day alone, I received two credit-card pitches, both dripping with "rewards" incentives. (Translation: Run up charges now, forfeit later.)

One thing that particularly irritates me about these come-ons is their emphasis on the word "deserve." As in get the car, house, boat, clothing, whatever, you "deserve." Not "want" or "wish for" or "lust after." Instead, this is something you are due, as if by birthright.

When suckers believe they "deserve" something, they're more apt to buy it—even if they don't stand a prayer of making the first payment.

"We had known Eddy and Linda for only sixteen hours, but they were the kind of people we'd love to have as friends," Tony told me, slowly shaking his head. "Then just like that, they were gone.

"It was the strangest sensation I've ever felt—a true 'Twilight Zone' experience. If we hadn't bumped into each other and introduced ourselves, their deaths would have been just another tragic story in the newspaper, the kind you read every day. Makes you wonder about the dozens of other faceless, nameless 'friends' you encounter all the time, doesn't it?"

Whew.

Perhaps it's a function of my age, but I do find myself writing more and more often about death. Comes with the territory. Even we savvy, wise, and hep Baby Boomers realize that nobody has found a way to beat the rap. Solemn as they may be, though, death stories don't have to be bleak. Quite the contrary. They can evoke the most tender, happy memories.

Even though my mother has been dead since 2003, I occasionally write about her—especially when I see purple iris in the spring. That was her favorite color of her favorite flower. Mine too. In fact, I can't recall a time when I wasn't stunned by the beauty of iris in bloom. Particularly purple ones.

Even as a rough-and-tumble redneck kid, with a baseball glove in one hand and a fishing rod in the other, I would set recreation temporarily aside and stare in awe every spring when "Maw's" beds were decked out in full glory.

They're such a fleeting flower, iris. A couple of days for each individual blossom, maybe three weeks for the season's complete run. Oh, but what unadulterated praise veritably shouts during that brief span!

Iris are at the same time tender and tough. The delicate flower unfolding from its tightly packed bud is part of a plant that can flourish under the worst of conditions.

Just like Maw.

Mary Elizabeth Spencer Venable spent her formative years in a most dichotomous world. The daughter of a steam engineer for the L&N Railroad, she lived weekends and summers in Chaska, Tennessee—a remote, can't-get-there-from-here hamlet tucked between the folds of coal country in Campbell County, just south of the Kentucky state line. Weekdays during the school year were spent in Knoxville. The family's home at Chaska was rather Spartan by today's standards but more than adequate for its time and place. It was a renovated boxcar, complete with separate sleeping quarters, a kitchen, and a screened-in porch—perhaps the forerunner of today's "modular home."

Although it had neither the electricity nor the modern plumbing of the family's more orthodox house in Knoxville, Maw loved it. She relished country life and regularly entertained her children with stories from the old days: everything from encounters with moonshiners, to bathing in the ice-cold swimming hole, to foraging for native plants with one particularly loquacious and learned "widder woman." Indeed, both Chaska and Knoxville provided fertile training. Whether she was roaming mountain wilderness or strolling city sidewalks, Maw learned to embrace whatever opportunities circumstance afforded.

Here was no high-maintenance woman by any stretch of the chic term. Like everyone else who came of age during the Great Depression, she made do with whatever resources were available. Let the Joneses worry about themselves, thank you; she never tried keeping up. Her beauty radiated from deep within, unfettered by such material nonsense as designer dresses or luxury cars.

She lived a life of love and learning. Of genuine interest in, and concern for, other people. Of travel to new places and meeting new faces and greeting each one as an old friend.

Maw was the human embodiment of the term "Tennessee volunteer," cheerfully toiling behind the scenes at whatever task was required. Girl Scouts, Cub Scouts, PTA, church, civic association—it didn't matter. She was there. Always. Working.

She adored children, her own and anyone else's. They became her calling. During an era when most women didn't even attend college, she earned undergraduate and graduate degrees, specializing in the development and creativity of young minds.

She taught university classes at one point in her long career. But her most rewarding vocational years were the ones spent setting up and running kindergarten programs. She helped implement Head Start, putting untold thousands of boys and girls from low-income families on the path to learning.

A massive stroke ended this marvelous story at ninety years. We buried her ashes atop the grave of our father, the love of her life, from whom she was widowed much too young. She left us a treasure chest of laughter and sweet memories—and purple iris that still sway in the breeze every spring.

There's another reason to visit the bleak side of life in print: It gives you the rare opportunity to spark positive change. In September 2010, it was my happy honor to complete the full circle of a saga that began as a chance meeting between two former U.S. Marines, Greg Walls and Tommy Rhoades.

I first chronicled their story in January 2008, shortly after Rhoades, a Knoxville truck driver, had backed his eighteen-wheeler into the loading dock of an auto parts factory in Kankakee, Illinois, and prepared to drop off his freight. In the process, he exchanged a casual nod and howdy with the trucker in the adjacent bay.

As Rhoades related to me: "That guy looked at me and said, 'I know you.' I told him, 'No, I don't think so.'"

It could have ended then and there, for the other trucker had to move his rig and check in with headquarters. But before walking away, he told Rhoades, "Stick around here for a little while. I want to talk to you."

Intrigued, Rhoades cooled his heels. A few minutes later, the other driver approached, stuck out his hand, and asked, "Were you ever in the Marines?"

Naturally, Rhoades responded, "Semper fi."

The quizzing went on: Were you ever stationed on the U.S.S. Guam? In Spain? Do you remember the helicopter crash?

By that time, cold chills were running up and down both men's spines. Seconds later, they were hugging and back-patting.

"We did everything but cry," Walls, the second driver, told me from his home outside Chicago. "Tell you the truth: When I finally got back in my cab, I shed me some tears."

Verily, the Lord works in mysterious ways. That's the only answer these men have for running into each other at a loading dock in Illinois, three decades after they participated in a harrowing rescue on the other side of the globe.

It was February 1978. Walls and Rhoades, who didn't even know each other at the time, were shipmates on the Guam. They were onshore, taking part in maneuvers, when the chopper crashed just downhill from them.

"Couldn't have been more than one hundred yards away," said Rhoades. "Something happened to the back prop. It went around in four or five circles, then fell. I ran down there to help. This other guy had just run up, too. He pulled back a big piece of metal and shoved me through a hole into the helicopter."

That "other guy" was Greg Walls. But this was no time to exchange pleasantries, for the wreckage could explode at any second. Covered in blood, sweat, aviation fuel, and hydraulic fluid, the two Marines pulled fifteen bodies, living and dead, from the smoldering wreckage. Nine ultimately survived.

Until their chance encounter at the auto parts loading dock, neither man had seen the other since. As it turned out, Rhoades had been awarded the Navy-Marine Medal shortly after the incident. Similar paperwork was initiated for Walls, but it never was completed.

After my first column ran, however, the American Legion began its own probe of the case and took it to the Department of Veterans Affairs. Marc McCabe, a service officer for the legion, handled the investigation.

"(Walls) had applied for benefits, but nobody at the VA ever believed him," said McCabe, who traveled to Washington, D.C., and Quantico, Virginia, and pored over volumes of paper files to document the evidence.

"This case became personal for me," added McCabe, himself a former Marine and three-tour combat veteran. "(Walls) served his country proudly and was wounded saving those lives. A great injustice was done to him all these years."

Not only did Walls ultimately receive the U.S. Navy and Marine Corps Medal, the highest peacetime award for heroism, he also found himself in line for back pay and medical compensation from the Marine Corps. Semper fi, indeed.

When you get to tell poignant tales like that, you sure don't need a silly dose of humor to carry the load.

THE CHICKEN HOUSE

First comes the news of illness in a dear friend. Then the shock of terminal diagnosis. Then the misery of watching him suffer and weaken by the day. Then the numbing grief of his death. And then, as time softens the pain and gilds the memories, comes the bittersweet job of combing through the detritus.

Which is why I am standing in the Chicken House, trying to make order out of Jody McKenry's waterfowl decoys.

Jody and I grew up together. We hunted and fished together. After cancer took his life in December 2008, I didn't know if I'd be able to bear walking through the doors of the Chicken House ever again.

The Chicken House is aptly named, for it once was a poultry rearing facility. That was eons ago—before the McKenry family, icons in the Knoxville chicken-and-egg business, moved out of south Knoxville and migrated "far away" to the banks of Fort Loudoun Lake in extreme west Knox County.

For more than forty years, the Chicken House served as storage central for boats, motors, trailers, blinds, decoys, rods, reels, rope, nets, kennels, cushions, batteries, paddles, push poles, hip boots, tackle boxes, and other trappings of McKenry & Friends who recreated on the water.

It was the gathering ground for excited men and eager dogs in the pre-dawn hours of blustery December and January mornings. It was headquarters for bird-plucking, call-tuning, gun-cleaning, and missed-shot postmortems at dark-thirty.

And now it's where a final inventory is taking place.

This is not collectible material. None of it. You won't find anything on any shelf cataloged by Sotheby's. Instead, what we have here is plain, honest, working stuff. The real McCoys—or McKenrys, as the case may more accurately be.

These fake ducks and geese are pocked by shot holes and stained with mud. A missing head here, a busted keel there. Some with anchors, some without. Paint more or less true to species. Monetarily, we're talking small numbers. I've already done enough online checking to get a handle on the meager prices commanded by used, mass-produced gear like this.

Which is fine.

A young hunter friend of the family has already approached Betsy McKenry about buying the entire lot of her husband's decoys to supplement his own spread. She's happy about that. She'll get a fair price. He'll get a bargain. Best of all, these old warriors will ride the waves once more.

But as I stand here, sorting Carry-Lite mallards from Victor black ducks, Plasti-Duk and Herter's bluebills from Flambeau pintails, wigeons, and gadwalls, my mind is far removed from the present . . .

It's half a lifetime ago, and I'm with "Jode" (rhymes with "toad") in Prater Flats on Fort Loudoun. Or Point Two and Muddy Creek on Douglas. Or Stump Island and Mossy Creek on Cherokee. Or Nickajack, Guntersville, Tellico, Watts Bar, Sweetwater Creek, farm ponds too numerous to recollect, plus the shallow prairie wetlands of Iowa and Nebraska.

The wind is howling. Pellets of sleet mix with snowflakes. We are alternately cussing frozen anchor strings and wayward Labrador retrievers. The gray eastern skyline is attempting to redden. A symphony of wings plays overhead. We climb into the blind, grabbing Commander calls, sloshing Thermos coffee, feeding three-inch fours into Remington pump guns, having the time of our lives . . . and then I blink and it's a sweltering August afternoon and I'm alone, staring at a mountain of dusty decoys.

In a few days, these old birds will fetch a couple of bucks apiece. But two hundred grand wouldn't touch the memories that go with them.

MAYBE IN ONE MORE CENTURY

Time for a history quiz. Choose which event occurred in 1908:

1. The Ford Model T was introduced.
2. Mother's Day was celebrated for the first time.
3. Robert Baden-Powell launched the Boy Scout movement.
4. A paper mill in Canton, North Carolina, began operations on the Pigeon River, sending brown, smelly, foamy, poisonous effluent into East Tennessee.
5. All of the above.

Those selecting Number Five get a gold star. Yes, every one of those significant events was birthed in 1908. And every one lives on, in one form or another, to this day.

Ford Motors, Mother's Day, and the Boy Scouts enjoy more of an international following than the pesky problem of putrid water in the Pigeon. But for those of us living below the paper mill's discharge pipe, this event trumps all others.

Thank heavens, the river isn't as filthy as it used to be. Slowly, and with exceeding amounts of regulatory arm-twisting, cleanup efforts began in the late 1960s and early 1970s. This, mind you, after more than a half-century of profit-taking by the mill's owners and despite the environmental havoc being wreaked downstream.

At every step along the way, mill operators and citizens of Canton cried tears of ruin and destruction: "No way can we clean up and stay in business!" To hear them talk, the western side of North Carolina would shut down faster than Interstate 40 after a rockslide.

I hold in my hands the *News Sentinel*'s Pigeon River file. Yes, hands, as in plural, because this thing is as big around as a country ham—and it only contains printed information up until the early 1990s. After that, everything we've published about the Pigeon has been archived electronically.

Included in these tattered pages, I found some choice words from two of the *News Sentinel*'s legendary columnists:

"I'll hold my nose and not my breath till the river runs clean again."—Wilma Dykeman, February 24, 1985.

". . . Don't get your hopes too high . . . We've lived with their dirty water long enough."—Carson Brewer, January 13, 1985.

Wilma and Carson were commenting on then-new environmental screws being tightened on the mill. A quarter-century later, the screws are being tightened again, as well they should. Even though the Pigeon shows promise of its pre-1908 self, the bilge churning out of Canton is a far cry from the fresh water flowing into the mill.

The Environmental Protection Agency has ordered stronger regulations aimed at addressing this mess even further. Either you fix it, EPA told North Carolina regulators, or we will.

Predictably, Tar Heel officials cried ruin and destruction.

"Technologically, it's possible," Sergei Chernikov of the North Carolina Division of Water Quality responded to an Associated Press inquiry. "Anything is possible, but the cost would be astronomical. It is not feasible."

Wow. You'd think *some*time, North Carolina would finally grasp the notion that folks over here are sick and tired of being on the receiving end of all that foul water. But after more than a century, I, like Wilma Dykeman, am not holding my breath.

Just my nose.

IT'S A CLEAR CUT ISSUE

If I might offer a bit of unsolicited but heartfelt advice to my Christian brothers and sisters in Sevier County and elsewhere: If you want to pray, then pray, for Pete's sake. Pray, as the Good Book says, without ceasing.

Pray from dawn's first light until long after the sun has set. Pray before meals, after meals, between bites. Pray at school, at work, while texting, when standing in line at the grocery store. Pray on the lake or at the bowling alley. Pray while washing the dishes or mowing the lawn.

Silent prayer is best. In fact, that's what Jesus recommended in Matthew 6:6. Audible prayer has certain limitations, not the least of which are noise ordinances that apply at golf tournaments, libraries, and other venues.

Your friends can pray with you, too. He, she, and thee are free to join hands and offer up all the prayers your collective lips can handle.

Pray, children, pray! It is your right, and no court in the land will stop you.

Ah, but I do have one caveat about this prayerfesting. So does the law.

Don't ask the government to pray with you or for you. Religion is none of the government's business. The courts have been very clear on this matter.

Recently, more than five hundred people turned out at the Sevier County Courthouse to pray. Fine. More power to them. I support their faith.

But I cannot support the reason they gathered.

These folks showed up to demonstrate against a threatened lawsuit by a group called Americans United for Separation of Church and State. AUSCS, headquartered in Washington, D.C., believes the Sevier County Commission's long-standing habit of starting each meeting with the Lord's Prayer is illegal.

I'm neither a lawyer nor gambler, but I recognize constitutional interpretation is, and always has been, a work in progress. My hunch is AUSCS will win this argument. I don't see how the county's position is defensible.

> **Rex E. Leuze of Lenoir City met Ruth Morris in 1945 while they were decorating for a Valentine's Day banquet. Romance bloomed. They were married for fifty-nine years. Ruth died the day after Valentine's Day in 2008. Rex died the day before Valentine's Day in 2009.**
>
> **Cupid certainly got his arrow's worth with this couple!**

County Mayor Larry Waters didn't start this practice. He says it was in place when he came into office more than thirty years ago. Again, fine. But that doesn't mean it's legal. It simply means nobody has called the county's hand until now.

A similar argument was made in December 2009, in Blount County, when a private citizen objected to a government-sponsored program that included the reading of the Christmas story from the Bible. The general sentiment was, "But we've always done it this way."

Perhaps. But, just as with the Lord's Prayer in Sevier County, that doesn't mean the practice hadn't been illegal all this time. Thus, the city of Maryville—

wisely, in my opinion—opted out of the program. If you will recall, another private citizen stood up on the night of the Maryville event and read from the Bible.

Excellent. If everyday Janes and Joes want to read the Christmas story in public or pray in public or express other manifestations of their religious beliefs in public, wonderful. The problem comes when it is sanctioned by a government body.

Why is this so hard to understand?

TRUE GRIT, COUNTRY STYLE

It was fitting that Kenny Carey's coffin at Smith Funeral bore a Marine Corps emblem, for they were burying a man's man. Here's a guy who packed more into sixty-six years than other mortals could have done in five lifetimes.

Kenny died in March 2009 while battling a brush fire at his home in Greenback, Tennessee. If you read news accounts of the tragedy, you might get the idea he was some ninety-eight-pound weakling, no match for strenuous activity. As the investigating officer noted in his report, Kenny, a heart surgery patient, was ferrying water to the blaze in five-gallon buckets. The exertion apparently took its fatal toll.

I don't doubt it, given the rush of the emergency and the state of his health. But allow me to share a bit more information about a fellow I knew and admired for more than thirty-five years.

I met Kenny in the early 1970s, shortly after I took the outdoor editor's position at the *News Sentinel*. I'd heard he was an ex-Marine who held a corps record for push-ups—1,025 in one session—and I immediately formed the mental impression of a swaggering blowhard.

Which proves how inaccurate mental images can be.

He was a chiseled specimen, all right. But inside that granite exterior happened to be one of the friendliest, genuine, aw-shucks country boys I ever encountered.

In those days, Kenny worked as a woodland lineman for the Aluminum Company of America. It was the perfect environment. No desk or pavement for him. He had just been discharged from the military and was a crack rifle shot. But shortly thereafter, he discovered archery. He, and the sport, would never be the same.

Kenny never did anything halfway. Over the years, he pulled a bow thousands of times. Tens of thousands. Hundreds of thousands. He shot with such intensity that he finally blew out his left elbow and shoulder. So he did what any Marine would do. He switched to his right. Those joints eventually failed him, too. Thus, he switched back to his left side, which by then had been surgically repaired.

This man suffered so many physical ailments they should name a hospital wing in his memory. Cancer. A stroke. Diabetes. Operations galore.

Yet he never stopped. Never quit his regimen of push-ups and pull-ups. Never quit jogging. Indeed, his daughter, Corky, brought a pair of Kenny's old running shoes to the funeral home. He had logged just shy of five-thousand miles in them.

Kenny's bow-hunting skill was the stuff of legends—so much that an Arizona archery company, Precision Shooting Equipment, sought him out to test its products.

The guy hunted like a wild animal: big game (more than one hundred deer), small game, it didn't matter. Kenny studied his quarry's habits, stalked like a cat, took his shots from mere yards away. I watched him do it any number of times—and marveled at his ability to blend in the background, pausing at just the right time, even in mid-stride if necessary, before narrowing the gap. He was pure poetry in slow motion.

Yet it was a deer Kenny bagged with a truly primitive weapon that I remember the most. A self-taught student of native lore, he learned to "knap" arrowheads out of flint. He once took an old, broken arrowhead—started hundreds of years earlier by an American Indian—reshaped it into a perfect point, attached it to a shaft, and killed a deer with it.

As he casually told me later, "Aw, I just finished the job that Indian started."

And I'd like to think these two old warriors are now swapping stories in their happy hunting ground.

A CLASH BETWEEN CULTURES

CROW AGENCY, Montana—At strategic locations in the Little Bighorn Battlefield National Monument, the National Park Service has posted small signs telling visitors they are walking sacred ground.

Given the potential for boorish behavior by Tom and Tammy Tourist, perhaps these reminders are necessary. But if someone truly needs etiquette lessons at the scene of historic carnage, a sign isn't enough. A dope-slap, maybe.

This sweeping grassland vista is more than the site of a military confrontation, fought to its visceral finish on June 25-26, 1876. Here, the U.S. Seventh Cavalry suffered some 260 dead, including its commander, Lieutenant Colonel George Armstrong Custer. Some were scalped, some disemboweled. Fatalities among Lakota, Cheyenne, and Arapaho warriors were believed to be 100 or fewer.

More significantly, this marks the spot where two radically different social cultures collided. Here is where the Northern Plains Indians won the battle but lost the war.

In truth, they—along with their brothers and sisters to the east—had been losing it for centuries. Aided and abetted by politicians who would sign a treaty one year and ignore it the next, settlers ceaselessly gobbled native territory. Neither side understood the complex lifestyle of the other. Ultimately, might morphed into right. And the beat goes on.

Belatedly, the federal government has acknowledged this tract signifies more than the culmination of us versus them. Even though designated a national cemetery in 1879, with a Seventh Cavalry obelisk erected on Last Stand Hill in 1881, it wasn't until 1991 that the name of this national monument was officially changed from "Custer" to "Little Bighorn" and a memorial to Indian participants was commissioned.

Today, the circular Indian memorial and the marble obelisk sit approximately 350 feet from each another. Behind fences, there is a profusion of markers denoting where Custer and the soldiers under his immediate command fell. Nearby are markers where fighters from both sides were known to have met their fate. And as with any killing field, surely the bones of many more unknown lie scattered, buried, lost to time.

It is a stunningly beautiful spring afternoon as I stand on this lonely hill, gazing southwest into the valley of the Little Bighorn River where approximately 7,000 Indians had been camped. Closer flows the river itself, across which Sitting Bull's warriors attacked.

Quiet envelops the land. The only sound that carries in the gentle prairie breeze is the lilting, melodious call of a western meadowlark. Nonetheless, I attempt—with utter failure, of course—to imagine the maddening din, the choking dust, the broiling heat, and the unbridled terror on both sides during those two days of savagery so long ago.

I need no reminder to remain reverent.

LOVE AND LETTING GO

It took Bill Alexander two years and two hikes to scatter the ashes of his beloved wife in Great Smoky Mountains National Park. If you can read his story with dry eyes, I trust someone will summon the coroner. Because you've crossed o'er the river yourself.

On May 23, 2006, less than a month shy of their thirty-fifth wedding anniversary, Mary Frances Bales Alexander died peacefully in her husband's arms as he recited the Twenty-third Psalm. She had bravely fought leukemia for six months.

"One of Mary's last requests was to have her ashes spread on a hill with a pretty view," said Bill, a retired environmental specialist with Oak Ridge National Laboratory. "I thought about it for a long, long time. We'd always enjoyed the Smokies, especially Cades Cove. I finally decided Gregory Bald offered the right mix of scenery and emotions for me."

Before you ask, the answer is yes; you can legally scatter ashes in a national park. You just need to get a permit first—and that's a requirement Bill almost sidestepped. Some background:

In addition to his professional work as a plant and soil scientist, Bill is a serious student of Southern Appalachian music, crafts, poetry, and folklore. He's the region's foremost authority on berry baskets made from tree bark. One of his friends, the singer-songwriter-biologist Jay Clark, was going to be conducting chestnut research in the Smokies during September 2008. The two conferred and planned to share a campsite atop Gregory Bald.

"I decided that would be the time to take Mary's ashes up the mountain," he said. "Just before I left Knoxville, I checked the regulations online and saw I needed a permit. I thought, 'Well, shucks; I'll scatter the ashes first and get a permit later.'"

He changed his mind when he saw a National Park Service vehicle parked at the trailhead.

"I said to myself: 'No, I'm gonna do this by the book. I'll take Mary's ashes up the mountain and back down for now, then get me a permit and come back later.'"

Bill was using his backpack, stuffed with spare clothing, for a pillow. It turned cold that night. During the wee hours, he put on the extra clothes. When he awoke, his head was resting on a pack that now contained only one item.

The small cardboard box filled with Mary's ashes.

"There she was, comforting me," he said. "One more night."

A week later, permit in hand, Bill made a lone trek to the bald. He poured himself a stiff bourbon. He ate Beanee Weenees and powdered doughnuts like he and Mary used to share on their hikes. Then released her cremains "just like Mary used to sow seeds. The wind caught some of the finer ashes, and they wafted off into infinity. It was a powerful moment, and I shed some tears. But there was also joy in knowing I had completed her final request and released her."

That's when these words formed in his head:

> On the way up to Gregory Bald, the load was heavy, Early
> Times, ashes and all. Her last request, my last to do, spread
> her ashes on a hill with a pretty view. The deed is done, al-
> ways be, with earth, wind, and sky, she is free.

A "TERRIBLY WRONG" MISTAKE

Perhaps Robert McNamara has finally found peace, along with the soldiers who
went before him.

The former secretary of defense, who died in 2009 at age ninety-three,
achieved great success in many facets of his busy life. But he will be remembered
by most in my generation as the architect of America's involvement in the hell-
hole of Vietnam.

It was a role he later admitted was a terrible mistake.

Hindsight is forever crystal clear. In McNamara's case, however, the clarity
is more defined. He recognized the Vietnam War for the debacle it was, yet refused to stop this waste of life and property.

In his 1995 mea culpa, *In Retrospect: The Tragedy and Lessons of Vietnam,*
McNamara blamed himself, President Lyndon Johnson, and other government
leaders for escalating and continuing the war that killed 58,000 American troops
and unknown hundreds of thousands of Vietnamese military and civilians.

I give the man credit for true confessions. Unfortunately, they came too late,
long after he could have helped change the course of world history.

For better or for worse, politicians are remembered for their sound bites.

Franklin D. Roosevelt's "nothing to fear but fear itself" and Ronald Reagan's
"Mister Gorbachev, tear down this wall!" will majestically reverberate through
the halls of freedom just as Richard Nixon's "I am not a crook!," Bill Clinton's "I
did not have sex with that woman," and George W. Bush's, "Brownie, you're doing a heck of a job" will be lampooned.

In McNamara's case, it wasn't so much his confession of "we were wrong;
terribly wrong" that will linger, but his 1962 assessment of the Vietnam strategy:
"Every quantitative measurement we have shows we're winning this war."

That was the problem. Vietnam was a guerilla war, not subject to quantitative measurement. And McNamara, the analytical, technological whiz kid who
viewed life as an orderly set of statistics, couldn't grasp this reality.

Vietnam became "McNamara's war." He couldn't, or wouldn't, convince
President Johnson otherwise. Makes one wonder if, three decades from now, an
architect of the wars in Iraq and Afghanistan will make a similar revelation.

Among his legions of critics was the late David Halberstam, who claimed in his book, *The Best and the Brightest,* that McNamara "did not serve himself or his country well. He was, there is no kinder or gentler word for it, a fool."

What a tragic legacy for a man who, by all other standards, got incredibly high marks for business success, personal achievements, and humanitarian outreach. Professor at Harvard Business School. First president of Ford Motor Company who wasn't a descendant of Henry Ford. President of the World Bank (after leaving the Pentagon), where he dramatically increased lending to impoverished countries. And unlike nearly everyone else in his position, cost himself untold millions of dollars by eschewing the speaking circuit after his days in the limelight ended.

Yet on the eve of his book's debut, McNamara broke down in tears on ABC News, acknowledging his "sense of grief and failure is strong."

How oh-so-very sad—for this man and his country alike.

RYO NOW, RIP LATER

Let the record show that the lungs of your obedient servant, once tarred by two packs of cigarettes daily, haven't been assaulted by The Evil Weed since 1979. Let the record further show that the owner of these lungs has no desire whatsoever to resume such a smelly, insane, unhealthy, and expensive habit until the ice covering hell is at least seven feet thick.

However—if I did ever take complete leave of my senses and fall off the wagon, I believe I'd smoke those roll-your-own cigarettes that are all the rage in tobacco shops right now.

You don't have to visit a specialty tobacconist to understand the impact of the roll-your-own (RYO) movement. Many area grocery stores, service stations, and delis are devoting shelf space to paper tubes and sacks of shredded tobacco.

Yes, cigarette papers have been available for decades. But you know and I know and everybody from the FBI to the Podunk County sheriff knows 99 percent of these products have been used for marijuana, not tobacco.

No more. Not only are individual papers, simple rolling machines, and bagged tobacco becoming big business, dozens of RYO "filling stations"—where customers can use the store's fancy equipment to crank out a carton or more—have opened across the land.

According to a recent story in the *Nashville Tennessean,* approximately fifteen hundred of these stations have sprung up nationwide, thirty of them in Tennessee, in recent years. By crafting their own, either one at a time or twenty to twenty-five per minute, smokers have a wider variety of tobacco blends to choose from. Plus, they save a bundle—at least half the cost of store-bought "ready rolls."

Janes and Joes patient enough to churn out single smokes also have a variety of small, inexpensive machines at their disposal. I checked a shop near the *News Sentinel* a few days ago and was amazed at how these things had made such a comeback.

When I worked for the U.S. Forest Service over four decades ago, nearly everybody in the woods, including His Stupidness, carried one of these "mousetrap" gizmos in his jeans pocket. You sprinkled tobacco on one side, licked the gummed edge of a paper, laid it down, and snapped the cover shut. Presto! Out popped a fresh one.

Quite a novelty for such a dangerous undertaking.

HIGH TIME TO JUST SAY "ENOUGH!"

A few months ago, my wife opened an email from one of her friends, glanced briefly at the contents, and said to herself, "Enough!"

Mary Ann doesn't recall the precise wording of the message, just that it was typical of the half-baked, mean-spirited, unresearched, sliver-of-truth, veiled-attempt-at-humor screed some people delight in forwarding to everyone in their address list—if, for no other reason, than it was forwarded-forwarded-forwarded-forwarded to them.

But instead of spiking it and moving on with her work, Mary Ann sent a reply.

"You and I both know there's no way this can be true," she wrote. "If you want to debate this or any other issue with facts, fine. Otherwise, please quit mindlessly repeating this nonsense."

Since that day, Mary Ann has sent the same message to several other email friends.

The result?

Some apparently have removed her name from their address list, for she has heard nothing more from them. Others, however, have taken it to heart.

"You're right," one person wrote back. "I'd never given this a thought. It's just so easy to forward a message these days."

Score one for civility.

Perhaps this is the way to ratchet-down the intense level of bickering that seems to have swept over this country. No need for new laws or massive government regulations. Just one calm voice at a time saying, "Enough!"

Ever since the tragic shooting of several people, including U.S. Representative Gabrielle Giffords, in Arizona, finger-pointing, name-calling, and blame-fixing have gone through the roof.

Is a 24/7/365 diet of bile and spleen responsible for causing a gunman to open fire at a political gathering, killing six people and wounding more than a dozen others? Heaven only knows. It's doubtful there's any one precise reason behind this attack.

Those on the left have been quick to accuse Sarah Palin, the former Alaska governor and 2008 vice-presidential candidate, of fomenting in-your-face ideology by using crosshairs to identify political opponents in her ads. Just as quickly, those on the right point out that none other than the Democratic National Committee used bull's-eyes on likely swing states during the 2004 presidential campaign. Thus, the shouting intensifies.

It's hard to utter the word "good" in the context of this awful event. But if anything positive can emerge, perhaps it's that decency will return to the national forum. We can only hope.

If such a miracle does occur, don't expect it to be quick or dramatic. It's going to have to come from the heart, one person at a time. One voice saying, "Enough!"

This isn't a radical concept. Certainly not new. The gist of it has been attributed to an Italian priest from the thirteenth century, Saint Francis of Assisi. The verse goes, in part:

> *Where there is hatred, let me sow love;*
> *Where there is injury, pardon;*
> *Where there is doubt, faith.*
> *Where there is despair, hope;*
> *Where there is darkness, light;*
> *Where there is sadness, joy.*

If I might be so bold as to add an East Tennessee corollary: "Where there is hollerin', a little bit of peace and quiet."

RICHER THAN WE REALIZE

Go gaze into a mirror, especially if it irks your social conscience that the rich keep getting richer and the poor keep getting poorer. You will notice that at least one of those despicable, heartless, money-grubbing pigs looks quite like someone you've known all your life.

That's the humbling feeling you'll experience after visiting the website globalrichlist.com.

Global Rich List is a London-based outfit that calculates and compares incomes based on statistics from the World Bank Development Research Group.

Its findings are sobering.

No matter what part of Knoxville you live in, no matter what type of car you drive, no matter what your income happens to be, no matter the shape of your retirement account, you're among the wealthiest in the world.

Do you make $35,000 per year? According to Global Rich List, that puts you in the top 4.62 percent of people worldwide.

At $40,000, the percentage shrinks to the top 3.17. Those earning $50,000 are in the top 0.98 percentile. For $60,000, the membership is even more elite: the top 0.91 percent. With a $100,000 income, you're among the top 0.66 percent wealthiest humans on earth at this very minute. And at $200,000, your circle comprises a tiny 0.01 percent.

What about the poorer side of this coin?

The U.S. Census Bureau says a four-person family with a household income of $20,614 is officially classified as living in poverty. Yet according to Global Rich List, such dire financial straits still ranks in the top 11 percent on a worldwide basis.

It's easy to criticize the mega-rich, particularly those who take advantage of the system.

In 2007, the *News Sentinel* carried results of a Scripps Howard investigation into fifty American billionaires who received millions of dollars in payouts from a government program designed to help poor, struggling farmers. These people—including banker David Rockefeller Sr., five members of the Sam Walton (Walmart) family, hotel czar William Barron Hilton, and Microsoft cofounder Paul Allen—neither till the soil nor struggle to make ends meet.

Neither do seven U.S. senators—Jon Tester, Democrat-Montana; Charles Grassley, Republican-Iowa; Sam Brownback, Republican-Kansas; Gordon Smith, Republican-Oregon; Richard Lugar, Republican-Indiana; Blanche Lincoln, Democrat-Arkansas; and Max Baucus, Democrat-Montana—who pocketed a total of $700,000 over ten years under the same program.

All of these payments were completely legal, albeit ethically questionable.

Please understand: I don't mean to insult the truly poor with disingenuous prattle about how need builds character, or if they simply work harder they'll achieve the Great American Dream. At the same time, I readily acknowledge that a rich and abundant life involves more than material possessions.

But it is worth noting that the vast majority of us *are* the Joneses, wealthier by far than any people who ever lived on the face of this planet.

A WAR SONG UNSTAINED BY BLOOD

I'm thinking of an oh-so-sad tune that has been played at countless funerals, memorials, and other somber services. You've probably heard the piece I have in mind. If so, I'll bet you ask yourself two questions the moment it opens with a mournful fiddle solo:

Isn't this from the 1860s? Does it have a title?

No and yes.

This isn't a Civil War number, per se. Although it has come to symbolize the bloody era pitting North versus South and family versus family, it wasn't composed until more than a century after Robert E. Lee surrendered to Ulysses S. Grant.

Its name is "Ashokan Farewell." And if you tear up upon hearing it, don't feel alone. Jay Ungar says about 30 percent of people do. Himself included.

"It was my own little secret for months," Ungar told me via phone from his home in the Catskill Mountains of New York. "I kept wondering, 'What's going on with me?' when I played it and cried."

Ungar has been a professional musician all his adult life (even though he holds a degree in anthropology). He and his wife, Molly Mason, tour throughout the United States and abroad. For well over than three decades, they have operated a summer fiddle-and-dance camp near an upstate community named Ashokan.

At the end of the 1982 season, Ungar recalled, he was feeling blue about "the transition from a secluded mountain camp back to traffic and telephones." He picked up his fiddle and began experimenting—first playing into a recorder, then listening, rewriting, changing, tweaking. Ninety minutes later, "Ashokan Farewell" was born.

A year would pass before the number found its way onto an album released by his band, Fiddle Fever. Except for a twist of fate, that's likely where it would have remained forever.

Enter legendary filmmaker Ken Burns, who was working on what would become a 1990 PBS blockbuster, "The Civil War." Burns heard the song and immediately was smitten. He not only used it as the theme for his documentary but wove it into the script twenty-five times. "Ashokan Farewell" plays a total of fifty-nine minutes and thirty-three seconds in the eleven-hour series. It's the only music in the entire production that doesn't date to the Civil War period.

In 2011, to mark the 150th anniversary of the start of that war, PBS rebroadcast Burns's award-winning series. With that in mind, I telephoned Ungar to see if there had been a resurgence of interest in the song—which did for his career,

Alan Williams, who lives on a houseboat at Fort Loudoun Marina, recently saw vivid proof of the adage, "When your number is up, there's no way to change it."

Walking off his boat, he noticed a large willow fly fighting for its life in a spider web. Doing his good deed for the day, Alan gently freed the insect and tossed it into the air. No doubt weary from its period of captivity, the willow fly fell to the water—whereupon it was immediately attacked by a small bass. But the fish missed it mark, and the insect was catapulted back into the air. Even then, its freedom was short-lived: A barn swallow, perched nearby on the mast of a sailboat, swooped down and caught the willow fly for a quick breakfast.

As the old saying goes, live for the moment—however fleeting it may be.

not to mention his bank account, what "Rocky Top" did for Felice and Boudleaux Bryant's.

"Actually, it never has let up," he replied. "I constantly get requests from people who want to use it. Plus, folks are always submitting lyrics they have written."

What?! Put words to this acoustic masterpiece?

"Well, I certainly don't intend to," he said with a chuckle. "But some day the right words might come along. After all, the tune for what we know as 'Oh, Danny Boy' was around for a couple of hundred years before somebody put words to it."

I wish armchair warriors everywhere would keep two things in mind any time there is talk of battle: Grainy photos of amputated limbs from the Ken Burns series and the haunting refrains of "Ashokan Farewell."

Perhaps then they wouldn't be so quick to pull the trigger.

HONOR IN THE FACE OF TRAGEDY

Among the heart-rending chronicles of death and destruction from Japan, one story was missing. And it's a sobering lesson for all of humanity. Based on everything I read, there seems to have been no looting after the country was ripped by earthquake and tsunami.

Contrast that to the scenes in New Orleans after Hurricane Katrina—or after any disaster in any other part of the "civilized" world. Hardly does the smoke clear before gangs begin ransacking what's left.

We're not talking about hungry, thirsty survivors scavenging necessary food and drink for themselves and their families. We're talking about the wholesale theft of other people's property, often by gun-toting mobs, simply because it's available.

I'm not naive enough to think no looting whatsoever has occurred in Japan. Surely a few took advantage of this horrible situation. But as a societal whole, the Japanese are the most honest people I've ever met.

In 1991, I spent eleven days in Japan as a chaperone for four high-school students. It was part of a cultural exchange program sponsored by Panasonic. One of the columns I wrote from that experience underscored how trustworthy these people are.

I'll never forget one particular sidewalk scene in downtown Osaka: In the midst of this bustling metropolis was a parking area for bicycles ridden to and from work by area residents. Not a few bikes, either. It was hundreds of them. Row after row. And there wasn't a padlock or chain in sight.

How long do you suppose an unlocked bicycle would stay put on a street in Knoxville? Or any other city in this country?

The honesty I witnessed on that trip went beyond "thou shalt not steal." I saw, firsthand, how total strangers looked out for each other.

One day, our guide inadvertently left his briefcase at one stop. It was an hour or two after the fact before he realized his mistake. Yes, he was worried. Not to mention embarrassed by the gaffe. While not containing vital materials like passports and money, the briefcase did hold important notes and travel plans. But thanks to those travel plans, everything was returned to our party by nightfall.

Seems someone had found the briefcase, looked inside for identification, read over the itinerary for details, and delivered the intact parcel to our hotel. Verily, you could have knocked me over with a feather. In the United States, that briefcase would have been emptied and tossed aside as soon as it was discovered.

I'm not the only visitor to Japan who has experienced this phenomenon.

"When my wife and I were there, we noticed that women would leave their purses open and on top of the table at a restaurant and go to the restroom with no thought that someone might steal from them," Bill Jones of Concord told me via email. "People in Japan live in an incredible culture of honesty and integrity."

Because their country is prone to earthquakes, the Japanese have led the way in developing methods of construction designed to withstand massive shocks. Now they're showing us how to survive with dignity and honor in the aftermath of unspeakable horror.

A WRONG HAS BEEN RIGHTED

In the category of "Most Explosive and Controversial Political Fight from 2010 That Will Now Fizzle into a Tame Non-event," my nomination is the repeal of "Don't Ask, Don't Tell" in the U.S. military.

Poof. Gone. This bogeyman has been exposed for the fraud he is. This Wizard of Oz has been revealed as nothing more than an ordinary man behind the curtain. Dark clouds of End Times do not loom on the horizon. It is time to move forward and leave a sad chapter of injustice in the dust of American history. Next order of business, please.

I'm not enough of a Pollyanna to believe armed forces will immediately adopt, let alone embrace, this directive like it was no more radical than switching brands of coffee for the mess hall. Surely there will be bumps and missteps along the way. Just as occurred in the early days of desegregation, the military will drag its feet initially. More than a few long-serving men and women will resign in protest.

None of which is surprising. In both the public and private sectors, social change tends to come slowly, painfully. But it does come.

Thanks to a forward-thinking majority in Congress and a president who made it one of his goals, the first steps toward righting this historic wrong are now securely in place.

There were good people on both sides of this heated debate. Passionate, knowledgeable, loyal people. In my humble opinion, however, those who clung to the old way of doing business were wrong.

Many of the arguments against allowing homosexuals to serve openly in the military were the same ones trotted out when racial mixing of troops was proposed.

"They" won't fight or follow the chain of command. "Their" presence will be disruptive. "We" cannot work with "them."

Sorry. Heard it all before. But it simply isn't so.

You don't have to agree. Indeed, you are free to insist you'd never live, recreate, fraternize, attend church, work, ad infinitum, with "them."

Guess what? You already do. And you have been all along, regardless of whether you realize or choose to acknowledge it.

I have no statistics to back up this claim—just six-plus decades of observing human nature—but I'll guarantee gay GIs have been fighting bravely alongside their straight comrades lo these many years. And will continue to do so in the future. Except now, they can serve their country without being forced to live a lie.

Like many in my generation, I grew up thinking homosexuality was a frailty of the depraved. There was something wrong with "them." This odd "lifestyle" was something "they" selected.

Life taught me different. If you're perceptive, it taught you the same thing.

Make no mistake: Sexual misconduct, gay or straight, should never be condoned—in the military or anywhere else—particularly when juveniles or subordinates are involved. But private behavior between consenting adults is nobody's business but theirs.

There are no atheists in foxholes, the old saying goes. I submit there are no homophobes, either.

SANTA'S SAD STORIES

Don't let the "ho-ho-ho" fool you. Sometimes Santa Claus is anything but a jolly old elf. In fact, there are moments when his eyes well with tears—and it sure isn't from pipe smoke.

"I was visiting an oncology unit," said Knoxvillian Jeff Peterson, who spent fourteen winters portraying Santa at malls and shopping centers across America. "One of the patients was a young mother about thirty years old. She was desperately ill but had told the nurses she wanted to be woken up if she was asleep when Santa came around.

"I gently rang my sleigh bells, and she popped up immediately. She was so excited to see Santa. I gave her some presents for her two little boys and visited with her a while. She seemed truly happy."

Peterson paused to clear his throat and collect his composure.

"She died two hours later. I was probably the last human image she ever saw."

Then there was a seven-year-old boy in Kansas City who "looked at me with the biggest brown eyes you ever saw and asked for only one present: 'I want my daddy to adopt me.'

"That one sure came out of the blue," Peterson related. "All I could say was, 'I'll see what I can do.'"

The lad's mother was nearby but hadn't heard her son's wish. Santa motioned her over, whispered into her ear, "and she cried into my fur like a baby."

Turns out the woman was divorced, had recently remarried "and this proved to her how much her little boy loved his new daddy. I would love to have been a fly on the wall in their house that Christmas morning!"

Even though he's commonly regarded as the king of largesse, Santa knows ridiculousness when he sees it: "I had one little girl ask for a hundred-dollar bill, two Super Bowl tickets, a BMW (full-sized car!), and a DVD player. I glanced at her dad and said, 'Oh, that sure seems like a lot.' Her dad shot back, 'She gets whatever she wants.'"

Again Peterson paused. He shook his head slowly: "I wonder if that little girl's not on drugs today."

Peterson has forsaken traditional mall and department store appearances. With good reason. During all those years of holiday travel, he logged tens of thousands of miles and listened to the wishes of (by actual count) 263,512 youngsters. Still, he sits for portraits during the Christmas season.

Peterson can still make children laugh with cheerful patter. He knows just the right way to respond to youthful requests, gently conveying "message received, but I can't promise anything." What's more, Peterson's stories about some of his unplanned, unexpected, bawdy experiences will have adults rolling on the floor—like the time a grown, well-dressed-but-drunken holiday well-wisher abruptly exposed herself in front of him and then passed out, falling smack dab into his lap. (Try explaining *that* to Mrs. Claus!)

But be forewarned: He's also got enough tearful tales to flood the Tennessee River.

HOPE IN THE MIDST OF HORROR

On April 5, 1968, despair and anger gripped this country. Late in the day before, Dr. Martin Luther King Jr. had been gunned down in Memphis, his dream of racial equality reduced to a nightmare.

A tall, bold headline on the front page of that afternoon's *Knoxville News-Sentinel* (before this newspaper began publishing on the morning cycle and dropped its trademark hyphen) spoke volumes: *Manhunt Pressed for King's Killer; Slaying Sparks Violence Across U.S.*

Fortunately, Knoxville was spared the rioting that turned many larger cities into smoldering ruins. But not the sorrow and the pain. In a memorial service that day at Knoxville College, President Robert L. Owens III said King "did more in his thirty-nine years than any other American. He was able to seek justice out of injustice, pluck nonviolence out of violence, and love out of hate."

Yet Owens and George Curry, a Knoxville College student leader, did more than revel in grief. Both of them challenged the audience to build on the foundation laid by the slain civil-rights leader.

"We must not let his words go unheeded," Owens said. "Each of us must make certain that this man has not died in vain."

Added Curry: "We have some unfinished business to look after. In his last speech, Doctor King said, 'Let us move on (and) make America the kind of country it should be.' We bear the burden now, and anything short of continuing Martin Luther King's work will be a betrayal to him."

The same theme was being spoken from political offices, pulpits, and opinion pages, here and across the nation.

President Lyndon Johnson prayed for an end to racial hatred "in our churches, in our homes, in our private hearts."

The Tennessee Diocese of the Episcopal Church called on its clergy to direct their upcoming Palm Sunday messages "to beseech God for grace upon our fractured and distraught state, peace in our time, unity for God's people."

Our newspaper noted in an editorial: "If the murderer was opposed to Doctor King's cause, his act will impel it to prosper more than ever."

Predictable sentiment, yes. Comforting. Challenging. All highly appropriate words in this terrible situation. Still, I wonder—

If you could travel back in time and relive that tragic day, do you think Americans truly believed what they were hearing and reading? Or was the collective sense of hopelessness so strong as to snuff any glimmer of harmony and equality for the future?

On April 5, 1968, could you have convinced anyone that by January 2011, African Americans would be serving as president of the United States and mayor of Knoxville? And that the third Monday in January would be a national holiday in memory of Martin Luther King Jr.?

Happily, we know the answers. They're the same words of eternal truth Henry Wadsworth Longfellow captured in a poem that later would become one of the world's most beloved Christmas carols: "The wrong shall fail, the right prevail."

Even in the worst of times.

WHY DO WE FOUL OUR OWN NEST?

Richard Karakis is an import from the Silicon Valley of California. He works in high-tech corporate training out of his home overlooking Tellico Lake. I assume he does rather well in this enterprise. But if he ever finds the answer to East Tennessee's most mind-numbing question, Karakis can quit the training business and relax by counting his billions.

This is a conundrum that has stumped many a native and newcomer alike down through the ages. To wit: "Why do the very people who recreate in this gorgeous patch of God's country do their damndest to ruin it with their own trash?"

Karakis posed that question to me in an email. Its arrival could not have been more coincidental. You see, exactly one day earlier, I'd been walking the shoreline of Douglas Lake, shaking my head in angry wonder—for the umpteenth time—at the same thing.

It happened like this: I had pulled into the parking lot of a TVA access area to eat my lunch. Something caught my eye on the rocky point below. Trash. A big pile of it. I remember thinking if this turned out to be what I suspected, I would be in favor of public flogging for litterbugs. Sadly, a quick walk from the vehicle proved my assessment correct.

Scattered about were the fresh remnants of a youngster's fishing kit. You've probably seen these things in stores. Maybe even bought one for your kids or grandchildren.

They're relatively inexpensive (this one had a tag for $19.95) and contain a youth-sized rod, reel and line, plus blister packs of hooks, lures, floats, and other accessories. Everything you need to introduce a child to a lifetime of recreational pleasure.

But obviously the dunce who did this teaching omitted one important lesson: Never leave a mess!

The entire packaging had been tossed aside. I spent four or five minutes rounding up the plastic sleeve, cardboard backing, and blister packs, carried them to my truck and brought them home for the trash can and recycling bin.

Arrrgh! Double-arrgh! $#@!

Karakis, his wife, Elaine, and other volunteers from Tellico Village probably said a lot worse than that when they conducted their annual cleanup of the lakeshore. They filled heaven-only-knows how many garbage bags with the usual offal: cans, bottles, cigarette packs, diapers, coils of fishing line, shoes, bait containers, you name it—all thrown aside by boaters, picnickers, campers, and anglers "enjoying" the lake.

"In a strange way, I can understand somebody driving down the road and tossing a bottle out the window," Karakis told me. "But the people who are out on the water? It blows my mind!"

Karakis knows something about outdoor recreation. While living fifteen years in the foothills of the Santa Cruz Mountains, he and his wife often hiked many of the local trails—"and we never saw the kind of crap that's all over the place around here."

Sigh. Welcome to East Tennessee. Slobville, USA.

A TALE OF TWO OLD VETERANS

Remembering two fine men who served honorably during World War II—one on the front lines, one at home:

Army Air Corps Lieutenant Charles Rainwater of Dandridge, Tennessee, was flying a P-40 over the Panamanian Isthmus on April 7, 1943. His six-plane formation ran into a sudden, fierce thunderstorm, forcing Rainwater and the pilots of three other aircraft to eject. He and another pilot hacked their way through jungle wilderness for six days, ultimately traveling forty miles before being rescued. He healed, returned to active duty, ultimately came back to East Tennessee, and enjoyed a successful business and civic career.

But what you don't know is something that occurred much later.

On December 1, 1998, Rainwater, seventy-eight, lay in bed, suffering the final stages of cancer. By then he was in and out of consciousness. Sometimes he recognized visitors, most times not. The last person who came calling was a neighbor and frequent golfing companion. Esther Rainwater is certain her husband was aware of the guest; just not a lot was spoken between them.

But as the man rose to leave, Rainwater did something quite unusual. He snapped a salute.

"In all the years I'd known Charles, I never saw him salute or heard him talk about saluting," Esther said. "I knew right then it was his final act. I broke down and cried. He was gone the next day."

Far removed from Dandridge—in Bourbon County, Kentucky—another old gent from the World War II era crossed the river as well. Unlike Charles Rainwater, however, Richard Hinkle, eighty-three, had never served so much as one day in the military—"and it bothered him until the day he died," recalled his daughter, Pat Sisson of Knoxville.

Two of Hinkle's brothers had been Army vets, one enduring conditions in the Philippines so hellish they triggered nightmares for decades thereafter. But the reason Hinkle was kept stateside had nothing to do with a traditional deferment. Instead, it was because he was blessed with a most unusual talent. He was an expert sheep shearer.

"He could shear one hundred sheep a day," Sisson said proudly. "The military needed the wool for the lining in flight jackets. Many of the farms he visited didn't have electricity, so he had to use hand-crank clippers. My mother used go with him and wind them so he could concentrate on shearing.

"The rest of his life, he used to say, 'I served my country, but no one will ever know.'"

Don't bet on it. Perhaps that's the buddy Charles Rainwater was saluting.

LET KIDS BE KIDS ON HALLOWEEN

Best I remember, I was in the fifth grade. Shortly before Halloween, I heard an appeal for youth volunteers to collect money for the United Nations International Children's Emergency Fund (UNICEF) as they made trick-or-treat rounds.

Sounded good. Based on the life lessons I'd been shown through example by loving parents, I knew folks should take care of each other. Look out for the little guy. Lend a helping hand. Heal the sick. Feed the poor.

So along with my candy bag, I carried a UNICEF jar.

The reception was good at most of the doors I knocked on. My jar was growing heavy with dimes, nickels, and quarters. Then I hit a brick wall.

At one house—I can take you down that particular road and show it to you to this day—the head of the family was happily filling everyone's bags with M&Ms or Tootsie Rolls or Mister Goodbars or whatever his Tooth Rot de Jour happened to be. After the doling was finished, I made my pitch for UNICEF.

I might as well have announced I was going to fling a bucket of herbicide across his lawn.

"The U.N.?!?!" he thundered. "Why, I wouldn't give a penny to that buncha comma'niss! You oughta be ashamed of yourself for doin' their dirty work!"

He ranted for another three or four minutes, spewing bile and spleen on anybody and everybody who might help attempt to alleviate human suffering under the umbrella of the United Nations.

This was my introduction to adult political agendas. Even though I was too young and too polite in that Norman Rockwell era to tell a grownup to shove it where the sun doesn't shine, I walked away thinking, "Mister, you're a jerk. If you don't want to give, just say no. I don't need your sermon."

That thought was renewed years later when I heard he had died. In one brief moment, this guy's radical persuasions had managed to suck the life out of a child's Halloween. I never forgot it.

The same goes on today. Maybe not against UNICEF, per se. But against something, anything, to dampen the excitement. Why do adults persist in ruining a holiday for kids?

If this runs counter to your religious beliefs, my apologies. You are free to raise your own children as you see fit. You are free to believe any doctrine you choose. You are free to quote whatever biblical verse that comes to mind. You are free to equate a *Star Wars* costume with devil worship.

But here's one believing, practicing Christian who doesn't buy it.

For Pete's sake, put a lid on your adult biases for one night. Resist the urge to be upset that somebody is enjoying plain ol' fun. Let kids be kids on Halloween. And have a Hershey bar on me.

SHE WALKED IN THEIR SHOES

Fame, wealth, and an Academy Award notwithstanding, the greatest tribute to actress Patricia Neal can be found on Clinch Avenue in Knoxville, wrapped in bricks, mortar, and human compassion.

It's one thing to know she founded the Patricia Neal Rehabilitation Center after suffering, and fighting back from, a series of strokes in 1965. And it's impressive to hear the center's familiar slogan of "restoring abilities and rebuilding lives." But when you talk to any of the thousands of people who owe their well-being to this institution and the woman behind it, you realize what a genuine legacy she gave to her hometown.

Neal, who enjoyed a long career on Broadway and in Hollywood, died in 2010. But her memory will live on whenever a stroke victim hears this challenge: "I survived it. You can, too."

One of them is Rick Davis, a former Air Force pilot who lives in the Watts Bar Lake community of Ten Mile. In early April 2003, Davis was the picture of health. Retired from the military, he was making a good living in airplane sales. To keep his private pilot's license active, he underwent regular physical examinations.

"Up until then, I'd been fortunate," he said. "The last time I was in the hospital was when I was nine, to have my tonsils removed."

On April 4 of that year, Davis's world turned upside down, the entire left side of his body abruptly imprisoned by a massive stroke.

"The total use of my left arm and leg were gone," Davis recalls. "I couldn't feel hot or cold."

He was admitted to the Neal center, stayed five weeks, took more than a year's worth of out-patient therapy, and worked out extensively on his own at home.

The result?

Davis laughs: "Oh, I still don't move my left hand all that well, and there's a little hitch in my giddy-up."

The guy's being modest. You should know that in 2005, he completed a half-marathon. This was only after his heart doctor advised he not run the whole thing in the Florida heat.

Davis is back at work these days. What's more, he serves as ambassador of goodwill, advocate, and source of inspiration for others so cruelly stricken. In 2006, Davis and other survivors formed a stroke club. It still meets monthly. He and his wife, Nancy, remain active in a peer visitation program, meeting, greeting, and encouraging the latest round of stroke sufferers.

"We let 'em know that I'm a survivor, I can walk, that there's light at the end of the tunnel," he said. "It means so much when somebody tells you he's been there, done that."

This pluck can be traced to a special visitor who knocked on Davis's own hospital door several weeks into his treatment.

"The paper said Patricia Neal made a point of visiting patients whenever she was in town," Davis told me. "That's exactly right. She spent a half-hour with Nancy and me. It was nothing like, 'I'm a movie star and you're not.' Instead, she was plain ol' down-to-earth folks."

They can teach acting, and no doubt Patricia Neal was a gifted student. But it's different with humanity. That can only come from the heart.

Throughout East Tennessee, "Patsy" Neal's will beat forever.

THE LATEST FALSE PROPHET

I have tried repeatedly to reach Allison Warden by phone. All I've gotten is a recorded message to leave my number. Which I have. Many times.

Not surprisingly, she hasn't called back.

Perhaps Allison has been too busy to check her messages. Perhaps she's out of town visiting friends. Perhaps she's too embarrassed to speak to anyone just yet. Or who knows? Perhaps she did get called to heaven, just as she predicted would happen when we talked several months ago.

Allison is (was?) one of the followers of Harold Camping, the California-based radio evangelist who went 0-2 in 2011 in his predictions about "The Rapture" and ensuing end of the world. Actually, he's 0-3. Camping first said this would occur in 1994. When planet Earth kept right on spinning, he claimed to recalculate his interpretation of the Bible and somehow came up with a new date in May 2011, then October.

Human communication has expanded exponentially since Camping's first "miscalculation." Thanks to the Internet and social media, he went from being a little-known whack job to a much-publicized whack job. Believers like Allison Warden—and who knows how many thousands of others?—swallowed his non-sense hook, line, and sinker.

Many gave away their possessions, left their jobs and, in some cases, their families to spend 2011 distributing pamphlets, granting interviews, and—surprise!—raising money that was funneled into Camping's empire.

For what result?

To paraphrase that old peace slogan from the Vietnam War era: "They gave an Apocalypse and nobody came."

The reason I wanted to speak with Allison was not to gloat or poke fun at her beliefs. I simply wanted to discuss her emotions, now that Camping's iron-clad prediction proved no more credible than a tuft of lint.

Does she feel betrayed? Used? Is she angry at herself? At Harold Camping? At God? Or, in some bizarre way has this strengthened her faith? Does she think Camping simply made yet another miscalculation and will come back with a new and improved can't-miss prediction in the future—one that she and other sheep will be more than happy to help fund?

As has been proven time and again through history, all religions have a way of getting distorted by misinformed, disingenuous, self-serving, and outright crooked leaders. In my book, Harold Camping—who, quite conveniently, didn't give his fortune away—sits at the head of this class.

According to 2009 tax filings, Camping's "nonprofit" organization raked in $18.3 million in donations. Assets were listed in excess of $104 million.

Think how many hungry mouths that would have fed, how many naked backs it would have clothed. Which, best I recall, is what Jesus instructed in the first place.

A DIFFERENT KIND OF PAYCHECK

A message to teachers at the start of a new school year:

I have always felt a special kinship to you and your profession. Both of my late parents spent long careers in the classroom. Collectively, Big Sam and Mary Venable devoted nearly seventy years to their students—kindergarten toddlers, to pre-teens in junior high, to doctoral candidates in college. When my father died suddenly in 1972, he was serving his umpteenth term on the Knox County School Board.

What's more, my wife is a teacher. My brother-in-law is a teacher. I have various cousins, aunts, and in-laws who are either active or retired teachers. (Alas, my sister used to be a teacher. But after repeated tests proved her IQ had fallen precariously, she was removed from the classroom and placed in administration. *Joke!*)

So trust me when I say I've got an inkling of what makes you tick—even though, thank heaven, I never received the call to join your noble ranks.

I know you didn't enter this line of employment seeking financial gain. Nor do you labor under the illusion that this inequity will change any time soon. In a just world, coaches in the classroom, not just those on the football field, would be knocking down lucrative salaries. But whoever said life was fair?

I also know that the vast majority of you pour your heart and soul into this profession, that you plan lessons carefully, that you explore creative opportunities for learning, that you abhor the few lazy, baby-sitting bad apples who sour your ranks.

And I know that—even with the excitement of a new year, new books, new students, and new challenges—you can't help but sometimes feel tangled in an ever-spreading web of rules, regulations, and procedures that rob you and your colleagues of precious time and scant resources.

Keep the faith nonetheless.

As a parent, grandparent, and taxpayer, I want you to know how much I appreciate your efforts. Always have. Always will.

I ask that you never forget the young minds you are shaping. On those bad days when lessons go unheeded and hormone-fueled hellions have just about driven you over the edge, please remember one thing.

The reason you're standing in front of a bunch of pupils right now is because you once were sitting in their place.

Perhaps the lessons weren't making sense to you, either. Perhaps it was a lot more fun to goof off. But then a teacher made the difference. A teacher turned on the lights. A teacher fueled your will to learn. Suddenly all those random pieces started falling into place.

You said to yourself, "Hey, I like this! Maybe I could do this job, too!" And at that moment, a new teacher was born.

It's not going to click with every kid on your roster. What works in Mister Smith's class might not work in Miss Johnson's. But I'll guarantee in that mass of faces, there is someone—a lot of "someones," in fact—who will be positively influenced by you. The debt will be paid forward. This year, every year.

Just a shame these riches can't be deposited at the bank.

Chapter **6**

A FEW EXTRA SLICES OF OUR DAILY BREAD

Silly me. For years, I thought food was for eating. Or dining or snacking or munching or whatever term might best describe the process of sending vittles down the human "swallow pipe." Little did I realize there are broader applications for our daily bread—along with our daily cheeseburgers, our daily barbecue, our daily hot dogs, our daily doughnuts, our daily pizza, our daily fries, our daily biscuits and gravy, our daily bacon-wrapped chicken livers, our daily ice cream, and other nutritious daily fare guaranteed to broaden the shadows cast by gourmands throughout Southern Appalachia.

Self-defense, for instance.

I discovered this rather unusual approach in the spring of 2009 after chatting with a Claiborne County woman named Wanda Bray. I had heard about her killer chili and called for the recipe.

"You just put tomato juice, hamburger meat, chili powder, chili seasoning, and chili beans in a pot and cook it," she said. "That's all."

No, that's not all. Seems it wasn't necessarily the ingredients that made her chili so special. It was the delivery. Wanda put some real juice on it, that little "something extra" separating her dish from all the others.

She served it hot. Very hot. And we ain't talkin' spices.

"I had just took it off the stove," Wanda told me from her home in Harrogate, Tennessee. "It hadn't had time to cool off none."

That's startling enough for an unprepared tongue, I suppose. But when the recipient of lava con carne is the entire *face* of an intruder, not just the mouth, it can be quite a hit. Indeed, a direct hit.

You see, Wanda took food delivery to new heights when she used her chili to fend off three would-be robbers.

"I had just sat down on the couch to eat and watch TV when they come bustin' in," she said.

("They," according to Captain David Honeycutt of the Claiborne County Sheriff's Office, are now three new guests of the government. No word if the Cross Bar Hotel serves chili for lunch or supper.)

"They come runnin' in here, shovin' their fingers in my face like they had a gun," said Wanda, who, by the way, throws right-handed. "I could tell it wasn't no gun. It made me mad. I was too mad to be scared. I reckon it was just a reflex action. One of 'em, he got right up in my face, and I hit him with the chili. He got scared and run out th'door. Then my granddaughter threw me a broom handle, and I went t'beatin' another fellow with it."

The intruders grabbed some of Wanda's medicine as they hot-footed out. Their getaway was slowed somewhat when Wanda's neighbors, alerted by her screams, began pelting them with rocks. Shortly thereafter, they were apprehended by Captain Honeycutt, who was investigating an earlier robbery at a nearby service station.

I asked Wanda if she had a name for her crime-fighting concoction. "No, I reckon it's just Grandmaw's Chili," she chuckled. "I can laugh about it now, but I sure couldn't laugh then."

Captain Honeycutt clearly was impressed by Wanda's spunk. "We might start a tactical chili defense class," he quipped, "and we may get her to teach it."

One year after Wanda's defensive chili toss, I realized food could also be used to perpetrate crime: A woman in Kingsport was arrested for domestic assault after she cold-cocked her boyfriend with a can of green beans. Police said she swung with such force it dented the can.

(Which, as far as I'm concerned, showed the shallow level of police investigations and news reporting these days. Who's to say this woman didn't buy the can already dented, on sale in the discount aisle, and merely gave her beau a love tap? Inquiring minds want to know.)

Anyhow, the story sent me to the canned veggie section of a Knoxville supermarket, where I spent a full two hours trying to find the perfect-sized container to carry into a fight. Ultimately, my search was in vain—illustrating how hopelessly out of touch with reality corporate America has become. Calories, carbs, sodium, and fat grams are fine. But doesn't the food industry realize consumers also need "fightability" information on the label in the event they're forced to open a can of whup-ass?

Right off the bat, I dismissed green beans—regular cut, whole, Italian, or French-style—in eight-ounce sizes. These cans are simply too small for an effective grip. Far better is the larger, fourteen-ounce package, which comes in a variety of brands.

I was particularly attracted to the Libby's label. It included a Spanish translation—"ejotes verdes cortadas"—which, I assume, means "cut green beans." But it's been forty-five years since I took Spanish. For all I know, this could be a subliminal knifing message to "eject Verd's cardboard tatas."

For those with an environmental conscience, Del Monte's organic green beans are a good option. According to the label, "They contain no preservatives or artificial ingredients—perfectly suited for the way you eat today!" Not to mention the way you fight.

But then I got to thinking: "Hey, why limit this to green beans? Aren't other cans of vegetables also capable of delivering the goods?"

Of course they are. Especially those with action names. Can't you just feel the riveting cadence of *"maters-taters-hominy-SQUASH!"* at the moment of impact?

For that matter, who says it's gotta be veggies? What about meat, the original heavy hitter?

Spam's no good; that flat can doesn't fit the palm. But I felt like Rocky Balboa when I wrapped my fingers around fifteen ounces of Hormel corned beef hash.

When all was said and done, however, my vote for the "champeen" cold-cocking clunkers were Green Giant asparagus and Allen's Popeye brand chopped spinach. The long, lean asparagus can was easy to grip, with plenty of striking surface on either end. And just the label picture of Popeye, that pugilist nonpareil, would likely settle any fight, food or otherwise, before it got started.

Wouldn't you know it, I then realized fresh produce, not canned, might be the ideal weapon of choice. In the fall of 2010, a woman in Helena, Montana, thwarted a bear attack by smacking the bruin with a fourteen-inch zucchini from her garden. I'm not kidding. I read an Associated Press account of the incident after hearing about it on National Public Radio. The Missoula County Sheriff's Office made a full investigation, although officials did not identify the woman at her request.

Naturally, that sent me to the phone to call Jerry Simmons, East Tennessee's "Zeus of Zukes." When you need straight answers, you go to the A-team.

"What's the best kind of zucchini to use if you have to whack a black bear in the head?" I asked as soon as Jerry came on the line.

"Straight-neck," he replied immediately. "You can get a good grip on it. And once it's dried, it can really pack a wallop."

Jerry and his wife, Ida, are Grainger Countians. They live in a 225-year-old house that sits on his late grandparents' farm near Bean Station. Jerry grows a lot of zucchini—although the term "a lot of" in matters of zucchini is redundant because this plant spreads faster than kudzu and fruits at a rate that makes rabbits look sexually chaste.

You know the old jokes about how to give away excess zucchini, don't you? Just bag it up, leave it on your neighbor's doorstep, ring the bell, and run like hell. Or else casually stroll the parking lot aisles of your local shopping mall until you find a convertible with the top down. Then deposit several bags of zucchini and make yourself scarce.

But unlike a stereotypic zucchini grower, Jerry doesn't have to resort to pleading, coercion, blackmail, or stealth to get rid of his produce. He turns it into jelly, and I swear on a case of Ball canning jars I'm not making this up.

Not only does he make zucchini jelly, which sells like proverbial hotcakes at the Grainger County Tomato Festival every July, it actually tastes good. Or, I should say, it tastes like whatever flavor he mixes in, such as strawberry, peach, black cherry, or green apple because—I realize this comes as no surprise to anyone who has ever bitten into this veggie—zucchini itself tastes vaguely like water-soaked cardboard. And I certainly hope I haven't offended cardboard lovers.

Anyhow, I asked Jerry if he had ever been forced to use zucchini for self-protection, either on the farm or during his fifteen years as a police officer in Morristown.

"Never thought about it either way," he answered with a chuckle. "About the worst animals I ever face in the garden are rabbits."

He pondered a minute and added: "Well, sometimes I do carry a .22 pistol when I go to the barn because of coyotes. But once I take a shot at 'em, they hightail."

Far be it from me to offer combat advice to a veteran farmer and cop. Nonetheless, black bears are on the increase in East Tennessee. Never know when you might bump into one. If it was me, I wouldn't stray too far from a hefty you-know-what.

Even if I do often tease about bizarre uses for food, you can bet a pair of XL sweatpants that Chef Venable knows plenty about the more conventional methodology—as in tooth, tongue, throat, and stomach. Like most aging Baby Boomers, I am a veteran of the Battle of the Bulge and have the midsection to prove it. This is commonly referred to as "Dunlop's Disease" because your belly "done-lopped" over your belt.

Such is a sad dietary fact of life in the South. Our specialty is "fried anything." You name the delicious food item—animal, vegetable, or Twinkie—and we'll show you a way to make it taste even better by being battered and bubbled in a sea of molten grease. If tap water could be fried, southerners would find a way to do it.

Yet there is one notable exception to this rule, at least as far as Chef Venable is concerned: there is no way under the sun to make a beet palatable.

You are welcome to disagree. Enjoy all the beets you can tamp down. But if you harbor any notion about changing my mind on this matter, save your breath, your time, and your postage. It ain't gonna happen.

I don't care if Aunt Hattie authored detailed recipes for beet pudding, beet soufflé, and beet casserole that have been jealously guarded in your family for six generations. I don't care if you know a great way to prepare fresh, frozen, or canned beets that has won cook-offs since Betty Crocker wore diapers. I don't care if you, your neighbors, your heirs, and assigns love the beet, the whole beet, and nothing but the beet.

I will not waver. There is no beet I will eat.

Beets are vile vegetables. When cooked, they look like lumps of blood, stink like sweaty socks, and taste like dirt.

The reason I'm so adamant is because I've been down this path any number of times over the last four-plus-decades-and-counting. You see, my wife dearly loves beets. Any and all beets. It is one of her rare character faults.

In the name of matrimonial harmony, I have attempted to convert. I've taken nibbles of this and pinches of that she has placed on my plate and done my utmost to comprehend how ordinarily rational people can enjoy something that tastes so positively putrid.

Every few springs, East Tennessee's red maple trees crank out an extraordinarily abundant crop of seeds. These little whirlygigs pile up in windrows on driveways, parking lots, and roofs. One year, reader Carl Porter found an Internet post about how to handle the crisis: Eat them.

"When cooked, these seeds taste like a cross between peas and hominy," it read." They also can be eaten raw or dried or throw into a salad." The piece went into dizzying detail about harvesting, hulling, rinsing, and cooking.

No thanks. Sound like way too much trouble. Besides I'm not too keen on the thought of a pea-hominy meal. But you never know what will attract the nation's taste buds—and you gotta admit "McMaple's" does have a catchy, down-home ring to it.

The closest she has ever come to success is beets in a thick orange sauce—and "closest" in this regard is twice the distance between Los Angeles and Manhattan. I'd just as soon gnaw on a muddy boot marinated in orange juice.

For better or for worse, this revulsion was captured in my DNA. Both of our children hate beets with the same degree of enmity as their father. But at least the standoff has spawned its share of family legends. I can't tell you the number of times, as kids and as grownups, Megan and Clay have given their mother cans of beets or packets of beet seeds on her birthday or at Christmas. Never let it be said that the woman is difficult to buy for.

Nor are Megan, Clay, and I alone in this loathing. It is a well-publicized fact that President Barack Obama is also a beet hater. Politics be damned! Any president who will go on the record as a beet basher is automatically elevated one step closer to sainthood.

I read about Mister Obama's disdain for beets shortly after he was elected. The story, in one form or another, ran for several days. This proves conclusively that today's keen-edged journalists know how to ignore peripheral fluff about war and the economy and concentrate instead on the truly important issues facing our sovereign nation.

A HEALTHY DISH OF MISERY

Never fails. About the time I develop a taste for healthy food, I discover it's deadlier than three packs of Camels.

Spinach happens to be the bad boy right now. It's the source of an E. coli outbreak that has killed one person and sickened hundreds coast to coast. As a result, store shelves have been cleared of standing stock. Farmers are plowing their crops under.

As a child, I would've greeted this news with unbridled joy. Back then I was force-fed tons of spinach. This was not a pleasant experience because it came canned or frozen and was always boiled to a stringy goo.

Then I discovered fresh spinach and got hooked. In the last few years, I've eaten enough of the stuff to send Popeye and Olive Oyl on luxury cruises for life.

Spinach is a superb salad green. Also a great sandwich condiment. Who else do you know actually eats spinach sandwiches? This is like a tomato sandwich minus the 'mater and mayo. Just take a couple of slices of light bread, a squirt of ranch dressing, pile on several handfuls of fresh spinach, give it a good mash (otherwise, the leaves fly out), and enjoy.

Even when spinach works its way back onto the "good" list, will it and I remain estranged? Or will we reunite like old lovers? To paraphrase Yogi Berra, I'm sensing culinary deja vu all over again. Seems like a food scare cycles around just after I've climbed aboard the bandwagon.

First was liver. My mother served up liver planks—you could've driven a nail with them—on a regular basis. As a teenager, I happily took revenge with a vow of liver abstinence.

Ahhh, but then I discovered liver doesn't have to be cooked to the consistency of a hatchet. I actually began enjoying it. At least I did until liver pole-vaulted from the "good" list to the "bad" list because of cholesterol.

Then there was mackerel, supposedly an exceedingly healthy fish because of its oil. Eat lots of mackerel, the food experts said. It's good for your heart—really and truly, not in a beans-beans-musical-fruit sort of way.

So I became a mackerelaholic. Broiled, grilled, canned, you name it. I ate enough mackerel to sprout my own gills. Naturally, mackerel was then yanked off the market because of mercury, PCBs, and other contaminants that tend to collect in its flesh. Goodbye, my finny friend.

Next came red wine. Hoo-boy. You ever had a red wine headache? I'm not talking about a hangover. I'm talking one of those tsunami-every-time-your-heart-beats cranium crushers.

Suffice to say the closest I come to any type of red wine these days is a sip from the communion cup at church. Any more than that and it feels like one of my mother's liver planks has hit me between the eyes.

Reversals are always possible, of course. Eggs have gone from "good" to "bad" and back to "good" again. So has coffee. No doubt spinach will as well. But in the meantime, I hear a dozen doughnuts calling my name. When it comes to dangerous dining, I say stick with the tried and true.

THE NEED FOR TRUTH IN ADVERTISING

It's time to add a new oxymoron to the English language. Right in there amongst such classics as "jumbo shrimp," "perfectly awful," "first annual," "even odds," and "long shorts," this glaring opposite begs to be included: "Seedless watermelon."

Those two words constitute a lie on par with "Yes, I'll respect you in the morning," and "Your check is in the mail."

Even the perpetrators of this "seedless" folly don't believe their own hoax. Just check the label slapped onto the skin of any of these green orbs. It says,

"May contain occasional seeds."

"Occasional?" Ha.

That's like warning someone who is wearing short pants—short-short, knee-length, or otherwise—that crossing four acres of waist-deep grass in the middle of July may result in an "occasional" chigger bite.

"Seedless" watermelons are most certainly not seedless. Not even remotely. I haven't compared them side by side, but my guess is that "seedless" melons and their "seeded" cousins contain the same number of pits. The only difference is that "seeded" seeds are mostly black and stout, while "seedless" seeds are mostly white and flimsy.

The black "seeded" seeds are easy to see and easy to remove because they tend to separate from the melon's flesh. Those pantywaist white "seedless" seeds stay hidden. Removing them is like trying to pick beggar lice off of wool pants while wearing thick gloves.

By now you should have come to the realization that I'm not a fan of "seedless" watermelons. Indeed, they are an abomination.

Mary Constantine, the *News Sentinel*'s food editor, says some people claim "seeded" melons are sweeter, a taste imparted by the seeds themselves—sort of how a pork chop or chicken thigh on the bone tastes better than one with the bone removed.

Perhaps this is true. But it's been my experience that sweetness, or lack thereof, has more to do with the variety of melon and conditions under which it was grown. In any event, I wish Congress would outlaw these ridiculous "seedless" monstrosities until they have been perfected.

If, somewhere down the pike, a truly seedless watermelon—attention food industry: this means no discernible seeds whatsoever—is developed, fine. If it can be further refined into one giant "heart" of firm red flesh—none of that soft, fuzzy mid-level stuff—also fine. But until then, keep these things where they belong: in the laboratory and off the market.

Admittedly, I am somewhat of a watermelon slob. Or slop, as the case may be. I prefer to clean an entire melon at the sink—seeds and rind removed and remanded to the compost pile, and succulent chunks of red flesh placed in a plastic bin for the refrigerator.

This results in a bit of watermelon waste, as my knife work grows sloppier as the job progresses. But the result is a mound of pure, unadulterated, heavenly eating. With no seeds. As in none, zero, zilch, ixnay.

Not even an "occasional" one.

SNACKING OUR WAY TO NUTRITION

Attention moms and dads. The next time you catch little Billy or Suzy clandestinely sinking their teeth into an apple or banana, resist the urge to scold. Instead, turn this unpleasant situation into a dietary lesson by offering them a nutritious alternative to junk food.

A scrumptious serving of potato chips.

Sure, Billy and Suzy might complain at first. We all know how hard it is to break poor eating habits. But given time and gentle encouragement, they'll develop a taste for the greasy goodness found only in potato chips. Then they'll come begging for more. And you, Mr. and Mrs. Proud Parent, will be happy to provide.

Don't take my word for this revolutionary news. Talk to an expert in the manufacture and distribution of health food: Frito-Lay, Incorporated.

I am not making this up. Indeed, I hold in my chubby little fingers a Frito-Lay advertisement from a recent issue of *Ladies' Home Journal*.

"Frito-Lay knows the goodness of simplicity and the importance of providing nutritious snacks for your family, but sometimes it's hard to know fact from fiction," the text begins.

I'm going to quote the next sentence verbatim, but I must take a long, deep breath. For two reasons. First is the fact that Frito-Lay's advertising copy writers, who obviously failed eighth-grade English, criminally violate Harbrace by joining three independent clauses with commas. Second is the sheer audacity of their commercial spin. Here goes:

"Take the potato chip for example, you might think it's 'junk food' but take a closer look, it's actually just three simple ingredients."

These three simple ingredients, the ad goes on to explain, are "One hundred percent North American farm-grown potatoes." Plus "a blend of corn and sunflower oil, with over eighty-five percent 'good fats' (mono- and polyunsaturated fats) and zero grams of trans fat per ounce." And "less than one-twelfth teaspoon of salt."

Of course, the ad does not mention that a 1.5-ounce serving of these three simple ingredients contains 230 calories, fifteen grams of fat, 270 milligrams of sodium and twenty-three grams of carbs. But let us not get sidetracked by boring details.

Instead, let us think of all the other wonderful health-food options available to Billy, Suzy, and their parents. Such as doughnuts, cookies, cakes, pies, and candy bars—all made from simple, natural ingredients like flour, sugar, and chocolate.

Ummmm-mmm, good! Separating dietary fact from fiction has never been more delicious! Thank heaven for companies like Frito-Lay that are bustin' a gut to keep supermarket shelves stocked with such wholesomeness.

So turn on the tube, plop down on the sofa, crack open a bag of crispy, fried goodness, and eat up, America! And be sure to tune in next time for our latest adventure in the wonderful world of healthy living: "George Dickel Whiskey—It's not just for breakfast anymore."

CHEW ON THIS

Somewhere in the great beyond, Geneva Anderson is having a conniption fit. It will be in a ladylike manner, of course. At least as ladylike as a fit—conniption, hissy or otherwise—can be had, for Geneva Anderson was Miss Manners personified.

> Oh, how I love it when the legislature debates the notion of legalizing horse meat for human consumption! Always gives me a chance to point out that the old gray mare truly ain't what she used to be—not to mention the fact that the common expression, "I'm hungry enough to eat a dead horse" might take on new meaning.

Nonetheless, I pity the fool who's dealing with her right now.

It's all because of research recently conducted at the Baylor College of Medicine. According to this study, children who chew gum make better grades than non-chewers. Up to 3 percent better in standardized tests.

The project was funded by the Wrigley Science Institute. Yes, *that* Wrigley, making me scratch my head, if not my jaw, about questions of credibility.

In any event, Dr. Craig Johnson, author of the report, believes the physical act of chewing improves concentration. As he told the *Los Angeles Times,* "There is research demonstrating an increase in blood flow in the brain during chewing."

Bully for the Baylor College of Medicine and Craig Johnson. They may cite statistics to their collective hearts' content. But I'll double-dog (or Doublemint, as the case may be) guarantee Miss Anderson would have none of it.

Miss Anderson was my senior English teacher at Young High School. Both she and the school are no longer of this realm. Young closed its doors in 1976 after sixty-three years of continuous service to south Knox Countians. Miss Anderson enjoyed an even longer run. She was seventy-nine at the time of her death in 1983.

Let me state unequivocally that here was the finest teacher I encountered through elementary school, high school, and college. She was challenging, demanding, a stickler for detail—the sort of tutor most students would immediately loathe—but her classes were such fun you forgot work was involved. I will forever love her for planting the first seed in my pea brain that writing, not forestry, was my life's calling.

But as delightful as she could be, there was one sure way to turn this warm demeanor into snow-covered granite.

"Now, cherubs," she would abruptly announce, "someone in this room is chewing gum. We will stop our lesson until the matter is resolved."

Then she would affix a laser stare until the miscreant walked the Bataan Death March to the nearest trash can and made a deposit.

I know this sounds outrageous in today's battlefield classroom environment, but a stare is all Miss Anderson needed to restore order. Would that every teacher had this skill at his or her disposal. Once Miss Anderson locked onto That Look, she could tame a tornado. As I columnized shortly after her death, "If you were never stared at by Geneva Anderson when she was in a testy mood, you never experienced primal fear."

I wish nothing but the best for Dr. Craig Johnson and his colleagues at Baylor College of Medicine. May they prosper and chart new educational horizons. But they better enjoy it, and their Bubblicious, while they can.

'Cause once they cross the river and come eyeball to eyeball with Miss Geneva Anderson, there's going to be hell to pay.

McHAGGIS ISN'T IN OUR FUTURE

The hottest news on the international front doesn't come out of Iraq, Afghanistan, Russia, or Pakistan. Instead, it's from bonny olde Scotland.

The Scots are asking the U.S. government to drop its importation ban on haggis.

If that statement causes you to say "Huh? *What*-is?" it's obvious your knowledge of sheep is limited to bawdy jokes about love-starved rednecks.

Haggis is a dish made from sheep innards, including the lungs, liver, and heart, combined with oatmeal, spices, and suet. These ingredients are then stuffed into a sheep's stomach—I'm assuming you realize the sheep is a rather unwilling participant at this point, having already been slaughtered, skinned, and eviscerated—and boiled for three hours. Traditionally, it is served with potatoes and mashed turnips.

Haggis is to Scots what hamburgers are to Americans. It's their national dish, proving that enough alcohol can make any food palatable.

Haggis imports have been banned in the United States ever since the European outbreak of mad cow disease, which is linked to Creutzfeldt-Jakob disease, a human brain ailment. But the Scots insist their meat poses no health hazards.

"It's safe, or we wouldn't eat it here," a government spokeswoman told Reuters news service. "We think there is a large market for it amongst expatriate Scots (in America)."

Maybe, maybe not.

I, personally, can attest to the relative safety of Scottish haggis because I ate some while touring there in 2003 and lived to tell about it. Mostly.

I credit this to an iron stomach, the above-mentioned ingestion of elixirs, and a proud Tennessee heritage of souse, chitlins, potted meat, and Spam.

What's more, I'm certain the spokeswoman is correct about the vast number of Americans, especially here in Southern Appalachia, who trace their roots to Scotland. She's also on the money about the growing U.S. market for kilts, bagpipes, tartans, Scotch whisky, and other products from the highlands.

But haggis? I think not.

Even if the import ban were lifted immediately, I can't imagine legions of locals flocking to restaurants and ordering it. Before I opened a haggis franchise in the United States, I would invest heavily in Enron, WorldCom, the subprime mortgage industry, and the Powerball and consider my chances of striking it rich exceedingly greater.

True, I've missed burgeoning culinary markets before. Years ago, you never would have convinced me egg rolls and tacos—let alone sushi—would appear on menus all over this meat-and-potatoes town. And don't get me started on the bottled water craze, which began when some genius brought in the first green jug of Perrier from France.

But trust your Uncle Tastebuds on this one: Even if it's rolled in seasoned flour, deep-fried, and layered with shredded cheese, haggis is still sheep guts.

In our part of the world, we call that catfish bait.

DO YOU WANT FLIES WITH THAT?

Except for mosquitoes, moths, midges, and various other winged beasties accidentally ingested while cruising after dark in a bass boat, I've never been much of a bug eater.

Oops, just thought of another exception. A major one. In 2004, when seventeen-year cicadas made their noisy appearance, I sampled several of Bob Hodge's culinary treats. Bob fried, sautéed, and broiled cicadas and brought them to the office. I like the fried ones best. Then again, as a proud native son of the South, I will eat dang-near anything fried. Even bugs.

Cicadas aren't scheduled to reappear in these parts until 2021, so it's going to be quite a spell before we get a chance to clamp our choppers around a mess of insects. "Mess" meaning a large quantity—not what's apt to erupt from the squeamish as they contemplate a platter of crispy critters.

Recently, three dozen scientists from fifteen countries gathered in Thailand to study the possibility of using bugs to alleviate famine, especially "during droughts and other emergencies." This was a conference sponsored by the United Nations Food and Agriculture Organization.

The group met in Thailand because bug-eating is considered the norm in many parts of Asia, as well as Africa and Latin America. As the scientists noted, caterpillars, grubs, and crickets are not only abundant, they're also high in protein and minerals.

Of course, trying to convince people elsewhere in the world—and we know who we are—presents a major challenge. We prefer our protein to have clucked, mooed, or oinked in an earlier life. Not buzzed.

In an Associated Press report about the meeting, Dutch entomologist Arnold van Huis said folks like us "are completely biased. They really have to change."

No doubt Prof van Huis is correct.

No doubt this attitude isn't going to change for a very long time, though. As they say down at the food court, you can have my McGrease when you pry it from my cold, dead hands.

All of which underscores just how strange our food fetishes truly are.

Most Americans don't blink about eating a hamburger made from ground cow. Or ground pig. Even ground turkey. But ground horse—which is routinely eaten in many developed countries—is shocking to American sensitivities.

My own meat prejudices are just as weird. I eat chicken, beef, and pork that has been killed, processed, and packaged by someone else. I also eat deer, ducks, geese, turkeys, and other wild animals taken by my own hand.

But as much as I enjoy venison—lightly grilled deer tenderloin stands up well against any beef you ever tasted—I cannot bring myself to eat deer hearts. Tried 'em once. Don't need to try 'em again.

Instead, I give my deer hearts to Bob Hodge. As he proved with cicadas, he'll eat anything.

SMELLS LIKE MONEY UP IN THE HILLS

Early each spring, many Southern Appalachians get downright "stanky." That's what happens when they eat ramps.

This small, hill-country plant is a wild leek (*Allium tricoccum,* if you want to get technical). It has an onion/garlic-on-steroids flavor that'll do more than give you an industrial case of morning breath. Ingest enough, and the vile scent will actually seep from the pores in your skin.

If someone eats a big bait of ramps for breakfast and hikes a few miles in sunshine, you can smell 'em coming down the trail. I'm serious. Even if the wind is blowing the other way.

But instead of reaching for a large bottle of Scope, folks are digging into their billfolds and paying for the pleasure. What used to be a quaint mountain culinary custom has blossomed into full-blown haute cuisine—to the point that natural resource agencies are starting to worry about wild stocks.

The National Park Service has banned ramp-digging in the Great Smoky Mountains National Park. In the Cherokee National Forest, visitors need a free permit to gather up to five pounds for personal use. Organizations may collect up to five hundred pounds in the national forest, at a charge of forty cents per pound.

In case you haven't noticed, ramp fests are everywhere.

There's the Polk County Ramp Tramp in Tennessee, as well as the "Feast of the Ramson" at the Richwood (West Virginia) Ramp Festival. Every April, you can choose from the International Ramp Cook-Off in Elkins, West Virginia; the Helvetia Ramp Supper in Helvetia, West Virginia; or the Graham County Ramp Festival in North Carolina. And in early May, of course, there's the granddaddy of Tennessee folk gatherings, the annual Cosby Ramp Festival at Kineauvista Hill in Cocke County. If you can't make that, try the Flag Pond (Unicoi County, Tennessee) Ramp Festival, or the Whitetop Mountain Ramp Festival (Grayson County, Virginia).

Chow down at all of those events, and you won't be bothered by people getting in your face for several weeks.

There are many ways to consume ramps: raw, scrambled with eggs, fried with sliced potatoes, chopped and mixed with ground meat. But until I recently spoke with Beverly Whitehead, I'd never heard of ramp cornbread.

Whitehead is chairwoman of the board of the Smoky Mountain Native Plants Association. She and her associates dehydrate ramps, combine them with stone-ground corn meal, and sell the mixture as fast as they can pour it into eleven-ounce bags. The outfit also packages and sells jars of ramp salt and ramp seasoning.

The native plants group has invested six years in ramp propagation. Members work with farmers toward the goal of creating a sustainable harvest of home-grown ramps, perhaps to help offset some of the loss from tobacco cutbacks.

Funny how things go around, isn't it?

Ramps once were the strict purview of poor hillbillies trying to grub something green out of the ground in early spring. Now, it's a different kind of green.

The Food Network recently featured ten ramp recipes. Included was succulence on the order of "roasted lion of Berkshire grass-fed veal served with roasted potatoes, with wild ramps and morel mushroom sauce." That was followed by a *New York Times* article about one wholesale produce market in the Big Apple that shelled out $29,600 for ramps. And now St. Lyon's Press has just come out with *Ramps: Cooking with the Best-Kept Secret of the Appalachian Trail.* This is a 114-page guide featuring dozens of recipes for ramps in meat, soup, salads, bread, and—I just felt a little spit-up form in the back of my throat—juice and jams. Will gastronomic wonders never cease?

If you had been sitting around a country-store stove anywhere in East Tennessee fifty years ago and prophesied such an economic forecast, the place was have exploded in collective laughter: "Tell us another'un, Bucktooth! I'll swan, you kin cook up a lie better'n anybody in these here parts!"

AHH, YEZZ; DON'T TOUCH THE STUFF

W. C. Fields, rest his curmudgeonly soul, had a lot to say about water. None of it good. His famous putdowns always started with, "I never drink water" and ended with gems like:

"—because of the disgusting things fish do in it."

"—because it's the stuff that rusts pipes."

"—because I'm afraid it will become habit-forming."

But if Mister Fields harbored such humorous contempt eighty years ago, imagine how he'd howl today as the world drowns in its addiction to bottled water. Here is a fifteen-billion-dollar (and climbing every year) industry that rivals the king's new clothes and snake oil for nutty illusion.

The Environmental Working Group, a non-profit research organization based in Washington, D.C., has just released another damning report on the matter. I say "another" because bottled water has been attacked on nearly every logical front.

First is its outrageous cost. Even in cheap store brands, it's more than one-thousand times more expensive, per unit, than water drawn from the tap.

Also, the Earth Policy Institute estimates that the plastic used in those billions-upon-billions of containers slurps up 1.5 million barrels of oil per year, enough to power one hundred thousand cars.

What about purity? Public health experts across the nation have long argued that bottled water is no safer than water from any approved municipal source.

But now, the Environmental Working Group's report says comprehensive testing has exposed "a surprising array of chemical contaminants" in ten popular brands.

"Unlike tap water, where consumers are provided with test results every year, the bottled water industry does not disclose the results of any contaminant testing that it conducts," EWG said in a 2008 news release. "Instead, the industry hides behind the claim that bottled water is held to the same standards as tap water . . . To the contrary, our tests strongly indicate that the purity of bottled water cannot be trusted."

What's a worried consumer to do?

Follow the advice of W. C. Fields, that's what: Drink hooch. This is the patriotic duty of every citizen, especially those of us blessed to be Tennesseans.

In January 2009, the Jack Daniel Distillery in Lynchburg set aside a special barrel of "Tennessee sippin' whiskey" to mark the inauguration of President Barack Obama. This whiskey will be closely monitored in coming years. When fully mature, it will be bottled and sold with all proceeds going to a charity selected by Mister Prez.

I am not making this up. I just got off the telephone with Mark Day, a spokesman for the distillery. He estimated the barrel will yield 240 bottles. Mark said this follows a tradition started by Jack Daniel himself, who always threw a party for the new president, regardless of political affiliation.

Hail to the chief, I say. Hale, yes!

Or, and the delightful Mister Fields put it: "A woman drove me to drink, and I didn't have the decency to thank her."

PARTY! PARTY! PARTY!

Holy hieroglyphics! All this time I've been an archaeological genius and didn't realize it!

So you'd better clear the phone lines. No doubt officials from Yale, Harvard, and the Smithsonian Institution will be calling for scholarly advice—which I'll be happy to provide for a nominal fee.

This startling discovery revealed itself while I was perusing a report from the scientific journal *Nature*. In the article, archaeologists said they had found evidence of the first "modern lifestyle" by human beings some 164,000 years ago. That's roughly 100,000 years earlier than previously believed.

Their theory was based on the uncovering of remnants from a beach party on the Indian Ocean in South Africa. I'm not kidding. Scientists said brown mussels, black mussels, saltwater clams, sea snails, and barnacles were harvested at the beach and carried to nearby caves. There, they were arranged on heated rocks. As the seafood cooked, the shells popped open, much as occurs during the modern steaming process.

While munching my way across the grounds of the Tennessee Valley Fair one brilliant autumn afternoon, I saw a food booth that was selling truth along with fat grams and calories. Instead of funnel cakes, the menu read "fried dough."

Then the meat was consumed by revelers—who, alas, didn't have a cooler of Bud Lights and Coronas to wash down their meal, tiki torches and citronella oil to keep mosquitoes at bay, or music by the Beach Boys for dancing. But everyone seemed to enjoy the festivities nonetheless.

One of the authors of the study, Curtis Marean of the Institute of Human Origins at Arizona State University, even simulated the process in his lab. He found the chow to be less moist than palates prefer these days but otherwise quite edible.

Forgive his boasting, but Professor Venable advanced a somewhat similar theory more than a decade ago. This was shortly after the discovery of a huge prehistoric site in upper East Tennessee's Washington County. When a road cut was being made near the Gray community, the bones of a mastodon, tapir, ground sloth, and crocodile were unearthed.

Scientists are still debating the hows and whys of this revelation. But on Friday, July 14, 2000, yours truly columnized his version in the *News Sentinel*: "I think a bunch of good ol' boy cavemen got together for a big-time barbecue and flung the bones into a pile as the feasting evolved. I can just see Ig, Ick, Org, and Ogg now, stretching out in the shade of an acacia tree, picking their teeth with a crocodile rib bone, patting their bellies, scratching, belching, arguing politics, talking sports, complaining about their bosses, and moaning to each other in blissful contentment."

In all honesty, Professor Venable must admit Professor Marean's research was a wee bit more involved. That's because Professor Marean speculated all the food was carried to the caves by women.

Professor Venable did not include such a minor detail in his study, naturally assuming the wives of Ig, Ick, Org, and Ogg thawed the mastodon, tapir, ground sloth, and crocodile meat; prepared the secret barbecue sauce; lugged everything to the grill; set the table, and made a salad—while the men argued about how much lighter fluid to squirt on the charcoal.

It doesn't matter if you're talking about Right Now or Way Back Then. Some truths are universal.

SOUNDS LIKE A FINE MEAL TO ME

The more I study the government's new guidelines for a healthy diet, the hungrier I become. Perhaps it would be best to order a pizza while I mull this thing over. Extra large with multiple toppings.

As you've probably heard by now, the U.S. Department of Agriculture recently scrapped its twenty-year-old "food pyramid" and replaced it with a dinner plate. This purports to illustrate what sort of chow—and how much of it—we should consume on a daily basis.

I perused some information about the new plan on the USDA's website and came away thinking I should have paid closer attention in algebra and geometry classes back in high school.

You see, the plate is divided into four colored sections. They are labeled fruits (red), grains (brown), vegetables (green), and protein (purple). Off to the side is a circle (blue) marked "dairy."

Unfortunately, the sections are not of equal size. So unless I can dig out my old geometry compass and remember how to use it, I'll never know how much of what to eat.

(Speaking of compasses, do they still use them in school these days? Probably not. The sharp pointy end surely violates zero-tolerance regulations. How strange. Back in the Dark Ages we didn't have enough sense to realize compasses were weapons of mass destruction. We considered them more as tools of vast boredom, capable only of drawing random, artistic curvy lines, not solving algebra and geometry problems. Or at least I did, which may explain my pitiful grades in algebra and geometry. But I digress.)

Best I can tell, the vegetable portion of the plate is larger than any other. Indeed, it and fruits make up half the dish. Meaning we're supposed to gorge on them.

"Fruits and vegetables are packed with fiber, essential vitamins, and photochemicals, which are cancer-fighting substances," Susan Levin, director of nutrition education at the Washington, D.C.–based Physicians Committee for Responsible Medicine, said on a recent ABC News broadcast.

Perhaps. But they might also send you to an early grave.

Ever heard of bean sprouts? Those apparently were the source of E. coli contamination that killed three dozen people in Europe during the summer of 2011. I say "apparently" because even toxicologists weren't 100-percent sure. At first they thought it was cucumbers. Then beet sprouts. Then bean sprouts. Whatever the case, veggies were to blame.

I contend the best way to avoid sickness is to fry vegetables in a sizable dollop from the protein side of the ledger. Bacon grease, ideally. And while you're at it, why not toss in a couple of strips of bacon itself? The more protein the merrier, I always say.

Then again, your frying agent of choice might be butter from the dairy circle. Speaking of which, if you want to mix up a good thick batter, starting with buttermilk, have at it.

Don't want to forget grains, of course. Aren't hops and barley grains? And would the cornmeal for the aforementioned frying batter come from grains or vegetables? You decide.

In the meantime, Chef Venable will pour himself a selection from the fruits department.

Chardonnay does go with pizza, doesn't it?

TRYING TO KEEP A LID ON OUR JOE

If coffee prices keep galloping along, we may all yearn for the good old days when the only thing to gripe about was the rising cost of gasoline.

Whether you buy it by the cup or the package, you've surely noticed coffee is skyrocketing. According to statistics compiled by the U.S. Department of Labor, the rate of coffee's escalation was greater even than that of petrol: 40 percent versus 37 percent, respectively.

Even worse, it's likely to keep right on climbing. And consumers will keep right on paying.

Don't take my word for it. Said a recent business dispatch by *The Associated Press:* "When money is tight, people may buy cheaper brands of coffee, but they won't give it up completely. Americans consumed 21.7 million sixty-kilogram bags of coffee in 2008, up from 21 million the year before."

This addiction isn't new.

"Even in pioneer days, people had to have their coffee," John Rice Irwin of the Museum of Appalachia told me. "No matter how poor they were, they usually found a way to scrape up enough money for coffee."

Sometimes they made-do.

"I remember (legendary mountain man) Alex Stewart once talking about making coffee out of wheat," said Irwin. "Can't imagine how bad that tasted. Of course, lots of people added chicory to give their coffee more flavor and kick."

You don't have to hold a PhD in American history to recall that southerners became quite inventive with coffee substitutes during the Civil War. I've long heard that acorns and cornmeal were frequently used.

But then a few tickles of the computer keys led me to research compiled by the University of Texas at Tyler. By gleaning articles from Civil War–era newspapers, historians found lip-smacking—or lip-puckering, as the case may be—concoctions that featured "coffee" made from beets, rye, asparagus seeds, okra seeds, parsnips, tree bark, field peas, sweet potatoes, red wheat, grits, sassafras, beech root, cotton seeds, persimmon seeds, and molasses.

Here's an entry from the *Augusta (GA) Daily Chronicle & Sentinel* on August 25, 1861:

> Take the common garden beet, wash it clean, cut it into small pieces, twice the size of a grain of coffee; put into the coffee toaster or oven and roast as you do your coffee, perfectly brown. Take care not to burn while toasting it. When sufficiently dry and hard, grind it in a clean mill. Take half a common-sized coffee cup of the grounds and boil with one gallon of water. Then settle with an egg and send to the table, hot. Sweeten with very little sugar and add good cream or milk.

Whew. That oughta put hair on your chest. Or, perhaps, take it off.

Next, try this acorn recipe from the *Little Rock (AR) True Democrat,* October 22, 1862:

> The (white oak) acorns should be hulled, cut up in the size of grains of coffee, well dried, then parched . . . A number of families have gathered acorns enough to last them a year, and we would not be surprised if acorn coffee should come into general use and favor.

Just don't tell the folks at Starbucks. They'll start selling it for twelve bucks a pop.

HONEY AND HOT DOGS DON'T MIX

You would think something as important as National Hot Dog Day would enjoy a degree of uniformity. And you would think wrong.

Halloween is always celebrated on October 31, Veterans Day is always celebrated on November 11, and Christmas is always celebrated on December 25. But the official day when Americans are encouraged to clog their arteries with massive doses of cylindrical lipids bounces around worse than tennis balls at Wimbledon.

I just did an Internet search and came up with at least three so-called "official" National Hot Dog Days for 2009 alone: July 19, July 20, and July 23. Perhaps there are others.

But no matter when National Hot Dog Day rolls around, I stand four-square behind the principle of it. I don't care if these puppies are packed with preservatives, carcinogens, fillers, and fats, there is a soft spot in my heart—not to mention a bulge in my belly—for them. I am, without reservation, a fan of franks, a devotee of dogs, a worshipper of wieners.

I feel the same way about hot dogs as I do about cold beer: There ain't no bad; just some a little better than others.

Well, yes, now that you mention it, I do wince when persons of Yanqui extraction refer to this fine food product as a "hut-dug." If they want to call 'em that in Detroit or Boston, fine. But Down Here, they are—repeat after me—"haat-dawgs." Go and sin no more.

There are as many ways to dress up a hot dog as there are excuses after the Tennessee Vols lose a football or basketball game.

Mustard-only is fine by me. In fact, that's my preference, especially if the dog is seated in a soft, white, chewy steamed bun that clings to the roof of your mouth. Chili, onions, and slaw also are worthy additions.

But I draw the line at ketchup.

It saddens me to admit this in public, but my wife, a southern belle of fine breeding, squeezes ketchup on her haat-dawgs. Yes, just like those Yanquis do to their hut-dugs. This has been the source of innumerable arguments around our place. I love her just the same, despite this serious flaw in her DNA.

Yet on vacation at the beach, I read about something even more repulsive than ketchup. Much more. It was in Tom Hanchett's food column in the *Charlotte*

Observer. He wrote about Luis Echeverry, a native Colombian who operates a Charlotte hot dog stand.

Echeverry will fix 'em any way you like. But his specialty comes from his South American homeland. To wit: First into the bun go potato chips, followed by the dog. Then crushed pineapple, crumbled white taco cheese, mustard, honey, a pink sauce called "salsa rosada," and more potato chips. Then the whole shebang is topped off with a hard-boiled quail egg. I, barf, kid you not.

Isn't Colombia a major player in illegal drug trafficking and use? Far be it from me to suggest a link.

JUST SMELL ALL THAT DOUGH

Les Clevenger, who lives on Melton Hill Lake, was breakfasting on his boat dock and watched a crow pick up a dead minnow from the shoreline, then fly to a piece of biscuit Les has tossed aside a few minutes earlier. The bird deposited the minnow atop the biscuit, crammed the whole shebang in its beak, and flew off.

"Sounds like southern lox and bagel to me," Les quipped.

If you thought bottled water was crazy, brace yourself for what's next: Canned air.

Yes, air—the stuff that's only a sniff away. Coming soon to nostrils near you will be air in bottles and cans.

Already there are a number of Internet sites where you can purchase canned air. I've seen prices ranging from five to thirty dollars—although, strangely enough, nobody seems to advertise exactly what size containers of air they're selling. I suppose this is akin to the old saw about expensive goods in exclusive stores: If you have to ask about details, you shouldn't be shopping in the first place.

This isn't pedestrian air, of course. Mostly, it's pure oxygen. It comes flavored in such vintages as "mountain mist" and "tropical breeze."

According to the airheads selling this material, a quick hit revitalizes tired bodies, promotes clearer thinking, improves energy, and increases metabolism. Plus, they say it's great for treating a hangover.

(Just wondering: If you were drinking bourbon-and-bottled, as opposed to bourbon-and-branch, shouldn't you not be hungover in the first place? Give me rotgut, thank you. If I'm destined to wind up with a throbbing head and queasy stomach, at least I'll have a good excuse.)

Of course, there are times when a dose of fresh air would be appreciated. Anyone familiar with cattle feedlots, sewage treatment plants, paper mills, and political debates has vast experience in this regard.

But for day in and day out snorting? I think not. Seems like such a ridiculous waste of money.

Still, I've been sorely mistaken before. Sure was with bottled water. Ten years from now, I don't want to start a remorseful column with, "What a dunce I am! I doubled up with laughter when bottled air hit the market a few years ago—and yesterday, shares of Tank o'Air Amalgamated were selling for five hundred bucks a pop."

So maybe I ought to quit poking fun at this fledging industry and invest heavily while the getting's cheap. Then I can retire to Bermuda and pay someone to serve me my water and air with gold-plated utensils.

If I do get into the canned oxygen business, though, I'm going to come up with more imaginative flavors than "mountain mist" (which could just as easily be Gatlinburg asphalt on a sultry August afternoon) and "tropical breeze" (downwind from a bait shop in Panama City, Florida, perhaps?).

Instead, I'll shoot for a sure-nuff winner. Show me a can of "Pizza Hut" air, and I'll show you what big money really smells like.

DON'T DIP DIRTY DOLLOPS

He's not a quarterback or a coach, band director, or radio announcer. Nonetheless, Dr. Paul L. Dawson is an important figure in modern football festivities. That's true for Big Orange Country and anywhere else in this sports-watching, snack-munching nation.

Officially, Dawson is a microbiologist and professor of food science at South Carolina's Clemson University. Unofficially, he is the dean of dip, the chancellor of chips, the crown prince of crackers. And after you learn about one of his latest research projects, you'll never feel the same about buffet browsing during a pre-game or post-game party—or any other gathering where vittles are there for the taking.

Remember the old episode from "Seinfeld" where George Costanza catches flak from other grazers after double-dipping a chip between bites? That was the inspiration for Dawson's study, which has been accepted for publication by the professional *Journal of Food Safety*.

Prof Dawson and a team of eight students replicated the "Seinfeld" scene under strict scientific guidelines. They tested with wheat crackers and three varieties of dip. I won't bore you with all the technical findings, but suffice to say they struck Cootie City.

In as few as three re-dips, subjects transferred upwards of ten thousand bacteria from their mouths into the communal bowl. Assuming there are multiple double- and triple-dippers in any given buffet line, that means the guacamole will soon become a green, gooey, gross glob of germs.

"It certainly made me less likely to hit the buffet line," Dawson said in a phone interview. "If you're at a party and see people double-dipping, you have to ask yourself, 'Do I want to kiss everyone else in this room?'"

Before you panic, please know the good professor isn't predicting plague.

"In the big scheme of things, this probably isn't a huge issue," he told me. "But during cold and flu season, it could certainly increase the spread of germs and disease."

This isn't the first time Dawson—who sounds like an educator who makes learning fun by blending scientific theory with real-life situations—has waded into a food fight. Some of his previous research into the spread of bacteria has disproved the "five-second rule" and the "blow-off rule" for spilled food, as well as the "alcohol will kill any germs rule" for spiked eggnog made with raw eggs.

"Maybe if you were taking a shot of whiskey between sips and swishing it around in your mouth, it would kill the bacteria," he laughed. "Otherwise, not."

The chip dip study has made Dawson somewhat of a campus celebrity. After the New York Times reported his findings, he became the subject of more than seventy newspaper stories and radio reports. He said one illustration in a British publication showed a giant set of lips blooming ominously from a bowl of dip.

But he refuses to take himself too seriously. I cited an upcoming Clemson-Alabama game and asked if Tiger fans would heed Doc Dawson's advice at their own tailgates.

"I'm sure they won't," he said.

NO FIRSTS, LET ALONE SECONDS

Men all over the world: Count your blessings you aren't living in Beijing, China, and dining at the Guo-Li-Zhuang restaurant. This is one food joint my shadow will never cross.

I'm not a finicky eater. Quite the contrary. I've spent a lifetime judging food by quantity, not quality. This proud tradition runs in the family. My late father answered to "Big Sam" long before "Little Sam" arrived and made the distinction necessary. When my grandson Max was an infant and being introduced to solid food, he would invariably screw his face into a frown at the taste of any new flavor—then promptly smile and open his mouth for more. In the Venable clan, Chow "R" Us.

All that being said, I can assure you nothing on Guo-Li-Zhuang's menu interests me in the least. In fact, it's all I can do to keep from cringing in sympathetic pain because the restaurant's bill of fare centers on one type of meat and one type only.

In deference to delicate sensitivities, suffice to say this main ingredient is an organ found solely in male animals. Oh, and I'm not talking about certain varieties of "oysters" you consumed at Uncle Earl's house out in the country. I'm talking about an organ that is packaged in units of one, not two.

Yes, my brothers. *That* organ.

You name the critter, and Guo-Li-Zhuang has a piece of it on the menu: dog, yak, oxen, deer, goat, horse, donkey, even seals.

I'm not joking. I hold before me an article from England's *London Daily Telegraph* that describes Guo-Li-Zhuang's exotic cuisine. Alfred Whitehead, a *News Sentinel* reader from Rockwood, alerted me to it.

(For the record, Alfred is cringing, too. Also for the record, so is the article's author, Richard Spencer, who opened with this sentence: "The menu at Beijing's latest venue for its growing army of gourmets is eye-watering rather than mouth-watering.")

In all honesty, I'd be squeamish about eating any part of a dog, donkey, or seal, let alone *that* organ. American palates simply aren't wired for some animals. But once you get over the concept of slaughtering any and all beasts for their flesh, I suppose it doesn't matter what winds up in the skillet.

What about the taste?

Spencer ordered the restaurant's signature dish, a medley of *that* organ from six different animals, boiled in chicken stock. His assessments ranged from "gamey" (dog) to "identical to gristle" (ox) to "the appearance and feel of overcooked squid tentacles" (deer and goat) to "light and fatty" (horse) to "firm color and taste" (donkey).

I'll take his word on it.

Spencer says Chinese men are gorging on *that* organ to improve their virility. How weird. As much as I enjoy fish, I've never eaten it to improve my ability to swim. Nor duck, dove, quail, grouse, or wild turkey in hopes of being able to fly.

If I wanted improvement in *that* department, I'd start with a "Vitamin V" prescription from my doctor.

Chapter **7**

THE SCIENCE OF SILLINESS

Be it known to all that I stand foursquare behind the principle of scientific research. Bring on the experiments, the tests, the studies, the investigations! Award lucrative grants! Bestow PhDs by the multiplied dozen! From the depths of the oceans to the vast realms of outer space, there's oh-so-much to learn about this planet we call home!

Meaning, of course, there is oh-so-much to poke fun at. This is the sacred duty of newspaper smart-asses, and I embrace the challenge with all my mind, strength, and will.

The size of a project, its scope, and its far-reaching implications to the betterment of humankind matter not one whit. I don't care if we're talking about huge, high-tech government research contracts, funded by so much federal money that employees of the Treasury Department are forced to sell their own blood plasma every month; or penny-ante stuff any decent office worker can easily hide on his or her monthly expense account. What's important for me is the chance to spin this serious, dedicated effort into 113 lines of daily drivel and get paid for it.

Perhaps this is a defense mechanism on my part because highly scientific, highly technical subjects—and by that I mean anything more complicated than the owner's manual for a three-battery flashlight—makes my head spin. (Speaking of which: Did you ever look at the schematic drawing that comes with any kind of equipment these days? Who draws these things? Why? Do they truly believe normal, rational people can follow all those zigzag lines to find the correct part when their equipment stops working? Don't they know it's much easier, not to mention more satisfying, to beat the offending equipment with a hammer and then go buy a new one? Sorry. I tend to digress. Where was I? Oh, yes, science and technology.)

Actually there's a plausible explanation for why I'm so scatterbrained right now: I've just lost track of time. Literally.

According to scientists at NASA's Jet Propulsion Laboratory, a 2010 earthquake in Chile slightly shifted the Earth on its axis. This resulted in a loss of approximately 1/1,000,000,000th of a second in a typical day. Frankly, it seems like an oxymoron to use the term "approximately" in the same breath as measurements of "one-millionth." But let us not dwell on petty details.

Truth be told, there's quite a squabble right now in the scientific community over whether this axis-shifting and time-loss business is even related to the earthquake. In a report on National Public Radio, various highbrows jousted with each other about the matter. Some claimed the earthquake was to blame. Others said these shifts and time changes are naturally occurring factors, completely unrelated to an 8.8-magnitude shake. Sorta like the he-said/she-said arguments over global warming.

But I say, "Who cares? Just be thankful there's a ready-made excuse if and when you screw something up." And I encourage my fellow citizens to think likewise.

Let's say you've got a big corporate meeting planned in a few days. All of the suits from HQ will be there. You, the boss, and everyone in the local office have rehearsed individual roles for the upcoming dog-and-pony show until you could perform them in your sleep.

Unfortunately, that's where your performance is taking place because you either forgot to set the alarm or slept through it. And now you're running late.

No problem-o.

Even if the meeting is well under way, and even if Mister Big is staring daggers in your direction as you saunter through the door, resist the urge to panic. Instead, take a slow, deliberate look at your wristwatch, then walk over to the clock on the wall and move its hands ever-so-slightly back. Then turn to the assembled masses and announce, with an air of unbridled confidence: "You folks can thank me later for getting us back on schedule. Let's get down to business. Time's wasting!"

Or let's say you've parked your car at a meter on the street, and as you're walking back toward it a cop is preparing to issue a ticket.

"There a problem, officer?" you inquire.

"Two of them," he replies. "The meter has expired, plus your car's parked outside the designated space."

Don't even flinch. Instead, whip out of a copy of the NASA report—you *have* downloaded it just for this occasion, haven't you?—and say, "Wrong, sir. When I left my vehicle, it was parked correctly and well within the lines. But the Earth's recent axis-shift has caused it to move. As for expired time? Pish-posh. As you can readily see, I still have 1/1,000,000,000th of a second remaining."

No doubt the officer will be so impressed by your knowledge he'll let you off with a warning. Well, yes; it may be a warning to his fellow cops: "Stay away from that guy! He's nuts!" But what the heck. Beats a ticket any day.

Since I've broached the subject of NASA and outer space, perhaps I should tell you about my latest real estate venture. Hate to brag, but I've just gained ownership of some very exclusive property. It's like nowhere on Earth.

Mainly because it's not on Earth at all. It's roughly 250,000 miles away.

Specifically, it's in Area F-4, Quadrant Charlie, Lot Number 008/1180, latitude thirty-three degrees west, longitude twenty degrees north, one square south and eight squares east of the extreme northwest corner. On the moon.

I'm not joking. I hold the official deed in my hands. Oh, and not only do I own the surface area of this valuable real estate, I also retain all the mineral rights. That document sits before me, too.

But wait, there's more. I also have a copy of the Lunar Constitution, complete with a Bill of Rights. It guarantees me the option to build on my property or consign it to someone else. Such a deal.

This vast acreage was a gift from my cousin Breck Grover, who lives in Denver. Breck purchased it from a British outfit called Moon Estates, which in turn has acquired all lunar property rights from one Dennis M. Hope.

Who is Dennis M. Hope? He is "The Head Cheese," as recognized by the United Nations. I quote from the official paperwork: "This is a transcript of the Declaration of Ownership document lodged by Dennis M. Hope with the United Nations General Assembly, the United States of America government, and the government of what was then known as the U.S.S.R. This document was lodged November 22, 1980, within the framework of the Homestead Act of 1862. Since the date of the signing of this document, November 22 has become known as the Lunar Day of Independence."

So there.

No, I haven't toured my lunar estate yet. These things take time. When you're a land baron, you can't just drop everything and go tramping off into the wilderness to inspect your latest acquisition. That's what hirelings are for. I'll get one of my assistants to do it. I have more important matters right now. Like maximizing profit.

The first thing I'm going to do is contact the folks at NASA and see if they have a lunar landing planned for Area F-4, Quadrant Charlie, Lot Number 008/1180 any time soon. If so, I expect rental fees. I shall instruct the director of my leasing operations to start negotiations at $25 million, minimum. Per mission.

If that doesn't pan out, no sweat. I have several other options in mind.

I'm going to call the Jims—Clayton and Haslam—and tell 'em if they want in on the ground floor of some exciting new expansion opportunities to get over here quick. With suitcases full of cash. Area F-4, Quadrant Charlie, Lot Number 008/1180 would be perfect for a mobile home park or a Pilot Travel Center. If neither Clayton nor Haslam is interested, there's always a Wendy's, McDonald's, KFC, Subway, Krystal, or Walmart waiting in the wings for immediate expansion and franchise licensing. And, if all else fails, Starbucks.

See? The entrepreneurial spirit is alive and well on Earth and beyond, thanks to science and technology. Because of the wizards who explore new horizons and test new ideas, Americans of the twenty-first century enjoy a lifestyle unmatched at any time in history. No longer are we chained to cumbersome, archaic machinery. Instead, we are chained to teeny-tiny machinery with screens so small I suspect the entire populace will be wearing jeweler's glasses by the year 2075. Not only that, but their forefingers and thumbs will be the size of turkey drumsticks. This is evolution in action.

The hottest ticket in scientific research right now is energy. If we can't drill our way to more oil—or invade our way into more oil-producing countries—then, by golly, we can study our way into more oil! And little did I know what potential gushers exist in my home state.

I speak of pond scum.

You immediately thought of politicians, lawyers, and newspaper columnists, of course. But in reality, there are experiments galore on how to turn common, everyday algae into fuel for the internal combustion engine. One of these projects is taking place in the state of Iowa as we speak. Through the use of a "photobioreactor" (an actual word every Scrabble player should commit to immediate memory), Iowa algae is being grown in massive amounts and then converted into biofuel.

But you know what I say?

I say ppfffft! Who needs photobioreactors? Here in East Tennessee, we've already got vast, fertile farmlands of this aquatic kudzu begging to be harvested. It's in the water all around us.

A few days ago I launched my bass boat into the fragrant waters of Fort Loudoun Lake and, while preparing to climb aboard, took time to peer into the murk. Yee-ouzers! Before me lay acres of ethanol-in-the-making. That's just one lake. When you think about the hundreds of miles of algae-rich rivers, streams, and creeks around here, it starts to smell like real money.

Why, there are even two algae bonanzas in my own back yard.

One is our ground-level birdbath, which is a misnomer because birds rarely bathe in it. However, it serves as the local watering hole for thirsty squirrels, chipmunks, skunks, possums, rabbits, and raccoons. Despite regular spray-washings and the occasional dose of bleach, it takes on a green cast from the start of warm weather until first frost and serves as proof positive that wild animals are blessed with guts of steel.

The other source is my wife's fish, frog, pickerel weed, and lily-pad pond, home of the most pampered thirty-cent goldfish in the history of aquaculture. At regular intervals every summer, Mary Ann wades into the morass on a mission. Imagine Moses parting the Red Sea with a fine-mesh seine instead of a staff. With deft sweeps, she brings slimy algal blankets to the surface, then hauls the entire dripping mess to the compost pile.

Any time my wife starts to download and print computer pictures at home— and I'm asked to fetch photo-quality paper from the closet shelf, I instinctively flinch when I realize the lights are on.

Sorry, but I spent too many years fumbling around darkrooms in the old days of newspapering. The thought of "photo paper" just sitting there, uncovered and unprotected? It ain't right.

Amazing. All this time Mary Ann and I have been fighting a losing battle against algae when we should have been cultivating it for fuel! Jed Clampett may have felt the same way when he was shootin' at some food and up through the ground came a'bubblin' crude.

Now think about this opportunity on a nationwide scope. Every year, Americans spend millions of dollars on bleaches and cleansers with tiny foaming bubbles, trying to rid themselves of algae—when they could be using it to put the pedal to the metal!

Imagine all the sources available at nearly every home in this region. Between seeps, birdbaths, wet basements, leaky hoses, shower stalls, mounds of used tires, and other breeding grounds for ooey-gooey gunk, we're our own mini-OPEC.

In fact, we might even come close to achieving perpetual motion.

You take your average East Tennessee Redneck Roadster, which hasn't been washed, waxed, or vacuumed since the Carter administration, slap one of those photobioreactors on the dashboard, and that puppy oughta run from K-town to Memphis. Back in the old days, your father may have driven with a tiger in his tank. But here in the modern era, we shall cruise with the ooze.

Economics research is another scientific endeavor that I (a) know nothing about and (b) frequently comment on. I don't have to have any knowledge of economics, thank you, because I know a couple of distinguished lecturers in this field: Janice Rogers and Betty Plemons.

Neither Prof Rogers nor Prof Plemons is fluent in the Consumer Price Index, the Gross Domestic Product, job growth, money supplies, NASDAQ, NYSE, Standard & Poor's, retail sales, building permits, Earnings Growth Rate, and other traditional indicators of boom and bust.

Indeed, Prof Rogers and Prof Plemons likely wouldn't know the Consumer Price Index, the Gross Domestic Product, et al., from a paperclip.

They do, however, have a keen eye for critical trends, thanks to their prestigious degrees in C.B.B.D.

Cracker Barrel Breakfast Dining.

Prof Rogers and Prof Plemons are sisters. They live in Lenoir City. Every Sunday morning, they share a table at the Cracker Barrel outlet in their hometown. They are particularly partial to pancakes and French toast. And therein lies the source of their incredible acumen.

"One day, we got to noticing that Cracker Barrel had changed its syrup," Prof Rogers explained to me. "They used to serve 100-percent maple syrup. It always came in 1.7-ounce bottles. But no more. These days, it's a blend of maple and other syrups. And the bottle size has been reduced to 1.5 ounces. That told both of us that the economy is in a tailspin."

I relayed this impressive discovery to the headquarters of Cracker Barrel Old Country Stores in Lebanon and almost immediately heard back from Julie K. Davis, senior director of corporate communications.

Guess what? The findings of Prof Rogers and Prof Plemons were correct! Well, sorta.

Cracker Barrel did indeed change its syrup formula in 2008, Davis admitted. The full-bore maple was diluted to a blend of 55 percent maple and 45 percent cane. But it had more to do with botany than economics.

Said Davis via e-mail: "There simply isn't as much maple syrup available in the world as there has been in previous years. Cracker Barrel never wanted to change the pancake syrup it offers and worked very hard to ensure that the new exclusive syrup meets our quality standards and, more importantly, the quality standards of our guests. No other restaurant company comes even close to having as high a percentage of maple syrup in their offerings."

Isn't high-brow research simply delici—er, I mean informative?

Of course, a callous person might suggest that Prof Rogers and Prof Plemons (1) are ingesting far too much syrup, maple or otherwise, (2) have a vast surplus of time on their hands, and (3) should engage in casual breakfast conversation about sports or the weather rather than poring over the fine print on the labels of bottles, whether they are 1.5- or 1.7-ounce in size.

But what right does a callous person have challenging the research methods of two dedicated economics experts like Prof Rogers and Prof Plemons? Especially if they offer to share a few bites?

LOOK OUT ABOVE AND BELOW

Handymen, amateurs and professionals alike, will tell you there's nothing more aggravating than a dropped or misplaced tool.

You're on a ladder, trying to reattach a piece of guttering to the house. You set a nail in place, but just as you start to tap it, the hammer falls from your grasp. It clatters across the rung and drops to the ground, fifteen feet away. There's nothing to do but climb down and retrieve it. *Arrrgh!*

You're changing bits in the power drill. One is out and another almost in when you bump your elbow on a chair, causing the new bit to fall silently to the carpet and bounce under the coffee table, where it will hide for the next twenty minutes as you search in vain. *Arrrgh!*

You're installing a new knob on the bathroom door when the bedroom telephone rings. En route to answering, you absentmindedly set your screwdriver on top of the medicine cabinet. Telephone conversation concluded, you return to the original chore—which now can't be completed because you can't remember where you put that (bleeping) screwdriver. *Arrrgh!*

If any of these hassles sound familiar, perhaps you can sympathize with occupants of the international space station. These folks are involved in an extensive, expensive, wild-blue-yonder maintenance and remodeling job. Naturally, there have been problems.

Astronaut Heide Stefanyshyn-Piper (who surely holds a record for longest name in orbit) was outside the spacecraft a few days ago, attempting to lubricate some gears on a rotary joint. A grease gun in her tool bag sprang a leak. When she tried to clean up the gunk, her entire kit—containing two grease guns, a putty knife, and some cleaning materials—drifted away.

This wasn't as easy to retrieve as a dropped hammer. In fact, it has been lost forever, one more bit of space litter. NASA estimated the cost at $100,000.

(Note to self: Holy mother of pearl! If newspaper layoffs continue, consider opening a hardware store for space travelers. Just sell a couple of tool kits, and you're set for life.)

But this is a minor setback compared to the task astronauts now face. They're about to start adding extra bedrooms, a kitchen, and a new bathroom to the space station.

Talk about the worst job on Earth! Or above Earth, as the case may be. I speak as a battle-scarred veteran of the home-remodeling wars when I say this exercise will be fraught with headaches.

It's one thing to take an incorrect measurement, run out of screws, break a saw blade, or cut the wrong board when you're on terra firma and there's a store nearby. It's a whole 'nuther matter when your neighborhood Home Depot is two hundred miles straight down.

That's not the worst of it, though.

The bathroom they're building includes a $154 million gizmo to recycle urine and sweat into drinking water. But it's not working. Engineers on the ground and in the air can't figure out what's wrong. I can only imagine what sort of "tests" they're having to run.

And to think I felt sorry for people in outer space because they had to drink that gosh-awful Tang.

A MAJOR MEADOW MISSION

The latest scientific research into cattle is finished, and the findings are astonishing—if not downright revolutionary. So get ready to be shocked.

This study had *nothing whatsoever* to do with bovine flatulence!

See? I told you it was big news. I have just perused the results myownself, and nowhere do the words "methane" or "gas" appear.

As you know, scientists have been measuring cattle toots since the Middle Ages. But now they have turned their attention to another riveting bovine question: Which direction does Bossie face when she eats?

I am not making this up. This research was conducted by German biologists, and the findings recently were reported in the Proceedings of the National Academy of Sciences in Washington.

Actually, it's a follow-up study. In 2008, scientists determined that cattle align themselves in a north-south direction when feeding. Now, they say that's not wholly accurate. Seems if high-voltage wires are nearby, it can disorient the animals, causing them to graze in different directions.

I quote from the findings: "When the power lines run east-west, that's the way grazing cattle line up, too."

There's more. If a power line runs northeast-southwest or northwest-southeast, it tends to throw a monkey wrench in things, causing the cattle to face in any of 360 degrees.

Of course, cynics would ask: Who cares?

What?! We all should care, for Pete's sake! If you can determine which direction a cow is turned, you'll know how to position yourself to avoid a blast of methane gas!

For example, if Bossie is facing due north, you should avoid her south end. Conversely, if she is facing south, you should steer clear of her north end. She's facing east? Then you should avoid the west. And vice-versa. Is this remarkable science or what?

Other power-line directions could prove problematic, however. If the wire runs northeast-southwest (causing Bossie to turn northwest-southeast), then you should realign your position accordingly—all the while keeping an eye out for fresh meadow muffins, especially if you're wearing good shoes.

Naturally, there can be extenuating circumstances. As the report says, "Wind and weather can also affect ways which cows choose to face."

Thus, if a power line is running northwest-southeast (causing Bossie to turn northeast-southwest), snow is falling, and the wind is blowing at, say, twenty-five miles per hour out of the north, you should—well, I'm not exactly sure what you should do, except I hope you brought along a warm coat.

If you think I'm making fun of this high-brow research, think again. This is cutting-edge stuff. In fact, I'd like to know where I can sign up for one of these jobs.

I can watch cattle with the best of 'em. What's more, my 1969 degree from the University of Tennessee is a "B.S. in journalism." Says so right there on my diploma.

Sounds like the pluperfect qualification.

IDK SQUAT ABOUT TEXTING

There is a cheat sheet in the top left drawer of my desk. It proves what a doddering, clueless croak I've become.

I assembled this guide out of necessity. It's the only way I can decipher some of the email I receive from readers.

Frankly, I should count my blessings because email communication is as high tech as I go. Meaning I've never text-messaged. And, the Good Lawd Hisself willing, never will.

It's bad enough that some fools feel so compelled to reach out and touch someone that they walk around with a cell phone at their jaw every waking minute. Or, even worse, with one of those hideous hands-free devices impaled in one ear like a cruel medical experiment gone awry. But at least these people speak honest-to-gosh words.

Caroline Burkey recalls a poem her father, a rural school teacher in upper East Tennessee, quoted from one of his students many years ago: "Spring has sprung; the snow has went. It was not did by accident. The birds have flew, as you have saw, back to the north by nature's law."

No doubt the author went on to enjoy a great career in English literature.

Not so in the world of text-messaging. Texters have a language of their own, and it's worming into everyday English.

My introduction to this nuttiness began when I started getting email from somebody named LOL.

Such as: "Your column today was funny! LOL"

Or: "Have you ever considered counseling? LOL"

Or: "Do they actually pay you to write that $#%*!? LOL"

I finally asked if anyone else in the newsroom was getting email from this LOL person. When the catcalls subsided, I was informed that LOL is text-speak for "laughing out loud."

(At this point, it is permissible for children to guffaw at Old Man Venable's utter stupidity—after they have looked up "guffaw" in the dictionary. Oops, my bad; kids don't know what a dictionary is these days. Forget I mentioned it.)

In any event, that's why I keep the cheat sheet. With it, I've become familiar with a few of the more common buzzwords, like IMHO ("in my humble opinion") and IDK ("I don't know").

Alas, some trick me every time. Whenever I see SWIM ("see what I mean?"), I instinctively think it refers to my morning habit of stroking laps in the West Side YMCA's pool.

Even worse are the emoticon doohickeys. I always have to consult the cheat sheet if an email contains an ":-)" or an ":-(" or an ";-)" because I never can remember which means what. For the sane who haven't bought into this New Age gobbledygook, those symbols translate to "happy," "sad," and "wink," respectively. I think.

Of course, it is incumbent upon any geezer-in-training to gripe about members of the younger generation. Their clothes are scandalous. Their music makes no sense. Their manners are atrocious. Blah-blah-blah. This has been going on since 400 B.C.

But it does trouble me that text-messaging marks yet another chapter in the dumbing-down of the masses. There's nothing wrong with short, simple declarations. Ernest Hemingway, who knew a thing or three about putting words on paper, was a master of brevity.

But imagine how the world of literature would have been robbed if Santiago, addressing his giant marlin in *The Old Man and the Sea,* had merely said "BFF, LY" instead of, "Fish, I love you and respect you very much."

PARDON ME WHILE I SCRATCH

Here's another reason to worry about global warming: As vile as it is today, poison ivy will be even nastier in the future.

At least that's the scenario envisioned by scientists studying the "greenhouse effect" created when massive amounts of fossil fuels are burned. Seems the resulting increase in carbon dioxide will provide ideal growing conditions for the plant we all love to hate.

According to a 2006 story in *Science News* magazine, researchers at Duke University erected elevated pipes so that trees and other plants growing in test plots could bathe in either (1) your basic, plain-brown-wrapper air or (2) air that was laced with extra carbon dioxide. Because plants take in carbon dioxide during the process of photosynthesis, it stands to reason that they might prosper from additional doses.

Did they ever, especially the nefarious P.I.! Poison ivy treated with additional carbon dioxide grew at more than twice the rate of its noxious cousins subsisting on standard air. All told, poison ivy's growth spurt was almost five times greater than other plant species.

Hold on. The picture gets worse. Researchers discovered that "urushiol"—the oily substance within poison ivy that causes so much misery to humans—

turned out to be as much as 30 percent more potent in the plants enhanced with carbon dioxide.

So what does this bode over the next half-century if carbon dioxide levels increase exponentially, as expected? It means we all need to grow sharper fingernails, for starters. Also, stock up on backscratchers, sandpaper, metal files, wood rasps, and other articles of abrasion.

Speaking as an expert who never met a chigger bite, 'skeeter welt, seed tick infestation, or poison ivy rash that couldn't be improved with vigorous clawing, I say let the digging begin.

Oh, sure. I've heard medical advice to the contrary. You have, too. Doctors and mothers have preached it for years. Don't scratch that bite, welt, rash, and infestation, they say. That just makes it worse, or else you'll get it infected. Just put some of this (insert name of preferred ointment here) on it and leave it alone.

Horsepuckey!

What good is skin irritation if you can't fight back? I say go down swinging. Or scratching, as the case may be.

About ten summers ago, I managed to attract the mother lode of seed ticks shortly before we left for vacation at the beach. Both of my ankles and both lower legs were covered. They itched like the proverbial fireball from hell.

But one day after a dip in the ocean, I discovered the perfect remedy: Walk ashore, coat your wet skin with fine powdery sand, sit down on your beach towel, rub your ankles violently against each other, then run back into the ocean and let the brine sting away at your bloody flesh.

What? You say that's about the nuttiest medical "advice" you ever heard? Yeah, that's what my wife was saying too—several weeks later, as the abrasions finally started to heal.

But, boy-howdy, it sure felt good at the time!

SOMETHING TO REALLY CHEW ON

At long last, mothers have a new hygiene warning to preach to their kids.

Out is: "Be sure to put on clean underwear before you leave home because if you have a wreck, you won't be taken to the hospital in dirty clothes."

In is: "Be sure to brush your teeth before you leave home because if you die and your body is discovered thousands of years later, people won't find old food in your mouth."

Clearly, some Neanderthal mothers didn't say that to their offspring. As a result—oh, the humiliation!—their children's teeth are being picked apart, literally, to see what they contain.

I'm not making this up. The story was first reported in an academic journal, *Proceedings of the National Academy of Sciences.* Ever since, it has been repeated by news agencies all over the world.

Seems that the choppers from three Neanderthals, discovered in Iraq and Belgium, were examined. They ranged between 36,000 and 44,000 years of age. Based on analysis of the plaque scraped from tooth surfaces, scientists think these folks ate much more vegetative matter than was previously believed. Not only that, the veggies had been cooked before ingestion.

Here's what anthropologist Amanda Henry, who led the research team, had to say in the scientific journal: "These data suggest that Neanderthals were capable of complex food-gathering behaviors that included both hunting of large game animals and the harvesting and processing of plant foods."

(Here's what columnist Venable had to say when he realized someone was actually prowling around in a 44,000-year-old mouth: "Aaakkk! And I thought morning breath was bad!")

But at least this gave me something to talk about with Tracy Queener, my dental hygienist, when I was sitting in her chair a few days ago.

Typically, my intelligent conversations range between "muhbshth thipsrhd" and "pwscbnhtr hysckltwzpt," depending on how many cotton swabs, metal probes, and fingers are protruding from my mouth at any given moment.

This time, Tracy stopped long enough to describe the various "scalers" and "jacquettes" people in her profession deploy when they're hacking away at dental buildup. During rinsings and spittings—when I was able to say something besides "muhbshth thipsrhd" and "pwscbnhtr hysckltwzpt"—I asked her, "Those things work sorta like a hoe, don't they?"

"Yes," Tracy responded. "There's even one called a 'hoe.' It's used for serious buildup, the really terrible stuff."

"Would it work on 44,000-year-old plaque?" I inquired.

"No," she replied. "You'd need a drill for something like that."

Arrrgh! The dreaded D-word! Frozen in fear, I was unable to speak further. In fact, it was all I could do to refrain from assuming the fetal position, let alone offer something witty, like "muhbshth thipsrhd" and "pwscbnhtr hysckltwzpt" during the remainder of the procedure.

Tracy seemed to understand. In 2013 A.D. or 40,000 B.C., dental people are accustomed to cowardly responses.

THE WORST ROAD TRIP IN HISTORY

Near the top of my List of Experiences I Can Happily Do Without—right up there with bullfighting, getting Tasered, and going three rounds with Mike Tyson, especially when he's in an ear-nibbling mood—is spending eighteen months sealed in a metallic tube.

There are six men who feel otherwise. These guys—three Russians, two Europeans, and one from China—have just been locked inside a space simulator in Moscow. They're making a mock journey to Mars.

I understand the scientific need for this weird experiment. It's all part of the training process. It's only a matter of time before some nation attempts a sure-nuff Mars mission, and unlike a comparatively short hop to the moon, this will be extraordinarily long and gruesome.

Imagine being a teenager and having to drive from Knoxville to Atlanta on a hot day, no AC, with your mom, dad, dorky little sister, and goofy Aunt Ida all singing "She'll Be Comin' 'Round the Mountain" nonstop. That's the kind of torture I'm talking about.

Based on what I've been reading about this project, every excruciating aspect has been considered. Consider:

The astronauts are housed in a contraption one of them described as "three or four Winnebagos connected by tunnels that you crawl through."

Crammed into this space is 520 days' worth of food, water, and other supplies and equipment.

There are no windows, not even one to peek out at tiny "Earth" in the distance.

All communication to and from mission control will incorporate a twenty-minute delay, just as it will Way Out Yonder.

Perhaps worst of all, these merry men will only be allowed to shower once a week.

Ouch. I assume clothespins were included in the necessary cargo. Either that or the participants were pre-screened for a faulty sense of smell.

As they go about their daily tasks, the astronauts will be monitored for physical and psychological changes. Neither should be difficult to detect.

Even with the services of a small exercise chamber—yeah, it's jammed in there with all the other gear—these folks are liable to turn into humanoid jelly by the end of the journey. But that would be the least of my worries. I get panicky in tight spaces for even a short amount of time. By Day Three I'd be so freaked out, my fellow passengers would vote unanimously to have me walk the plank.

Even if these guys are ideally suited for lengthy periods together, you know tensions will fester and boil at some point. One "Says who?" will lead to a "Says me!" and the next thing you know, fists will be flying. Not to mention any and all items not securely bolted down.

Which probably explains why windows aren't included on this buggy.

WE WEREN'T BITTEN BY THIS LIST

Here's a celebration we can really sink our teeth into—mainly because our choppers are up to the challenge: The Top Worst-Teeth Cities list has just been announced, and Knoxville is nowhere to be found.

What a relief.

Usually when some disgusting hygiene rating comes out, K-town finds itself thrown into the mix. Like what happened in 2003, when a deodorant company ranked us the forty-eighth sweatiest (translation: in bad need of underarm protection) city in the nation.

This time, the survey was done by a New York outfit, the American Society for Dental Aesthetics, and announced by a Web site called TotalBeauty.com. These folks enlisted the services of one Irwin Smigel, DDS, who, coincidentally or otherwise, is founder and president of the society.

(Is it just me, or does Doc Smigel's name sound like it belongs on some fancy designer toothpaste? "Brush with Smigel for a smile that shows you care about what goes in your mouth.")

Antique tractors and other mechanized farm equipment from days gone by are immensely popular these days. Do you suppose one hundred years from now, grizzled-face geeks will sit around and show off their IBM Selectric typewriters, PC Juniors, and Apple II computers, while trading floppy discs and listening to music on their Walkmans?

"Factors such as regular dentist visits, not smoking, minimizing coffee, tea, soda, and red wine intake, and of course brushing and flossing, are on top of every dentist's list," the groups said in a news release. "There are other factors, such as living in an area with hard water or a dry climate, which can stain teeth, create a dry mouth, and cause bacteria," leading to a mouthful of pure-T ugly.

The capitol jewel of cruddy choppers, according to Doc Smigel, is Biloxi, Mississippi. According to his findings, "Biloxi is like a perfect storm for bad teeth: Number fifty-one in dentists per capita, number fifty-two (he's including the District of Columbia and Puerto Rico) in dental visits, number fifty-one in exercise, and number forty-nine in fruit and vegetable consumption. As if that weren't enough, it's also number seven in tooth loss and the third smokiest city in America. Teeth don't stand a chance here!"

Number two on Doc Smigel's list was Huntington, West Virginia. Rounding out the rest of the top five were Mobile, Alabama; Tulsa, Oklahoma; and Baton Rouge, Louisiana. Even though Knoxville was spared, one Tennessee city did get nailed; Bristol came in at number six.

"Bristol is the second smokiest city, according to *U.S. News and World Report*," Doc Smigel said in his analysis, and "smoking can cause major staining of teeth. Plus, the tar can contribute to gum disease. The state is number three in most teeth lost (according to the Centers for Disease Control) and number forty-seven in amount of exercise, which means residents have two strikes against them."

In all, Doc Smigel named fourteen bad-teeth cities. How weird. Whoever heard of a Top Fourteen list for anything? Aren't these things supposed to break in groups of five?

Hmm. This is purely a guess on my part, but maybe this bizarre numbering has something to do with adults having thirty-two permanent teeth, but generally losing four of the wisdom variety, leaving twenty-eight—fourteen upper and fourteen lower.

And, if brushed regularly with Smigel, they're sure to stay strong and pearly white for a lifetime!

STEP ONE: BEAT HEAD ON WALL

Yes, children, there is a hell. It is called a new computer system.

Our newspaper recently got redesigned. Part of the process involved tossing out our old computers and bringing in "new and improved" (insert hearty laugh here) ones.

I should be accustomed to this shell game by now. So should anybody who works in an office environment. About the time your equipment starts feeling comfortable, the suits decide you need something else. Such is life.

But this SaxoTech gizmo—it oughta be called WhackoTack—has taken the learning curve to new depths.

Oh, sure; all the functions we had before are still there. They've just been moved, repackaged, changed, rearranged. And slowed to sloth speed.

Imagine you wake up one morning and begin getting dressed. You open the sock drawer, only to find hammers and screwdrivers from the garage.

"What are these doing here?" you ask the geek who has been assigned to assist your transformation. "I expect to find socks in my sock drawer, not tools."

"It doesn't work that way in the new system," the geek says. "Your socks are now in the hall closet."

You start toward the staircase, but the geek interrupts: "You can't go that way anymore. Under the new system, you need to climb out your bedroom window—please note we have installed an OSHA-approved ladder—then walk around the house, enter through the front door, and proceed down the hall to the closet."

Like a good Stockholm-syndrome sufferer, you follow the new orders obediently. Sure enough, there are your socks. Except they're paired black-white, brown-blue.

"Why aren't they paired by the same color, like before?" you naively probe.

The geek smirks: "I knew you were going to ask. Just highlight them, double-click and drag."

After a yawning moment, the socks finally are regrouped by same color.

"Why go to all that trouble?" you inquire. But before the geek can reply, you already know the answer: That's the way it works under the new system.

Thus the humanoid reprogramming continues.

The only thing that has gotten me through this wretched week is a cheat sheet. I wrote it on real paper with a real pen. It takes me, step-by-step, through the intricate process of making a template, which I then fill with words and forward to a cyber-drooler somewhere. Assuming I don't ship it to Jupiter by mistake.

Yes, the time will come when I get comfortable with this beast. That will occur approximately six weeks before the suits decide we need an even newer computer system.

I sure could use a beer right now. Maybe there's one in the microwave.

YOU DON'T HAVE TO TAKE IT WITH YOU

Recalling a "Dennis the Menace" cartoon strip from long ago: It begins with Dennis and his young friend Joey digging in the freezer. Out they come with a fish—its eyes "X-ed" in cartoonist style to signify deader-than-a-doornail. They carry the frozen fish upstairs, fill a bathtub with water, toss it in, and watch for results.

Donna Heffner has a fully functional manual typewriter on the counter at her Spirit of Red Hill nature art shop in Rugby, Tennessee. She always keeps a sheet of paper in it, encouraging customers to hunt and peck on the keyboard and return the carriage when the bell dings.

"One girl, probably nine or ten years old, caught on quickly," Donna said. "She called out to her mother: 'Mom! Come look at this! It's awesome! You don't even have to wait for the printout!'"

"See, Joey," Dennis finally announces. "It's like I told ya. Once they're dead, they're dead."

Perhaps for fish, but not humans. Despite what you've previously heard about the certainty of death and taxes, I'm here to tell you that one part of this age-old equation ain't necessarily so.

Well, sort of. A company in (where else?) California has just launched a computer plan that "allows people to easily manage their 'virtual' presence after death."

This is true, so help me. I hold a news release from an outfit in Palo Alto called I-Postmortem Limited. It announces the formation of two online services "that will expand the boundaries of the Internet by allowing every human being to build his own immortality and leave a trace of his presence on earth."

To accomplish this goal, I-Postmortem has created a "World Virtual Cemetery, the resting place of the virtual memory of deceased people from all over the world." The release goes on: "I-Tomb is a multimedia memorial made of photos, videos, texts, music, and documents that encapsulate the life of a deceased person, telling the next generations who they were, what they believed in, and what the world they lived in was like."

Actually, there's nothing new about this concept, although the technology is radical. People have been "speaking" from the grave for generations—via memoirs, paintings and, more recently, photos and home movies. Computerization and digitization simply take it one step farther along. But I gotta wonder: At what point will technology really make it possible to communicate with folks in the Great Beyond?

I'm not sure I want to know. Imagine:

"Herb? Herb? HERB! It's me, Phyllis. Your late wife."

"Uh, hi, Phyllis. What's shakin'?"

"I'll tell you what's shaking: ME! Or maybe 'rolling' and 'tossing' is more like it. I knew you'd go off and marry that hussy Janet the moment I was in the ground. What in the name of common sense do you see in her?"

"Uh, well, uh . . ."

"Quit stammering! You look like such a dork when you do that—even from this distance. Now, listen to me, Buster—"

See what I mean? Dennis the Menace had it right. When fish—or folks—are dead, that's the way they oughta stay.

BURIED IN A PILE OF PASSWORDS

Every so often, I get one of those "high-importance" emails, complete with a red exclamation point, from the geeks in charge of technology at our office. The exact wording varies, but their ominous message is always the same:

1. Never reveal your password to anyone.
2. Change your password on a regular basis to prevent it from being compromised.

Frankly, the second message makes no sense because we have a built-in security system that demands a new password on a regular schedule. I think it's a ninety-day cycle. But don't hold me to that because I'd have to remember the password I used to access our security system guidelines, and I've long-since forgotten what it is.

Which highlights one of the nuttier aspects of the allegedly advanced era in which we live: People are supposed to memorize dozens of different passwords for dozens of different programs. And these passwords require frequent changing.

You gotta have a computer password. An email password. A pharmacy password. A bank account password. A charge card password. A health insurance password. Password here, password there, here a password, there a password, everywhere a %$#*! password.

What began as an innocent, easy-to-remember system for privacy has morphed into a monster. We've become a nation of technological slaves, shackled to a cyber chain every bit as cumbersome and unwieldy as those basketball-sized key rings warehouse custodians carry on their belts.

Oh, and before I'm inundated with sales phone calls and sales emails: Yes, I know there are online password memory and protection programs, available for a small fee. But they also require a password, which makes about as much sense as hiding the key to your house inside a special lock box which also requires a key.

Recently, Mary Ann and I consolidated some of our mega-passwords into a single one only she and I understand. This has worked with some success— and I realize every cyber security guard who just read those words has broken out in hives and is now breathing in fits and jerks: *"You've done what?! What if someone cracks your code? Run! The sky is falling! Aaaa-iii-eee!"*

But even our simple system needed tweaking. That's because the required password updates for different accounts came on a staggered schedule. Thus, when we changed a letter or a number, we had to make certain the other person knew. So we did what any rational couple would do when they realized the rest of world had gone completely mad.

We wrote everything down on real paper with a real pen.

Now, if we only had a password to remind us where we hid that hateful piece of paper.

GETTING THROUGH THE NIGHT

Please hang on while I do a little ciphering.

Let's see, now: 16,500 divided by 125 equals 132. And 132 multiplied by 2 comes out to 264. Furthermore, 30 multiplied by 6 is 180, and 264 divided by 180 is 1.47.

What does this math exercise prove—other than my twelve years of Knox County public schooling and four years at the University of Tennessee qualify me to operate a pocket calculator?

This: There's some strange "research" going on at a U.S. research station in Antarctica.

You see, the 16,500 I mentioned above are condoms. They have been delivered to 125 scientists and staff at the McMurdo base station to help these folks endure the six months (or 180 days, give or take) of the dark Antarctic winter.

I double-dog swear on a box of Trojans that I'm not making any of this up. I got the information straight off a dispatch from the Reuters news service.

(Quick geography lesson for those who slept through school or were able to throw a football accurately: Even though it's summer in the northern hemisphere—where most of Tennessee is located, although the jury is still out on Red Boiling Springs—and even though it's hotter than a depot stove Up Here right now, it's colder than a well-digger's butt Down There. That's because Antarctica is located in the southern hemisphere, where the water drains backward. I forget the precise reason why, but I think it has something to do with the Monroe Doctrine. Or maybe the Pythagorean Theorem. Just take my word that the seasons in Antarctica are 180 degrees reversed from ours. But I digress.)

Reuters quoted Bill Henriksen, manager of the McMurdo station, who said the condoms would be available free so staffers wouldn't be embarrassed to buy them. "Since everybody knows everyone, it becomes a little uncomfortable," he said.

True. It's bad enough when you're a modest teenage lad in a town of twelve-hundred and awkwardly slink into a store for The Purchase, and the girl behind the cash register sits beside you in Algebra II—even though this unsettling situation has the potential to reap abundant fruits, if you catch my drift. But a community of 125 is tiny indeed, and I'm happy these shy staffers are well fortified for the bleak winter ahead.

Still, I gotta wonder . . .

The 132 figure above represents the average condom distribution per person. There was no mention in the Reuters story about gender breakdown, but you gotta assume each twosome will only need one per session. And since they've only got six months until sunlight becomes a twenty-four-hour-a-day affair—oops, poor choice of words—that means there's a whole lot of activity taking place. Roughly 1.5 sessions per couple per day. On average.

I know it's bitterly cold in Antarctica. And I know you gotta do whatever it takes to stay warm under severe conditions. But speaking as one who has spent a fortune over the years on goose down, wool, Gore-Tex, Thinsulate, and other winter materials, I never thought condoms would be classified as cold-weather protection.

Al Gore can theorize all he wants. But if a few dozen folks in Antarctica are using 16,500 condoms to make it through winter, I think we've just discovered the real source of global warming.

ANSWERING A CHILLY QUESTION

When it comes to handling excess water, are you a "drainer" or a "retainer"?

No, not *that* kind of water. I'm talking about ice chests, not Depends.

Every year when summer rolls around, along with it comes debate about the proper way to store soft drinks, lemonade, fruit juice, and certain other beverages—especially those of the foamy variety—in a cooler during journeys away from home.

Frankly, I never realized there was much to discuss about this matter. I was raised a drainer. Meaning I, and others of my ilk, discharge the water out of our coolers as the ice melts. But I've come to discover the retainers also have a valid argument.

This issue was raised to me by Chuck Estes, a civil engineer who lives in Oak Ridge. His brother Larry, also a civil engineer, lives in Clinton, Mississippi. On a recent family outing, they got into a discussion about the relative merits of draining versus retaining. Being engineers, they decided to settle it the gentlemanly way.

They dueled with slide rules.

Just kidding. The only use for a slide rule these days is for kindling, swatting unruly children, and propping windows open. Since engineering majors no longer walk around college campuses with a slide rule dangling from their belts, it's a mystery to me how they distinguish themselves from other students on college campuses.

What Chuck and Larry did was consult eng-tips.com, a website touted as "intelligent work forums for engineering professionals."

Sure enough, someone already had posed this question. And it kicked off all manner of scholarly arguments.

"I'd say drain it," noted a mechanical engineer whose Web name is mintjulep. "Convective coefficient between water and inside wall is much higher than between air and inside wall."

"I've always kept the water because you are dumping cooling," replied dcastro, a chemical engineer. "The ice chest is supposed to stop the heat transfer."

One thing led to another, and before anybody could say, "When in the course of human events"—oops, that's what historians would say; anyhow, you get my drift—the back-and-forth raged for fifteen full computer screens.

The majority of the arguments were rife with professional jargon. Boring stuff like "R-factor" and "delta T" and something called "28 W/m^2" kept popping up.

The more I read, the more I realized (1) why I studied journalism in college instead of engineering and (2) my own drool was draining in massive amounts.

But then I came upon an excellent opinion offered by a mechanical engineer named mechengdude: "Drink all beer before ice melts," he advised. "Use a funnel if needed. Have fun."

I'm going to conduct my own experiment to answer this question once and for all. Just as soon as I can hide two brand new Coleman coolers, twenty pounds of ice, and four cases of beer on my expense account.

In journalism school, that was called "creative writing." Best I recall, I got an A.

A SCENIC TRIP BACK IN TIME

I've been trying to understand how the Hubble Space Telescope can look millions and billions of years into the past.

Not that I claim to comprehend even the basics of physics, astronomy, and other branches of science involved with the Hubble project. When I hear the words "Milky Way," I think of heavenly nougat, caramel, and chocolate, not an odyssey into the heavens themselves.

Nonetheless, the dried nougats of my pea brain have been rattling loudly since the nation's top scientists announced that Hubble had ripped a few bazillion-quadrillion pages off the calendar and taken a look-see at the earliest image of our universe.

For proof of this startling discovery, the American Astronomical Society released a picture. We published it in our newspaper on January 6, 2010, and I studied it intently. What I saw was a crisp, clear image of a black blob, fifteen blue dots, and an orange flash. Either that, or my particular copy of the newspaper had suffered an unfortunate ink malfunction as it rolled off the press.

In any event, the caption said the photo "shows the earliest snapshot yet of the universe, six-hundred million years after the Big Bang."

Gosh. If I had waited six hundred million years to take a picture, I sure hope it would come out better than a black blob, fifteen blue dots, and an orange flash. Then again, I never claimed to know much about photography.

So tell me this, Mister and Missus Big Shot Astronomers: If this was an accurate look into the fledgling years of our universe, where in that picture is Fred Flintstone? Or Wilma? Or Barney and all the other residents of Bedrock? For Pete's sake, I couldn't even find evidence of Conan the Barbarian or Alley Oop.

Not that I'm willing to dismiss this high-brow information out of hand. I kinda like the idea of looking over my shoulder. Except I don't need to scroll billions of years in reverse. Just a few hundred would suffice.

I'd like to see my grandfather, big Artemus Venable, a typesetter for the old *Knoxville Journal,* who died a decade before I was born. I'll guarantee he and I could enjoy some knee-slappers about how this nutty biz has changed since he was tickling the keys of a Mergenthaler Linotype machine.

I'd also like to see Knoxville in the late 1800s and early 1900s, especially the forested ridge where I live. Hmm. Except judging by the age and size of the trees growing today, I suspect my ridge was rather clear way back when. I had to have a humongous white oak taken down in 2006, and I was certain it must have been at least 150 years old. Nope. Best estimate I could determine after trying to count the growth rings—some were so close they blended—was between 90 and 100.

I'd like to see the Tennessee River before its path was blocked by concrete. Not to mention the woodlands of the Great Smokies, the Cumberlands, and Cherokee National Forest before they were laid bare by chestnut blight.

In fact, I can think of dozens of images from the Great Beyond I'd like to view, up close and personal. And I bet my snapshots would show a lot more than a black blob, fifteen blue dots, and an orange streak.

Chapter

VERY IMPORTANT DATES

I used to be one of the most addicted calendar watchers in the history of office work. But not for reasons you might expect.

There was none of this business of flipping ahead to June or July on a dreary, snow-patched February afternoon and happily daydreaming of summer vacation at the beach. Nor was the object of my calendar-gazing ever one of those fancy photo collections featuring twelve months of sporting scenes, close-up wildlife images, or vast wilderness landscapes.

Quite the contrary. I didn't need pictures. Instead, my eyes stayed glued to the single-sheet, plain-Jane, numbers-only calendar on my cubicle wall for a very practical reason: I had to make iron-clad certain I identified the exact publication date for upcoming columns. Nearly everything I write is done at least one or two days in advance, often more, so it was important to keep the dates properly aligned in the computer's inventory.

Back in that innocent era, everything I cranked out was "slugged" in the message line with a simple code—month, date, year, my name—so copy editors and page designers would know which column was supposed to run on what specific day. For example, if the slug read "051711sam," that meant the piece should be directed to my column slot on May 17, 2011. If I decided to hold the column for a while in favor of a more timely topic, it was an easy task to "re-slug" the line as "051911sam," "052011sam," or whatever date was necessary.

This process was so easy and so effortless, even a newspaper columnist could figure it out. But then we changed computer systems, and everything went to hell. I won't get into the technical jargon—mainly because I don't understand one iota of it—but what I do these days is build a "SAM" template and then try to coordinate it with an itty-bitty, one-line calendar entry buried deep within the bowels of my computer. The process is slower than the last day of school and requires roughly five bazillion keystrokes. This is called progress.

Thus, I don't glance at the calendar on my cubicle wall—or virtually any calendar in the newsroom, for that matter—like I used to. I miss this little ritual. True, the computer's calendar is just as accurate as the paper sheet on my cubicle wall. But it doesn't give me that friendly, subtle reminder of where I am at any given time: early month, mid-month, late month. If you haven't guessed by now, I don't handle changes in my routine very well.

Still, I have a sixth-sense feel for the evolving seasons and the ever-changing holidays, even without seeing them posted on a cubicle wall. All newspaper people do. Virtually any moment of the year, we just "know" when a special time is nigh because it affords us an easy column. All you gotta do is tweak a sentence here, jiggle a phrase there, and you have re-invented the wheel—or the season and holiday, as it were. (How do you think I was able to "cover" the opening day of trout season, duck season, deer season, turkey season and heaven-only-knows what other seasons for fifteen straight years as outdoors editor? It's not like they keep score in these things like they do in football: Hunters 35–Deer 0.)

I enjoy both the constant and the change of seasons and holidays. Their long-standing traditions, moments, and celebrations are like old friends when they show up, right on schedule, year after year. Just as thankfully, they don't hang around long enough to get stale or wear out their welcome—with the possible exception of Christmas. Geez. Thanks to modern aggressive sales tactics, it's Christmas season on almost any page of the calendar. Sorta like the National Basketball Association's eleven-month, twenty-nine-day schedule.

Some holidays naturally lend themselves to humor; others don't. You can crack wise all you wish about Valentine's Day, for example, but the mood must remain somber on Memorial Day. And every now and then, fate plunks one squarely into your lap.

In 2010, October 31 fell on a Sunday. Based on calls and emails to our office from frantic parents, you would've thought this matchup had never occurred throughout the history of Halloween—or else it was a secret plot by godless communists at the United Nations to destroy Life as We've Always Known and Cherished It.

Some wanted to know if it was permissible to trick-or-treat on Sunday. Or should this activity take place on Saturday night? Monday night, perhaps? Was there a government office to call about such things?

As immune to sheer stupidity as I think I am, this blithering nonsense floored me. I always figured that October 31 was, well, October 31—no matter what day of the week it happens to occur. We're talking about a simple, fun time for grown-ups to behave like kids and kids to shake down grown-ups for candy. How hard is this to figure out?

Plenty hard.

Maybe it's because I came of age during the anti-establishment '60s—a time when nobody was going to tell us what we could or couldn't do. Then again, maybe it was because of my second-nature smart-ass reflex. Whatever the case, I created a government official, straight from the ivory towers of City Hall, to address these concerns.

I called him I. M. "Completely" Nutz, supervisor of an agency known as When Halloween is Allowed to be Celebrated in Knoxville—or WHACKO, as it is known in local bureaucratic circles. It was his duty to enforce the laws, rules, regulations, and requirements of all Halloween activities in the twenty-first century. Obviously, this was a busy season for Mister Nutz. But he took a few minutes out of his schedule to meet with me and go over the fine points of Halloween protocol. Here's how our "conversation" went:

SV: *First, please tell me about your unusual nickname.*

IMN: *No offense, pal, but you're pretty slow—even for a newspaper columnist. When your last name is Nutz, you just naturally pick up a nickname like mine. Sorta like how guys whose last name is Rhodes automatically become "Dusty."*

SV: *Oh, I get it. Anyhow, back on topic—what's this I hear about how and when Halloween can be celebrated? Isn't this a matter of tradition and common sense?*

IMN: *Maybe back in the Stone Age when you were a boy. But this is 2010, an era when nothing happens without rules.*

SV: *So when should the kiddies go trick-or-treating this year?*

IMN: *Depends on who they are and where they're planning to visit. If their last name begins with A through L, Saturday is their only option—and then only at even-numbered street addresses. Sunday is reserved for M through Z and odd-numbered street addresses. No exceptions.*

SV: *You're telling me that if, say, your grandchildren's last name is Phillips but your street address is 116, they can't come trick-or-treating to your house at all?*

IMN: *Well, there is one loophole. If a male trick-or-treater hops exclusively on his left foot—right foot for females—throughout the prescribed trick-or-treat route, either evening is acceptable.*

SV: *That's ridiculous!*

IMN: *Hey, I don't make the laws. I just enforce 'em.*

SV: *I never realized Halloween was so complicated. Is there anything else?*

IMN: *Are you kidding?* (He holds up a book thicker than the Yellow Pages.)

Check out a few of these: Devil costumes are not allowed on Church Avenue, Church Street, Church Hill Road, or Churchwell Avenue. Anyone dressed as a vampire must carry a health card. Cowboys and cowgirls are restricted to Rodeo Drive, Rifle Range Road, and Palomino Way. Paper trick-or-treat candy bags must be approved ahead of time to make sure no endangered tree species were used in their manufacture. Plastic jack-o'-lanterns must be certified PBA-free.

You know what's truly weird? Last time I heard, a few parents were still trying to contact Mister Nutz for elaboration—proving conclusively that some humans should not be permitted to procreate.

On the other hand, sometimes it is the lesser-heralded moments, ones that don't always lend themselves to strict confines, that I enjoy the most. For instance, forget what the calendar says in late June: In my mind, summer never can be declared present and accounted for until the sultry night air hangs thick with katydid music.

OK, so this isn't music in the instrumental-vocal sense. These insects, members of the Tettigonioidea family, create their delightful "songs" by rubbing their wings, not actually giving voice. Tettigonioidea contains thousands of individual species, and I do believe there are nights when half the entire clan is represented in the symphony that plays in the treetops around my place.

Traditionally, they strike up their band on or around the Fourth of July. It can vary a few nights either way, but trust your Uncle Entomology: If fireworks are in the air, get ready for a katydid concert. Often, everything starts with a quiet creaking here and there in the canopy, followed by a period of quiet. As my friend and fellow katydid listener Ann Hassel puts it: "It's like the first ones are surprised and shocked by their own sound."

But, brother, once they start in earnest—wow! It's a full-fledged racket that goes on for hours. When katydids are knocking the tops out of the trees at night, and cicadas are droning endlessly during the heat of the day, I know the wait is over. Summer has officially arrived.

People in other parts of the country also take their seasonal cues by sights and sounds. And have done so throughout the ages. One of them was a dear old friend, the talented midwestern nature writer John Madson (1923–1995). Among many books left in his wake is a collection of essays, published in 1979 by Winchester Press, simply called *John Madson: Out Home*. It contains a story, "North Again," that addresses this yearning. But instead of katydids and summer, "North Again" chronicles the return of migratory waterfowl to their Canadian breeding grounds in early spring.

Writing to his buddies shivering in "Saskatoon, Moose Jaw, and Portage la Prairie," Madson says hundreds upon thousands of ducks and geese are "bringing spring up from the Gulf Coast and will be with you directly. Hang in there. The Grand Passage is under way. Spring is being delivered by our most dependable airline."

How well I understand—for there is a tiny brown bird, the Swainson's thrush, that heralds spring for me just as certainly as mallards, pintails, and snow geese did for John Madson. These secretive songbirds migrate through East Tennessee every May, but you'll need ears more than eyes to detect them. Gerald Dinkins, an avid birder who owns a biological consulting firm in Powell, calls them "ghosts of the woods."

Dinkins told me he's only seen four or five in his life. Sadly, the only Swainson's I've positively ID'ed was a dead specimen that crashed into the bay window at the back of my house. But Dinkins and I and other members of our exclusive fraternity always know when these dainty fellows have arrived because of their delightful music.

I can't accurately describe it in print, other than to say it's a lilting, flute-like melody that fairly vibrates through the cool morning air. Look up "Swainson's thrush" on any bird Internet site, click the audio, and listen for yourself.

"It's my favorite bird song of all," said Dinkins, who comically called it "ethereal flute music on drugs."

What with wild and cultivated flowers bursting into bloom, trout and bluegills biting, turkeys gobbling, my heart explodes with joy every May. And when I hear Swainson's thrush symphonies, all is well with my soul.

That being said, however, fall is the most welcome season of them all. Would humanity ever tire of the kaleidoscope of oranges, browns, reds, and yellows in the forest canopy? Or that first smell of wood smoke?

A few nights ago, I celebrated the arrival of autumn by lighting the season's first fire.

I take my firewood seriously. Chainsaw it myself. Haul it myself, with occasional

Nearly every autumn, I get calls and letters from readers warning of an impending brutal winter because hornets and wasps have built their nests (1) higher or (2) lower than usual. I've never been able to establish a correlation to either—leading me to believe that wasps, hornets, and winter behave as they dang-well please.

son and son-in-law assistance since back surgery. Split it myself—with ax, maul, and wedge, thank you; not one of those sissified hydraulic cheats. And stack it myself under a metal-roofed shed I built myself.

Stack it precisely, in fact. So precisely that when editors of the Tennessee Farm Bureau magazine, for which I occasionally write, needed the photo of an oaken Taj Mahal to illustrate an article on firewood, they knew where to turn.

Of course, owning such a trove can lead to jealousy and cruel remarks from the unwashed. More than one alleged friend has made derisive comments about my fortune in firewood. Every time he comes up the driveway and sees all those neat rows, David Etnier utters a snide remark involving the word "anal." Many years ago, Marvin West told me he'd steal some of my inventory "except I'm sure you've got it serial-numbered."

Marvin was wrong. I don't serial-number my firewood. Wayne Doster does. He actually drove to the house one day and inscribed "BR549" on several log ends with a Sharpie pen. Yes, I immediately noticed the marks—and promptly sent Wayne a terse letter about vandalism.

I can't help it. Firewood has been part of my life since childhood. I take pride in still swinging my father's double-bit ax, circa 1950. Thus, on the occasion of fall's first blaze, I tend to make somewhat of a production. By late February, my nightly fires will long have become a matter of rote. But in October, they tend to be ritualistic.

The first fire must include special wood—bits and pieces that have unique meaning. This time around, I placed on the grate:

- A slice of tamarack from Powell Ranger Station in Idaho, where I'd worked in 1966 and revisited in 2008.
- A wedge of rock-hard dogwood, chainsawed off a hollow log that came from a dead tree at my brother's house, the house where I grew up.
- The remains of a gnarled apple stump, given to me last spring by Morgan Simmons and from which I busted a box full of chunks for meat-smoking.
- A twist of barber-pole maple I foolishly attempted to split earlier this year. Arrgh! I'd rather attempt cleaving concrete. Watching fire consume those cursed, crooked cells brought a wicked smile to my face.
- The hollow top of a long-dead sourwood stump that reminded me of a chimney when I sawed it down while clearing a spot for Mary Ann to plant rose bushes.

I kindled all these offerings the same way I do every October: with hand-fuls of cedar shavings that accumulated at my feet as I whittled during folk fes-tivals. Then I poured whiskey and a splash, parked myself in Maw's old chair, and rocked contentedly as the flames danced and climbed through the sourwood "chimney."

Later I walked outside, inhaling the perfume of sweet smoke. I stood alone in the dark, listening to the hoots of a great-horned owl on the west ridge, ac-companied by the feeble chirps of a remnant cricket beneath the deck.

Not a bad way to send summer packing.

A CARD-CARRYING CONUNDRUM

Just in time for Mother's Day, my normally low-maintenance wife suddenly de-veloped expensive tastes.

You know what she requested this year?

A pair of large shiny rocks, for starters. Plus a new set of wheels! Plus a chunk of real estate!

Obedient husband that I am, I acquiesced on all fronts.

I bought the two stepping stones she'd been wanting for her flower bed. Also a two-wheeled cart to carry her gardening supplies. Also a bag of potting soil. Am I Husband of the Year material or what?

But the toughest part of the entire celebration was finding an appropriate Mother's Day card. I shopped early and often, trying to procure the perfect ex-pression of sentiment. It simply did not exist.

What I wanted was an all-inclusive card that addressed Mary Ann's three roles: wife, mother, and grandmother.

No such thing exists. Of approximately 878,539 selections I thumbed through, that exact combination was not to be found. Here are some of the Mother's Day cards I did locate:

For new mothers. For stepmothers. For Nana, aunt, sister, sister-in-law, nurse, godmother, friend, "someone special," "almost like a mother," and "any mother."

I also found Mother's Day cards from a variety of sources. Such as: From daughter. From son. From daughter-in-law, son-in-law, granddaughter, grandson, and other relatives up and down the family tree. Even (I swear) the cat and dog.

I found Mother's Day cards with bookmarks. With magnets. With recorded music.

I was particularly puzzled by all the Mother's Day cards that were catego-rized as "funny" and "religious"—and couldn't help but think there must be

A story in the October 2008 issue of *Better Homes and Gardens* dissed the popular folklore notion that the brown-and-black color bands on wooly worms are accurate portends of winter weather. Has nothing whatsoever to do with climate, the magazine said; instead, this color pattern indicates the age of these critters, which are the caterpillars of the Isabella tiger moth.

Bah! Next thing you know these smarty-pants "experts" will claim thunder has nothing to do with how long a snapping turtle stays clamped to your finger.

polar-opposite selections that are "non-funny" and "sacrilegious." If so, they weren't on display. Maybe they're kept under the counter.

To compound the problem, I was also searching for a birthday card for Bill Henry, the talented wood whittler who's turning eighty in a few days. In the store where I shopped, rows of birthday cards stretched out like spokes of a giant wheel. No telling how many forests were shorn to make them.

There were birthday cards "for her." "For him." For bosses, sons, daughters, cousins, aunts, uncles, nieces, nephews, and friends, ad infinitum. But none for wood whittlers.

I did find one for an eightieth birthday. It was among a vast inventory of cards celebrating the following numeric birthdays: Thirteenth, sixteenth, eighteenth, twenty-first, thirtieth, fortieth, fiftieth, sixtieth, seventieth, eighty-fifth, ninetieth, ninety-fifth and one-hundredth. Presumably no one deserving a card lives beyond one hundred.

But the lone eightieth-birthday card I found was so boring and so lame, I couldn't bring myself to insult Bill's keen sense of humor by purchasing it. Instead, I picked out one with a ribald theme, totally unsuited for polite company. I'm sure Bill will like it because his appreciation of weird humor is almost as sharp as mine.

At least I hope he likes it. You never want to get on the wrong side of a guy who handles sharp knives with flair and aplomb.

DOOMED FROM THE GET-GO

What might happen if the first Thanksgiving was set today instead of 1621:

PLYMOUTH, MASSACHUSETTS—Proponents of a festive civic dinner here were forced to cancel the event because of massive protests, legal wrangling, and financial setbacks. The program had been designed to celebrate the harvest, recognize a mixture of cultures, and give thanks to providence. But it was saddled with controversy from the start.

"It seemed like such a great idea at the time," said a visibly distraught Governor William Bradford.

Resistance began as soon as initial plans were announced in late summer. Radio talk show host Rush Limbaugh assailed the notion as "the very essence of socialism" and urged his listeners not only to boycott the effort but also appeal to officials to cease their support.

Limbaugh's campaign was mirrored by another conservative commentator, Glenn Beck, who said, "I personally counted 93,578,284 protestors who showed up in Plymouth and waved Lipton tea bags in anger."

Furthermore, former CNN newsman Lou Dobbs led a large delegation opposed to the inclusion of what he termed "illegal immigrants" on the agenda: "What right do these so-called 'Indians' have interrupting a celebration by the people who lawfully came here from Europe? Let's see their birth certificates! I say we build a fence around Plymouth to keep them out."

There were problems on the left, as well.

The group known as People for the Ethical Treatment of Animals filed several lawsuits, claiming turkeys, deer, fish, and ducks should not have been included on the menu.

In addition, the American Civil Liberties Union secured a temporary injunction, arguing Governor Bradford had exceeded his legal authority when he issued an executive order asking citizens to "give thanks to God."

More hurdles were posed by the Massachusetts Division of Wildlife, which claimed the turkeys and deer in question had not been procured through proper licensing channels. Also, the U.S. Fish and Wildlife Service was able to obtain a court order confiscating ducks and geese scheduled for the dinner to make certain they had been killed with steel shot instead of lead.

Legal problems and protests notwithstanding, Governor Bradford pressed forward with his Thanksgiving plan until he met an insurmountable problem.

"The money simply ran out," he said. "We had put together a consortium of public and private donors and thought we had secured one million dollars, sufficient to hold a dinner like this. But when Bernie Madoff's empire crashed, we tanked right along with it."

In addition, Governor Bradford said the lack of a marketing strategy helped doom the effort.

"You'd think a simple name like 'Thanksgiving' would cover it," he lamented, "but all the experts told me that's not flashy enough. They wanted to call it 'Black

Friday Eve: Where Profits Begin.' They also said we needed a catchy slogan like, 'Pumpkin: It's not just for pie anymore.'"

Governor Bradford then left for a quiet weekend in the woods with his friends Squanto and Samoset (their last names were not made available to the media).

"Thanks for nothing," he sighed.

FORGIVE US IF WE SIN BY LAUGHING

Maundy Thursday is a very somber day in a very somber week of the Christian calendar. It commemorates the final meal Jesus of Nazareth shared with his disciples before his execution the following day.

I reverently appreciate the significance of Holy Week. But, forgive me, Sweet Lord, I can't hear the words "Maundy Thursday" without chuckling. If I'm in the presence of any of my younger siblings, the chuckling soon escalates to full-born laughter. Such occurred a few days ago when I was talking to my brother Rick about his plans for Easter. One of us mentioned Maundy Thursday. Naturally, we had to relive the situation one more time.

You remember that hilarious Ray Stevens song, "Mississippi Squirrel Revival"? This is that sort of thing. Except we call it "The Maundy Thursday Grandmother Brought the House Down."

For the record, let me stress that I understand the trauma of dementia and the wicked toll it exacts from its victims. Typically, dealing with the effects of this insidious disease is fraught with emotion for all concerned. But sometimes, you gotta laugh to keep from crying.

My paternal grandmother, Angie Anderson Venable, was a sweet, intelligent, vivacious lady with the proverbial heart of twenty-four-karat gold. Tragically, her mind began to betray her late in life. Perhaps it was the onset of Alzheimer's—although nobody knew it by that name back then.

Grandmother was a stalwart in the tiny church all the Venables attended in those days. My father and his brothers were scattered across the region with young families of their own by then, but it simply wouldn't do for anybody to be parked anywhere on Sunday morning other than the pews of Fort Sanders Presbyterian. The church folded half a century ago. Its building, now called Laurel Theater, still stands at Laurel and Sixteenth Street in Knoxville.

Eclectic, Fort Sanders was not. We had services once a week. On Sunday morning. Period.

Then a young preacher came to town and began instituting all manner of new and diverse programs. One was a Maundy Thursday service (which all of us kids thought was weird enough or else it wouldn't be called "Monday-Thursday," right?)

Anyhow, everyone—all thirty-five or forty in the congregation—had dutifully gathered in the small ground-level fellowship hall. To milk the full effect of the moment, the young preacher opted to begin his presentation in total darkness.

Everybody was prepared for the lights to dim. Everybody except my grandmother.

The instant the room went black, Grandmother's frantic whispers grew progressively louder. My mother took her hand and tried to calm her down. To no avail. Indeed, the only sound permeating the gloom was Grandmother's concern, which escalated in volume with every draw of her breath: *"Mary Elizabeth! The lights just went out! What's going on? Stop it, Mary Elizabeth! Stop! Aaak! MARY ELIZABETH, YOU'RE PINCHING THE BLOOD OUT OF ME!"*

Neither Rick nor I could remember how long it took for the ensuing bedlam to die down so that the young preacher—who himself was laughing fit to choke—could continue. But we both recalled it was the first and only Maundy Thursday service Fort Sanders Presbyterian ever attempted.

WELCOMING SPRING WITH A BANG

The Swiss have given us fine chocolates, exquisite cheeses, secret banking, precision timepieces, and pocketknives bristling with saws, pliers, tweezers, toothpicks, corkscrews, awls, and scissors. But these advancements pale in comparison to exploding snowmen, and I say we rectify the situation, East Tennessee style.

I hold in my hands a report from the Swiss Broadcasting Corporation describing the "Sechselauten" festival in Zurich. This celebration is held every year to "drive out persistent winter and welcome spring."

I quote details from a recent Sechselauten: "The festivities culminated at the stroke of 6 P.M. when a three-meter-high effigy of a snowman atop a pyre was set on fire. It then took only eleven minutes for the explosive-laden head to blow off, much to the delight of tens of thousands of onlookers. Legend has it that the quicker the head bursts apart, the better the summer will be."

Now that, children, is a seasonal legend! Here in America, we've got this hohum groundhog custom that occurs weeks before spring. A bunch of old men in top hats stand around the entrance to a groundhog's burrow, patiently waiting to see if the animal casts a shadow when it emerges. Boorr-ing.

But in Switzerland, they send winter packing and welcome spring with a bang. Literally. And I propose we do the same.

Not with a snowman, however.

In the first place, that would infringe on Zurich's idea. Expanding on some-one else's civic fun is one thing; outright copycatting crosses the line.

In the second place, East Tennessee isn't exactly snowman country. We get enough white stuff in a typical winter to give just about everybody the experi-ence of bringing Frosty to life. But North Dakota, we ain't.

Thus, for a highfalutin hillbilly Sechselauten, we might want to detonate an old station wagon, a dumpster, a surplus Army vehicle, or maybe a huge pump-kin grown the previous summer and preserved for this sacred ceremony. Or we could go whole hog and blow some derelict building or bridge to smithereens. That never fails to make the 11 o'clock news.

Frankly, the "explodee" really doesn't matter. What matters is that it goes BOOM on command. Trust your Uncle Pyromania: You advertise a civic ceremony that culminates in a yee-haw demolition, and thousands of screaming rednecks will show up to watch. What's more, they'll gladly pay for the privilege.

That oughta put K-town on the cultural map, fer shore.

AMID THE COLD OF WINTER

Somewhere in the dark recesses of a file cabinet at my home office—note to self: I will organize that thing some day; second note to self: yeah, right—is a photo-graph I shot in December 2007.

I keep meaning to turn it into the family's Christmas card. But I haven't for two reasons.

First, my computer-geek wife is much more disciplined than I am. She actu-ally gets tasks like this accomplished.

Second, Mary Ann consistently arranges a boffo family portrait, like the one from last summer's beach vacation. Our friend Matt Mowrer caught us perfectly in the setting sun: casually yet symmetrically standing against a sand dune, sea oats waving in the background, glimmering ocean in the distance. It's one of those rare pictures in which all smiling adults have their eyes open and no tod-dlers are picking their noses.

Still, hope clings eternal. One of these years, I'll get around to my card. Ab-solutely. Positively. Well, maybe . . .

My impromptu photo was snapped one bitterly cold morning as I draped garlands of fake greenery across the rustic fence in front of our house. One end of this emerald faux fir dangled from a fence post, to which I was attaching a red bow. Down on the ground, something brilliant caught my eye.

It was a tiny rosebud, coming to life in the dead of winter. Just like the words to my all-time favorite Christmas hymn: "Lo, How a Rose E'er Blooming." It plays constantly at our house during the Christmas season. It's selection number five on a CD of sacred music performed by the Cambridge Singers and Orchestra, directed by John Rutter. It was recorded in 1997 in the Lady Chapel of England's famed Ely Cathedral.

My taste in holiday music runs a broad gamut, secular to religious: from "Please, Daddy, Don't Get Drunk This Christmas" to "O, Holy Night" and everything in between. But "Lo, How a Rose" trumps them all. As Mary Ann frequently laments, "You *know* there are other selections on that CD besides number five, don't you?"

Really? I'll get around to playing them about the time I do that card.

This is a hymn of German origin, circa sixteenth century. No one knows the original author, although the English translation was composed by Theodore Baker (1851–1934) in 1894.

One of the most moving performances of it I ever saw was broadcast years ago by WBIR-TV. Videographer Doug Mills, genius behind the "Heartland Series" lens, recalls shooting it for a news program. The choir from Kentucky's Cumberland College was at the Museum of Appalachia that day, singing from the front porch of an old log cabin. At the start of "Lo, How a Rose," a gentle snow began falling. I can still see the scene in my mind, still hear those words wafting through the chilled air:

> *Isaiah 'twas foretold it, the Rose I have in mind.*
> *With Mary we behold it, the Virgin Mother kind.*
> *To show God's love aright, she bore to men a Saviour,*
> *When half-spent was the night.*

If you don't get goose bumps from a glorious hymn like that, there just ain't no hope. You probably won't get a visit from Santa, either.

DUAL THANKSGIVING DAYS

If you think Washington is the capital of the State of Confusion these days, you should have been around in 1939.

Way Back Then, we didn't have one Thanksgiving Day. We had two.

Well, no. Now that you mention it, your humble correspondent wasn't around Way Back Then. I was minus-eight years of age. But the *News Sentinel*'s microfilm machine is handy, and I have availed myself of its services.

In 1939, Thanksgiving was celebrated on November 23. At least it was in twenty-five states. Not so in the remaining twenty-three. In those rebellious outposts, including Tennessee, T-Day didn't arrive until November 30.

(Right now you're rolling your eyes and saying, "What a goof Venob is. You add twenty-five and twenty-three and it comes to forty-eight. Doesn't he know there are fifty states?" To which I reply: "Neener-neener. Hawaii and Alaska hadn't even been invented Way Back Then! It wasn't until 1959 that a pineapple was discovered in an icebox owned by some old coot named Stewart, forcing Congress to ratify the Gettysvue Amendment. As a result, this guy named Ross sewed a flag with fifty stars, signifying Hawaii and Alaska could be visited by American tourists, but only if they purchased souvenir leis and mukluks." At least that's the way I recall it from history class.)

I'm not joking about twin Thanksgivings in 1939, however. It came about because of spatting between the president and Congress. Sound familiar?

Although Thanksgiving had been observed on various dates, the last Thursday in November was proclaimed by President Abraham Lincoln in 1863.

Such an arrangement worked well for a while. But then the pre-Christmas marketing rush came into vogue. By the time 1939 rolled around—accompanied by a November with five Thursdays—President Franklin Roosevelt felt November 30 was too late to launch the Christmas shopping season. So he decreed T-Day would be the fourth, but not necessarily final, Thursday.

You would have thought FDR had ordered tofu be served instead of turkey. The aforementioned rebellious states screamed, "No way!" and continued to observe the last Thursday. This controversy likely would have erupted every few years. But in 1941, Congress stopped it by officially designating the fourth Thursday. Period.

Based on vintage newspaper accounts I've read, the whole thing boiled into a humongous fight. Indeed, the FDR Presidential Library in Washington contains many of the irate letters, telegrams, and editorials it sparked.

Oh, for the good ol' days when that's all politicians had to argue about!

WHO DARES CALL THEM "WEEDS"?

In the vegetative cornucopia known as East Tennessee, nothing says "autumn" like a hillside of hardwoods, ablaze in Jack Frost foliage.

Nothing says "winter" like a freshly cut spray of holly, green leaves, and red berries all decked out for Christmas.

Nothing says "spring" like a sea of dogwood blossoms, gently dancing in the cool breeze of a dewy April dawn.

And nothing says "summer" like the multi-purple display of ironweed and Joe Pye weed, standing tall and proud at the fringe of a meadow.

I use the term "multi-purple" because these two native wildflowers own the patent on every variety and interpretation of that color. With the exception of iris, they dare any other plant to come close.

Ironweed's purple is as bold and royal as you can get. The sort of purple you'd expect on the robe of an Old World monarch. Indeed, ironweed's purple is so rich, it can't be broadcast willy-nilly. Rather, it is limited to small patches of blooms at the top of each branch. Anything else and OSHA would demand the wearing of protective glasses.

Joe Pye's purple is much more muted, its intensity cut to somewhat of a rusty pinkish-purple hue. Thus, it can afford to be more showy, culminating in a huge, flowing dome at the top of the stem.

Four times every year, I publish the dates of that particular quarter's "Ember Days." According to mountain lore, these are ideal times for cutting brush because the offending vegetation won't grow back.

Each time, I always caution readers that if they follow my Ember Day advice and it works, I will happily accept their praise as a botanical-folklore genius.

And if it doesn't work so well? What gullible dolts they are.

Ironweed and Joe Pye weed are as common as crows in this part of the country—if you'll allow me to mix my biology, if not my metaphors, and fling ornithology in there amongst the botany. I'll guarantee you've seen them, even if you never knew 'em by name.

If you aren't immediately familiar with these two late-summer gems, avail yourself of any decent field guide. You'll slap your head and say, "Oh, so *that's* what I've been seeing the last few days!"

Just look along rural road rights-of-way, unkempt medians, edges of wetlands, fence rows, pasture borders, creeksides, any piece of open, relatively moist territory that hasn't been stung by a rotary blade.

Which brings me to a plant pet peeve. How in the name of Carl Linnaeus did these two gorgeous specimens ever get demoted to "weed" status?

True, the stem and root of ironweed are tough as a ten-penny nail. And from what I've read through the years, "Joe Pye" emerged from a Native American word for typhoid ("jopi") because it was used to treat the disease.

But "weeds" in the modern context? What blithering idiocy! Ironweed and Joe Pye are weeds in the same sense that Dom Perignon is rot-gut stump blower, overpriced at two bucks a gallon.

Oh, well. Let the sun bear down mercilessly from cloudless, windless heavens. Let the thermometer flirt with ninety-eight every afternoon. Let the humidity flood off the charts.

As long as I can see ironweed and Joe Pye weed in bloom, the world remains on its axis.

A PARTING SHOT AT CHRISTMAS

You know the holidays are officially over when Janet Hart reaches for a gun and starts blasting away at her Christmas tree.

On second thought, mayhaps "blasting" is a bit of exaggeration since Hart's weapon of choice in these matters is an air rifle. "Plinking" is a more accurate term, from both grammatical and ballistic standpoints. When you're a seasoned Christmas-tree shooter, accuracy is of foremost concern.

"Shooting of the Christmas Tree" has become quite a tradition at the Anderson County home Hart shares with her husband, Tony Powers, and their children. It comes complete with fancy invitations, one of which I hold in my hands at this very moment.

"We always do it on New Year's Eve," said Hart, an environmental engineer who works for the Knox County Office of Air Quality Management. "Rain and fog can hold the crowd down somewhat. But we always put up a shelter in the yard so nobody gets wet."

Please understand: This is not a casual shot across the bow—or bough, as the case may be. This is a complete fusillade that commences around 8:30 P.M. and doesn't conclude until after 11:00 when more than one hundred glass ornaments and numerous strings of lights have been shattered. Then everyone repairs back inside to dance, make merry, and welcome in the new year.

In case you were wondering, the answer is yes, there's a reason behind this bizarre celebration. Hart's mother died in 2000, and that first Christmas without her was a sad one. Post-Christmas depression is bad enough under the best of circumstances, but this one was particularly tough to endure.

Then Hart recalled a tale her mom had handed down across the decades.

"It was one of those family stories everybody always talked about," Hart related to me. "It happened more than fifty years earlier, before Mom and Dad even had kids. My aunt and uncle were over and everyone was bored. So they actually shot a few ornaments off the tree. I got to thinking about that and turned to my son Sam and said, 'Where's your BB gun?'"

Thus, a tradition was born.

The tree is ceremoniously carried into the yard. A tarp is put down to collect the rubble. And the firing begins.

"I always get to take the first shot," said Hart. "I look up and say, 'Mom, this one's for you.' Our guests bring their own BB guns, and we shoot till nothing is left."

Naturally, this calls for fresh supplies on an annual basis. Hart scours the after-Christmas sales to stock up on glass balls and lights for the following year's festivities.

"One year before Christmas, our daughter Emily and I were in a store, and she saw this gorgeous ornament. She said, 'Oh, Mom, let's buy it, but please don't shoot it off the tree!' I don't know what the rest of the people in the store must have been thinking!"

This being gun-totin' East Tennessee, probably envy.

MR. AND MRS. APRIL FOOL

Paul and Marty Hamilton have been hearing it since 1969: "Oh, c'mon; what's the *real* date of your anniversary? Who would get married on April Fools' Day?"

"We did—really!" Marty says with a laugh. "I reckon we were the biggest fools of all."

Unusual date notwithstanding, nobody would argue with this couple's success. More than four decades later—plus four children, five grandchildren, "and a lot of love, sweat, and tears, but no blood," she quipped—the Hamiltons are still together.

You can't pick your parents or your birthday, but there's usually a bit of latitude involved when deciding when to say "I do." Except in this case.

"Paul was in technical school and working part time," she explained. "April 1 was the only day he could be out of class and off work at the same time."

By most measures, then or now, this was a recipe for quick and certain matrimonial failure.

"He was nineteen. I was seventeen. We drove over to Bryson City (North Carolina) and got married in front of a judge. That was when the term 'Here come da'judge' was all over TV. I remember Paul whispering that to me when the judge came walking up to meet us. A popular song then was the movie theme from 'The Good, the Bad and the Ugly,'" she added. "To this day, whenever Paul hears it, he says, 'That's our tune!'

"Oh, we were poor! Paul had to sell the tachometer off his car to scrape together enough money for us to get a motel room."

She laughed even harder: "And we've been broke ever since!"

Suffice to say that when the new Mr. and Mrs. Hamilton returned to their native Sevier County, the home crowd was not overly pleased.

"Neither of our parents liked it one bit," she recalled. "Paul's daddy said to him, 'Why, you can't afford to feed one mouth, let alone two!' But they let us move in with them. It was a challenge for all of us, to say the least."

Paul joined the Army and served in Vietnam. Marty continued her studies at Gatlinburg-Pittman High School, graduated, and completed nurse's training. After Paul was discharged, they both worked, off and on, at Paul's father's weekly newspaper, *Tri-County News,* which he had founded in 1947.

Later, they served as Christian missionaries in Africa, eventually coming back to East Tennessee and joining the family business. Harry Hamilton died in 1993, and the second generation took over. Covering events in the region where Knox, Blount, and Sevier counties blend, *Tri-County News* remains one of the oldest, continually published weeklies in Tennessee journalism history.

"Our kids threw us a big wedding on our twenty-fifth anniversary, then another one for our thirtieth," said Marty, who served as a Sevier County commissioner 2002 to 2006, the first woman in county history to be elected to that office. "We sent out printed invitations to our friends—and both times, everybody thought it was an April Fools' Day joke."

Comes with the territory. Out of the entire calendar year, that's not the date most people would select for such a momentous occasion. But, as she pointed out, "At least it's easy to remember your anniversary."

And with their kind of track record, the only fools—April or otherwise—are the ones who doubted it would last.

HUMMING A FEW BARS WILL SUFFICE

If you feel like breaking into Christmas carols, fine. Make all the music you wish. Far be it from me to ruin your holiday fun. Indeed, join your friends and neighbors, traipse house-to-house, and sing yourselves silly.

It's just that I've been mulling over the lyrics to some of the season's favorites—"Frosty," "Jingle Bells," "Sleigh Ride," and the like—and I gotta tell you I've scratched a furrow in my head trying to get them to make sense.

Maybe I'm too literal, but—*c'mon!*—don't you really think:

There's no way a new mother would give permission for some kid to start banging away on a drum set just as her baby was drifting off to sleep?

Any kid named Will who'd asked for computer games would be really ticked off if all he found in his stocking was "a hammer and lots of tacks, also a ball and a whip that cracks?"

The only people who run around deliriously shouting, "Let it snow! Let snow! Let it snow!" are meteorologists or grocers?

If you walked down the street and said hello to "everyone you meet," you'd be accused of being a perv?

Christmas is a weird time for "scary ghost stories and tales of the glories?"

You'd melt in embarrassed laughter if a girl sat down next to you and introduced herself as "Miss Fanny Bright?" (What *were* her parents thinking?)

When people are searching for the perfect Christmas tree, they're more interested in price than "how steadfast are thy branches?"

Anybody who claims to have seen a deer with a bright red nose (1) is pretty well-lit himself and (2) has no business in the woods with a gun, bow, or knife.

The Village People must be in concert nearby when some folks are donning gay apparel, others look like Eskimos, and city sidewalks are dressed in holiday style?

Anyone named Brown who goes into the ministry would take whatever dietary steps are necessary to make certain he's never confused with a snowman in the meadow?

If your true love produces five golden rings, there's a good chance he's guilty of bigamy? Or at least is laundering drug money?

Children are listening for the ringtone on their iPhone instead of sleigh bells in the snow? And as for those sugarplums? Bah! What about gift cards to Mickey D's?

Seven swans a'swimming, six geese a'laying, four calling birds, three French hens, two turtle doves, and a partridge in a pear tree would make one hellacious mess?

Homeland Security agents would come running, Glocks drawn, if they heard people were conspiring by the fire?

Anybody who would climb atop a snowy roof and try to squirm down the chimney with a fat man wearing a red suit has click-click-clicked past the eggnog bowl a few times too often?

Your wife would look better in bed wearing something from Victoria's Secret instead of that lame ol' kerchief?

Figgy pudding sounds like something the Grinch would eat?

Yeah, I tend to wander as I wonder about these things.

EVERY FALL HATH THIRTY FINE DAYS

Tomorrow I say goodbye to a dear old friend. It's never easy. The only comfort is knowing this friend will revisit—again and again and again.

I speak of November, one of my favorite pages on the calendar.

Let poets wax eloquent in June. Let songwriters compose silly verse during those lazy, hazy, crazy days of summer. Let merchandisers and the party crowd celebrate throughout December.

No contest. November holds sway over them all.

Please understand that I rank months of the year the same way I do brands of beer: There's never been a bad one made; some are just better than others.

That's November in a nutshell. From the dawn of All Saints Day till the clock strikes midnight on the thirtieth, November is a pleasure to the senses. As Goldilocks discovered with Baby Bear's porridge, November's not too cold, not too hot. It's *juuust* right.

OK, so maybe April runs a close second. That's especially true if we've endured one of those drizzly, chilly Marches that clings to the woodlands like gray glue. In the nick of time, April wafts in on southerly breezes, bathing the landscape in sunshine and dotting the forests with dogwood, trillium, and bloodroot in full flower.

But let us not think of spring at this moment. Let us savor the final days of fall. Real fall.

Not the faux fall of September—which, in reality, is summer in disguise. Or the alleged fall of October—which applies principally to Vermont, Maine, New Hampshire, and the covers of L.L. Bean catalogs. Agreed, the East Tennessee foliage extravaganza debuts before Halloween. But invariably it waits until trick-or-treat candy is gone before ripening into sure-nuff, eye-popping, breathtaking maturity. Anyone who tires of this performance ain't human.

What's more, November offers a preholiday laziness, a calm before the Christmas storm that's as comforting to the psyche as a second helping of pumpkin pie, or third, is to the belly.

Perhaps I wouldn't feel this way if I had to spend Thanksgiving week inching along some distant interstate or standing in lines at crowded airports. Such are the benefits of being a native in November.

Havilah Babcock (1898–1964) understood this seasonal euphoria completely. During his twenty-seven-year tenure as head of the English Department at the University of South Carolina, Babcock wrote copiously about the joys of autumn in the Southland. One of his most memorable volumes is a book in my office library. Rarely does a fall go by that I don't take it down, pour a tumbler of elixir, poke at oak logs glowing in the fireplace, and reread Babcock's essay that lent its name to the title—*My Health Is Better in November*.

So is mine.

SIX MONTHS OUT OF SYNCH

"Just hear those sleigh bells jingling, ring-ting-tingling, too. Come on it's lovely—"

Oops. Sorry. Didn't realize anyone was listening. I'm in such a holiday mood, I can burst into full throat without thinking.

As you can tell by my choice of song, it's not Independence Day that I'm celebrating. Nothing against the Fourth of July, you understand. For Yankee Doodle's sake, I stay red, white, and bluing through early July. When you're blessed with friends who host barbecue bashes every July Fourth, and that's also your wife's birthday, the middle of summer is a non-stop, eat-a-thon, drink-a-thon throwdown. Yowzer! Let the good times roll, and pass me another chicken leg.

Yet there happens to be an antidote for such festive excess. Truth be told, I've been holding it back for six months. A seasonal ace in the hole, you might call it. Happened like this:

During the winter of 2009, when holiday TV specials were stacking up faster than sugarplums, I asked my wife to record "Christmas with the Mormon Tabernacle Choir." It aired December 20 on PBS.

I made a point of not watching it during the Christmas break. Nor at New Year's, Valentine's, Easter, and other special holidays, either. Instead, I told Mary Ann I was going to keep this show on ice until the middle of summer, then crack it open and judge its effect.

I'm weird like that.

On the darkest days of mid-winter, I'm bad to gaze at beach photos, if for no other reason than to remind myself that thawing will, in fact, occur. Conversely, a dose of December in the thick of summer can be an equally bizarre ride. In the parlance of old hippies, this might be considered tripping without the drugs.

And an interesting trip it was.

While fireflies blinked and fireworks exploded outside the den window, I settled in for an hour of white lights, trees decorated to the nines, fake snow, garlands of holly, strings of cranberries, and a shingle-blasting choir of women in blue, sequined evening dresses, men in tuxedoes. Sprawled on the sofa in my shorts, T-shirt, and sandals, I felt downright naked. Perhaps straitlaced Mormons would agree—and also harrumph at the contents of the glass in my hand.

Winter or summer, though, what a show!

The rich baritone of actor and vocalist Brian Stokes Mitchell boomed throughout the performance. You put a gift like that in front of the Mormon Tabernacle Choir—to the accompaniment of strings, brass, woodwind, and hand bells—and the result is a blend of musical talent audible halfway to Mars.

On a more muted side of the broadcast, actor Edward Herrmann was at the top of his game with a reading of the Christmas story from Saint Luke. Ditto his poignant rendition of "Longfellow's Christmas" that ended with a stirring rendition of "I Heard the Bells on Christmas Day" by the choir. Real goosebump stuff, that. It was such an enjoyable, time-warp experience, I hopped into bed thinking Santa Claus might come during the night.

Nope. All that greeted me the next morning was a shaggy lawn that begged to be mowed.

Perhaps next July Fourth, I'll videotape barbecues, Mary Ann's birthday party, and fireworks and save 'em until the following December.

Like I said earlier, I'm weird like that.

CHRISTMAS TALES FOR TELLING

There's nothing like a wonderful family story during the Christmas holidays.

Some of them are old—such as a "Christmas chair" tale from the late 1920s that I recently heard from Ann Russell Mullins, who grew up in Nashville but has lived in Knoxville most of her adult life. Others are relatively new—like a "fish for Christmas breakfast" epic from Oak Ridger Elizabeth Busteed that only had its origin in 2009.

Doesn't matter. As long as families continue to gather and share holiday memories, these stories, and countless others like them, will live on.

Actually, Ann Mullins's story dates back a wee bit longer ago than the 1920s. Indeed, all the way to the Old Testament book of Jeremiah. There is a passage in chapter ten, verses two through four, that some Christians interpret as a prohibition against Christmas trees.

The exact wording varies depending on which Bible is quoted, but here's what it says in the Revised Standard Version: "For the customs of the peoples are false. A tree from the forest is cut down and worked with an axe by the hands of a craftsman. Men deck it with silver and gold; they fasten it with hammer and nails so that it cannot be moved."

Ann's father took the Jeremiah passage literally. Thus, there was no Christmas tree the entire time she was a child.

"But my mother wanted us to have something, so they worked out a compromise," Ann said. "She bought a string of eight colored lights and wrapped them around a small chair. That's what we had every year. We thought it was beautiful."

> My all-time favorite Halloween treat is candy corn. I've tried growing it in the garden but can't get the dang things to sprout!

Indeed, she never had a full-blown Christmas tree until marrying James Mullins in 1943. She and James enjoyed fifty-eight Christmases together, complete with trees, until his death in 2000.

"I still have a tree, even though it's a small artificial one," she told me. "It's usually up and decorated by early December."

Elizabeth Busteed's tale doesn't have biblical roots. Nothing about loaves and fishes, you understand. But it does bring to mind certain passages about manna from heaven.

She was in West Tennessee, staying with her son at his home on Kentucky Lake. Her great-grandson, Will Stanley, age eight, of Chattanooga had received his first gun for a Christmas present, and all the men and boys of the family went outside for the inaugural firing.

"My son's family is fortunate to have several bald eagles around their home during the winter," she said. "One was flying nearby, with a fish in its talons. About that time, Will shot at the target they had set up on the ground. The blast apparently startled the eagle into dropping its catch. The fish fell right among the crowd, much to everyone's surprise. It was a four-pound bass and was perfectly delicious for our breakfast."

And I'll guarantee the family will be feasting on that story for many Christmases to come.

Chapter **9**

SPORTS OF SORTS

Although I played varsity football—ineptly, sloppily, and without one scintilla of skill—throughout my years at Knoxville's Young High School, I've never been much of a fan of organized sports.

Oh, I follow baseball in early fall and usually know which teams are headed for the World Series. And I watch enough college and professional football on TV to keep up with who's who in their respective championship quests. Beyond that, pretty much zilch. You could hand me a list of players from the National Basketball Association and National Hockey League, and I couldn't tell you which athletes belonged to what outfits. (Then again, perhaps I *could* guess the NHL guys, since it's a requirement that hockey players have strange surnames, like "Vltchiklsvchwokd" and "Swzyplkuntro," largely devoid of vowels.)

I suspect the root of this noninterest lies in my loathing of statistics—those mind-numbing, brain-blowing sets of numbers sports fans are expected to cite by rote. It is impossible to carry on a conversation with these people because they speak only in numeric tongue. If you happen to casually mention around the office coffee pot some Monday morning that quarterback Peyton Manning threw for two touchdowns the previous afternoon, the stats squad strikes like a pack of jackals:

"True, but his overall efficiency rating was down by 15.74 percent based on other games played when the temperature is above sixty degrees."

"Perhaps, but remember that both of those passes came on two rare first-and-short situations from his own 36, which he is going to hit 87.35 percent of the time when throwing into a wind of less than fourteen miles per hour."

"Also, the average weight of blitzing linebackers was down 21.9 pounds, giving his blockers a superior advantage in keeping him protected. This only occurs once in every 66.3 games during months not ending in '-r'."

Arrgh! Enough! I can't stand this mindless gibberish! *Statistics, staschmistics!*

Truth be told, though, I do owe statistics a huge vocational debt of gratitude. A failure to comprehend numeric relationships, aka Statistics 201 at the University of Tennessee in fall quarter 1966, made me realize I had no future in the forestry profession. Well, yes, that and Chemistry 213 two quarters later.

Whatever the case, I had to settle for a degree in journalism, a profession that requires no expertise in numbers whatsoever—which is why newspaper reporters and radio-TV commentators can enthusiastically engage in learned debate about millions of dollars here, billions of dollars there, and trillions of dollars over yonder without the slightest idea of what these figures actually mean. This is a talent we share with politicians.

Over time, I discovered it's permissible to write about organized sports without mentioning the dreaded "s-" word because the odds critical to the story are so outlandish as to be incalculable.

Such as a bizarre set of circumstances that played out in Florida, March 2006, at a preseason baseball game between Detroit and Houston. For the record, the Astros prevailed, 13-3. But that didn't matter, for a much larger story occurred in the stands. I learned about it from Carl Rietman, a retired executive from the U.S. Department of Housing and Urban Development who lives in Knoxville.

Carl and his wife, Sarah, were vacationing in Florida. He was glancing at the local paper one morning and noticed that his beloved Tigers would be playing that afternoon. So he drove over to the ol' ballpark to take in a game.

"It was one of those spur-of-the-moment things," he told me. "My wife doesn't care about baseball, so she stayed at the time-share. I bought my ticket in the parking lot."

Carl found his seat and settled in. Pretty soon, a couple sat down next to him. Carl and the other guy started shooting the breeze. "How ya'doing?" "Great weather, ain't it?" "Where are you from?" That sort of thing.

Said Carl: "I told the fellow I was from Knoxville. Turns out we both had time-shares in Florida. He said he was from Michigan originally. I said, 'Oh, yeah? What city?'"

When the other fan answered "Holland," Carl did a double take.

"I grew up in Holland, too," Carl said. "What's your name?"

"Hopp."

Carl chuckled. "I once knew a guy named Hopp from Holland, Michigan," he said. "In fact, I was in the Army with him. His first name was Sherwin."

The other fan stared at Carl for a moment. Then he said, "I'm Sherwin Hopp. Who are you?"

And that, dear hearts, is the moment Korean War–era veterans Sherwin Hopp and Carl Rietman reunited for the first time since they parted company at Fort Knox, Kentucky, more than a half-century earlier.

"I never would have recognized him, and he never would have recognized me," said Carl. "There are over five thousand seats in that stadium. If we had been even three or four seats away from each other, this never would have happened. We ended up hardly even watching the game, just sat there talking, filling in the gaps, and catching up with our lives."

Here's the scoop: Four boys from Holland got drafted at the same time: Ken Lemmon and Sid Lankie, along with Sherwin and Carl. They stayed together until Fort Knox.

"Sherwin heard that a cooking school was opening, and he applied for it," Carl said with a laugh. "The rest of us weren't that smart. Turned out that Sherwin stayed at Fort Knox, while the rest of us got shipped to Korea. We had some pretty rough times. Guys were dying all around us."

Happily, they all survived. After the war ended and the boys came home, Hopp, Lemmon, and Lankie stayed in Michigan. Rietnam, a high-school dropout who had earned his GED in the service, went on to get a degree in construction engineering from Michigan State. He spent his career traveling all over the map for Uncle Sam, including assignments in California and Florida, before retiring to Tennessee in 1971. He had long-since lost contact with the old gang—until a happenstance meeting at a spring-training baseball game.

Find *that* in a statistics list!

By and large, I enjoy participating in, and writing about, sporting events that don't require strict adherence to numbers. Sports like hunting and fishing. Except for details such as length limits and creel limits in fishing, and shooting hours and bag limits in hunting—not to mention an occasional foray into bass-weight and deer-antler recordkeeping—you are free to enjoy unencumbered.

Meaning you get to lie a lot.

Just kidding. I don't mean lying as in the technical, legal, do-you-swear-to-tell-the-whole-truth sense. The type of lying hunters and fishers engage in is more of a "truth massaging" exercise. It calls for the skillful manipulation of certain numbers, if for no other reason than to throw overly inquisitive questioners off the trail.

If someone asks whether the crappie fishing is any good on your favorite lake, an answer of "I've caught a few" could mean everything from "It stinks, but I'm not about to admit failure" to "They're jumping in the boat, and I don't need the likes of you messing things up."

The level of lying, and the finesse with which it is deployed, tends to ratchet up or down depending on the perceived skill of the questioner. It's like chess: the next move you consider often is predicated by what you assume your opponent *thinks* you will do.

Thus, if someone wants to know if there has been much turkey-gobbling activity in your neck of the woods, your casual answer of "naaa" is, in fact, an exceedingly calculated one because you know it will be subjected to intense analysis and scrutiny.

Internally, the quizzer is thinking: "Does 'naaa' truly mean 'naaa'? Or is he just saying that because the birds are gobbling wildly and he wants to hide it? Or is nothing going on, but he knows if he says 'naaa' I'll think he's lying and waste the next two morning prowling around in *his* silent woods while he's hunting *my* birds?"

Riverboat gamblers have nothing on serious hunters and fishers.

On and on it goes with lies about special baits, secret lakes, and hush-hush game territories. Multiple layers of tangled webs get woven, underscoring the necessity for liars to have good memories. There's nothing worse than having a well-crafted lie turn on itself and bite you squarely in the butt because you forgot certain "facts" about your own prevarication.

In fact, I'm so confused right now about outdoor truths, half-truths, and untruths, I'm in desperate need of R&R and must head to the water. Don't ask for specifics; I'm fresh out of lies for the moment. Instead, I leave you with one fishing fact you can take to the bank: If you want to be the best angler in the United States, forget the latest lures, lines, rods, reels, boats, motors, and other nonsense.

Just have the right name.

No, this name is not "Izaak," as in Walton, the seventeenth-century English writer whose *Compleat Angler* is believed to be the first book on the sport. Nor is it "Santiago," as in Ernest Hemingway's main character in *The Old Man and the Sea*. Not "Peter," "Andrew," "James," and "John," as in fishermen disciples of the New Testament, either.

Instead, it's "Mike," as in "McClelland."

I came to this learned conclusion after perusing a Bass Pro Shops advertising flyer and tickling computer keys.

The brochure I was reading contained a list of fishing experts who were hosting seminars across the United States. One of them, scheduled to appear in Alabama and Georgia, was named Mike McClelland.

"Wonder if that's the same Mike McClelland I met, and spent several days fishing with, in South Dakota in 1982?" I thought to myself. "He was a professional walleye fisherman back then, but maybe he has switched to bass."

So I looked up his bio on the Internet. Nope. The picture didn't look anything like the Mike I knew. Besides, it turns out that bass Mike McClelland, who lives in Arkansas, is only forty-five years old. He would barely have been a teenager back then.

Out of curiosity, I Googled "Mike McClelland walleye fisherman." Lo and behold, up popped "my" Mike.

He still lives in Pierre, South Dakota, still fishes for walleyes, and is listed as the all-time money leader in professional walleye circles with earnings of more than half a million dollars.

Wow! What are the chances—See? It's those incalculable odds once again—that two professional fishermen would be named Mike McClelland?

Better than I imagined.

Tickling the keys further, I turned up yet another professional angler named Mike McClelland. He specializes in trout. I kid you not.

Trout Mike McClelland is a native of California, lives in Colorado, guides high-dollar clients to secret waters all around the world, and owns a travel company called "Best of New Zealand Fly Fishing."

Wonder what sort of lies would be told if bass Mike McClelland, walleye Mike McClelland, and trout Mike McClelland bumped into each other at a baseball game?

LOVE IN ALL THE WRONG PLACES

In the years he served as the *News Sentinel*'s police reporter, John Stiles occasionally wrote about kinky sexual encounters—recreational, commercial, and otherwise. But he telephoned me the other day with a situation outside the realm of human experiences.

"I've got a goose that keeps tryin' to get it on with my lawnmower," he said.

Stiles has become a gentleman farmer in retirement. He lives on a six-acre spread near Kingston Springs in Middle Tennessee. He and his wife have a menagerie of furred and feathered critters. They sell eggs and Cornish hens for the market.

Recently, they took in a wild Canada goose—John named him "Shadrack"—with a strange idea about its role in the birds-and-bees thing. Whenever John fires up the mower, Shadrack falls in love.

"It doesn't happen when the mower's turned off," Stiles told me with a laugh, "just when it's running. If I turn it off and walk away, so does Shadrack."

Even though male and female Canada geese look alike, John and I agreed

> **The fragrant waters of Fort Loudoun Lake have long been famous for their offal. But at least Knoxville-area boaters and anglers don't have to worry about things that go boom.**
>
> **In June 2009, the *St. Petersburg Times* reported a fisherman caught a "rusted supersonic AIM-9 Sidewinder heat-seeking missile" while trolling in the Gulf of Mexico. His "catch" was immediately claimed by the U.S. Air Force.**
>
> **And you thought snagging an old Michelin was bad.**

Shadrack has to be a guy. Why else would he be so (a) dumb and (b) infatuated with machinery?

"You ever heard of a bird this weird?" John asked.

Yes, I have. Usually, it's a case of one male bird fighting the reflection of his "enemy" in a mirror or window pane. Cardinals and mockingbirds are particularly susceptible, although we once had an indigo bunting at our house that pecked himself to death in pursuit of "that other guy."

A couple of years ago, Jefferson Countian David Rivers told me about a male wild turkey that fought its reflection in the hubcaps of his car. For weeks, any time David pulled up, the gobbler would rush out of nearby woods and attack the shiny suitor.

I've also heard of, uh, "more personal" confrontations. Seen 'em, too.

You don't have to take my word for it, either. My dear wife will vouch for me.

This occurred three or four springs ago, the time of year when the fancy of wild animals turns to an activity besides eating and sleeping. The wild turkeys on our ridge were going through their usual displays of courtship. The males greeted each morning with loud gobbling. They were strutting and puffing their feathers, hoping to entice sweet young she-turkeys to join them in the business of making little turkeys.

The women, as usual, weren't interested.

"Those gobblers remind me of some loud-mouthed jerk at a bar," Mary Ann once observed. "You know the kind—with a hairy beer gut, his shirt opened nearly to the waist, two or three gold chains around his neck, drenched in Brut, running his jaw, and thinking the women love it. All the while, the women are rolling their eyes and thinking to themselves, 'Oh, *paa-leeze!* What a loser!'"

Anyhow, Mary Ann and I happened to be looking out a side window one morning when the spectacle was playing out. A gobbler in full strut kept trying to pirouette around a hen. Except there was one problem. A small log kept getting in his way. It was a crooked piece of white oak I had tossed aside months earlier while cutting firewood.

The poor ol' gobbler kept tripping over it as he turned, first to the left, then to the right in his courtship dance. He must have clambered across it five or six times.

"That dummy!" I chuckled as we watched. "You'd think he'd step to one side and get away from that log."

Nope. But finally he did do something else.

The log.

Yes. He mounted and bred that piece of white oak. So help me. The hen stood there, seemingly in shock. If I'm lyin', I'm dyin'.

Mary Ann shook her head in amazement: "And that's the bird you claim is so smart!"

Sometime after the sizzling session was over, I fetched the log from the woods, took a photograph of it, and sent it to my Mississippi friend Will Primos, who makes game calls, decoys, and other hunting accessories.

"There are millions of dollars to be made with this revolutionary concept!" I told Will. "Just make a plastic model of this log, like those plastic antlers you sell for deer rattling. Tell hunters to set it out on the woods, go hide, wait until a gobbler comes along to make love to it, then shoot him."

Will said he'd consider it. Just as soon as he quit laughing.

THE OL' COACH STILL HAS IT

With all due respect to current and former coaches at the University of Tennessee, the most famous coach in the history of Knoxville football is alive and well and still on the recruiting trail.

That, of course, would be Billy Joe Tom Bob Parker, head coach of the Fightin' Possums at Clyde Clod University.

If you're a longtime Knoxvillian, you immediately recognize this coach's name. You're familiar with his reputation. You remember some of his epic games, especially the annual rivalry with Nashville Country Club. If you moved here after 1995, however, and are wondering, "Billy Joe Tom Bob who?" you have my pity. You don't know what you missed.

Coach Parker, the Fightin' Possums and CCU were the brainchild of Curtis "C.P." Parham, one of the funniest personalities to ever grace Knoxville radio waves. He's been off the air since Bill Clinton was in office and says it's been at least ten years since he performed his Coach Parker shtick in public. But when I telephoned Parham at his production company the other day, he picked up the Billy Joe Tom Bob patter like he'd just been cued from the control room:

"I was out in the country, lookin' for a big strong lineman and saw this young man plowin' with a mule. I stopped and asked directions. When he picked up the plow and pointed it, I knew I had me a prospect."

I made my call on National Signing Day, the most frenzied moment in all of jockdom. This is the day gifted high school players select from the many universities that are tripping over themselves to offer a scholarship and sign on the dotted line. Assuming they know how to write.

I'm kidding, of course. The vast majority of these prospects can at least make their mark on paper and compose intelligent text—like "lol, c u 2 nite"—on an iPhone.

In the midst of this nationwide nuttiness, it was oh-so-refreshing to hear Parham's voice as he parodied college football.

"We went 8-4 last year," he said.

"Wow," I replied. "Eight wins and four losses isn't bad at all."

"No, I mean eight arrests but only four convictions."

Coach Parker also told me he had been UT's second choice to run the Vol football program after Lane Kiffin's abrupt departure to Southern California.

"Who was first?" I inquired.

"Everybody else."

"What does your upcoming season look like?" I asked.

"This will be the fortieth year of our rebuilding program," Coach Parker said. "Fortunately, we're going to have a lot of returning veterans.

"There's Booka Matches, a linebacker. He's hard to get started on rainy days, but once he gets lit, he's a regular ball o'far.

"And then there's our running back, Lance Boil, the ol' red-head. I expect him to hook up quite often with our great wide receiver, La'Fronia "Wineglass" Jackson.

"Also coming back will be Cumberland Plateau, our two-footed placekicker. His longest last year was from eighty-four yards."

"Pretty impressive," I said.

"Not really," the coach replied. "That's only forty-two yards per foot."

A WEIRD WAY TO CELEBRATE

In all of professional jockdom, baseball players have to be the dumbest.

I'm not talking about on-the-field smarts. When it comes to knowing who's on first and what kind of pitch will likely be offered to encourage hitting into a double play, every millionaire on each team is a PhD.

Yet they're overtaken with a serious case of ignorance by celebrating with champagne if they win their division, their league's pennant, or the World Series. I was just watching the jillionth episode of this seasonal nuttiness a few nights ago, shortly after the New York Mets secured the National League's East Division title. From outfielders to pitchers to batboys to the manager, everyone in the clubhouse was soaked with bubbly. Even as some of the key, albeit drenched, players were being interviewed by a TV sportscaster, others could be seen in the background, shaking green bottles and hosing everything and everybody within spray range.

Far be it from me to be a spoilsport. Quite the contrary. I'll party with anybody, anytime, for any reason. And the more hooch, the better. Whoo-hoo! Chug-a-lug, chug-a-lug!

But that's the problem. *Ain't nobody chuggin'!*

Perhaps it's just me, but aren't you supposed to drink this stuff instead of squirting it all over the room?

Baseball isn't the sole purview of this beverage blasphemy, of course; it's just that baseball has been around longer. I've seen televised champagne showers in the aftermath of pro football championships, particularly the Super Bowl. I suppose they do it in the National Basketball Association, too, but the last time I endured an entire NBA game, Jimmy Carter was contemplating a run for the White House. Nonetheless, it's safe to say baseball is where drinking champagne during celebrations is about as common as sauerkraut and Swiss cheese on peach ice cream.

Oh, well. This would be a boring world indeed if every sport handled triumph with a stiff upper lip. Nothing yawns like the umpteenth fitting of that green jacket at the Masters. So if lads of the diamond want to behave like fraternity brothers at a homecoming bash, fine by me. I just hate to see all that marvelous joy juice go to waste.

And now that I think about it, there's something else about baseball that's as predictable as champagne dousing. It's the verb always used to describe the divisional victory process. Invariably, this milestone is "clinched."

Amazing. Sportswriters and broadcasters own vast warehouses of colorful verbs to convey victory and plumb them with zealous regularity. Even the greenest intern can describe how a team was "whipped," "mauled," "shellacked," "manhandled," "tripped up," "keelhauled," "clobbered," or "crucified."

But for some reason, this rich inventory evaporates at division title time. Only "clinched" need apply. If I ever read a baseball story about how a team "won," "claimed," or "captured" this honor, I'd be inclined to celebrate with a bottle of champagne.

One slow, delicious sip at a time.

THE MOST EXPENSIVE DOVES EVER

Let's talk money—specifically missed opportunities. Between the "if I'da only knowns" and the "wudda-shudda-cuddas" making the rounds these days, there's enough grist to jump-start talk for months on end.

The particular discussion I have in mind has nothing to do with stocks, bonds, mutual funds, the Dow, or Nasdaq. Instead, it involves one Theophilus Nash Buckingham, who died in Knoxville on March 10, 1971, at the age of ninety.

If you have even a remote interest in sports, you're familiar with that name. I don't need to tell you "Mister Buck" was a giant in American sporting literature. Or that he was an original Tennessee Volunteer, captain of the 1902 football team. Or that he was a pioneer conservationist whose name was linked to nearly every major environmental initiative during the first half of the twentieth century.

Don't bother going to your local library to study Nash Buckingham. His nine books—the originals, not reprints—are in such demand as collectors' items you won't find them on open display. Instead, check eBay or Amazon.com. Cling tightly to your billfold when you do, for merely a "Nash Buckingham" byline on the cover of a vintage magazine increases its value astronomically.

Buckingham was born May 31, 1880, and spent most of his life in Memphis. He directed one of the nation's first wildlife restoration programs for Winchester Arms and was a founder of More Game Birds for America, forerunner of today's internationally renowned wetlands conservation organization, Ducks Unlimited.

His stories enjoyed a wide following from the 1930s through the '50s and into the early '60s. Then audiences shifted to a different style of writing. His name eventually faded from print. Late in life—his own health failing and his wife confined to a nursing home—Buckingham moved to Knoxville and lived with his daughter and son-in-law, Irma and Roy Witt.

Buckingham's fame almost immediately rebounded after his death. Indeed, it multiplied exponentially. By any standard, he is considered one of the lions of the American conservation movement.

Which brings me to my gaffe.

In 1970, at the tender age of twenty-two, I was hired as outdoors editor of the *Knoxville News Sentinel*. One early assignment was to interview the legendary writer. Mister Buck, dressed in coat and tie as always, was the perfect gentleman. He was deaf by then (a lifetime of shooting will do that), so our "interview" was conducted via pen and note pad.

A few days after my article appeared, Buckingham sent a box of shotgun shells to my office as a token of thanks and esteem. Sometime thereafter, I took them dove hunting and fired all but one, which I kept as a souvenir.

The first time I told my friend Larry Cook that story, his mouth flew open: "You did *what*?!"

A banker by profession, Larry is a broker of sporting antiques, particularly those of the Buckingham era. More than once, he has pointed out that if I'd kept those three-dollar shells and gotten Nash Buckingham to autograph the box in his trademark flowing script, it would easily fetch five thousand dollars today. Quite possibly much more.

Mercenarily and sentimentally, I kick my own butt every time I think about it.

A SEW-SEW SORT OF JOB

I'm tempted to start this exercise with a stern warning: "Don't try this at home!" But that would be self-defeating, because Gary Harding did try it at home. More so, he succeeded.

Shortly after arriving at the office one gorgeous spring morning, I returned phone calls left on my recorder by a pair of dear old friends—one in Sevier County, the other in Knox County.

And do you know what? Both of those sniveling, hateful, low-down, rotten $#&#s had the audacity to answer via their cell phones WHILE THEY WERE FISHING!

Sevier Guy even set his phone aside long enough to make a catch while I stewed in silence at the other end. Knox Guy kept jabbering about the ideal conditions while counting the vast assemblage of slab crappies sloshing in his livewell.

Forthwith, I sketched stick-figure images of each guy and drew sharp, pointy objects at crucial anatomical regions. Not that I was envious or anything.

I have seen the evidence myself. And while I'm not medically qualified to assess these things, it sure looks good to me.

"It" is a thin white scar, roughly two inches long, that arcs from Harding's nose to above his right eye. If you didn't know it was there, you might not even notice.

This scar is the result of a freak accident Harding suffered one morning while deer hunting. More on that in a minute. What's far more amazing is how he treated the situation.

He closed the wound with a needle and thread.

By himself.

Looking in a mirror and working "backwards."

Ten stitches.

Without anesthetic.

"It was pretty intense," said Harding. "But I figured if Rambo could sew up his own wounds (as depicted by Sylvester Stallone in the 1982 hit film *First Blood*), I could, too."

Harding, who lives in Rockford, was deer hunting on his next-door neighbor's property. He glanced out one corner of his blind and saw a nine-point buck.

"I guess I got a little excited," he recalled. "I had to turn and shoot at an angle. Plus, I guess I didn't have the butt of the gun tucked into my shoulder tight enough."

When he squeezed the trigger and the rifle recoiled, it slammed the telescopic sight into his face: "I saw the deer go down, but then all I could see was blood. It was running down my face and dripping off my nose."

Harding immediately realized the seriousness of his wound. He walked back home and took matters into his own hands. Literally.

"I don't have any medical insurance," he told me. "I'm a Vietnam vet and have to rely on the Veterans Administration for medical treatment. I knew I couldn't drive to Johnson City bleeding like that. Plus, I had a dead deer to take care of. I told my wife to start boiling water."

It might help to know that Gary Harding does have some experience stitching flesh. Just not living flesh, nor human. For the past quarter-century, he has worked full time as a taxidermist.

"I use surgical needles in my business," he said. "I knew they had to be sterile for something like this. That's why I boiled them and the thread.

"The first stitch was the worst. I just gritted my teeth and did it. Actually, I was surprised that it didn't hurt as much as I thought it would. It didn't hurt near as bad as the gash itself. The hardest part was watching myself in the mirror and realizing that when I 'pushed' I was actually 'pulling.'"

Harding kept the wound clean. He regularly applied a topical antibiotic and changed bandages.

"I've got a neighbor down the road who's a nurse practitioner," he said. "A couple of days after I'd done it, she took off the bandage and looked at it. She said I'd done a real good job. She told me I should have been a doctor."

All's well that ends well. As Harding said with a smile: "The cut is healed, I've got deer steaks in the freezer, and I'm ready to go hunting again next season."

Note to self: Never pick a fight with this guy.

HOW TO KEEP FROM GETTING LOST

Daniel Boone, a man who knew a thing or three about the boondocks, always proudly claimed to never have been lost. However, as he told an interviewer late in life, "I was bewildered once for three days."

I understand completely.

True, my prowls in the outback are quite tame compared to Daniel's. Today's wilderness, wild and remote as it may be, is decidedly less wild and less remote than it was two centuries ago. (Why, they didn't even have public restrooms along the interstates back then! Can you imagine the inconvenience?)

Nonetheless, I've been known to get "bewildered" a few times myownself. Once to the point that, after emerging from one section of the Cherokee National Forest via a different route than I entered, I actually went to the trouble of consulting a map. That's when I discovered—*gasp!*—I'd come within one watershed of exiting on the North Carolina side of the mountains, not the Tennessee. Several friends actually called me "Mister Bewilderedness" for a while after that embarrassing episode.

Of course, I've never been worried about getting truly lost, as in hopelessly AWOL. That's because I always check to see which side of McDonald's the moss is growing on. This always keeps me on course. Nonetheless, if I'm correctly interpreting the latest scientific news, a lot of folks are about to become bewildered. Especially if they rely on a compass to go from Point A to Points B, C, and D.

You see, the Earth's magnetic north is shifting. I swear on a Northstar Model 8000i GPS navigational system—list price $5,369.05, and at such an outlandish cost I have no idea why they bother with the stupid nickel—that I'm not making this up. The McClatchy-Tribune Information Service recently filed a story about the phenomenon and its repercussions on the navigational industry.

Experts says there's nothing new about this shift. It's been going on since Ig consulted his compass and told Og to bear left at the next cave, but before Og could say, "Kiss my saber-tooth," they careened into a tar pit and were never heard from again.

It's all due to the hot, liquid core of our planet constantly rolling and churning, like Earth ingested six beers and a giant pizza before going to bed and is now facing the consequences.

"Magnetic north is shifting all the time," said Jeffrey Love, a geophysicist with the U.S. Geomagnetism Program in Golden, Colorado. "It's a continuous process, not an event."

Perhaps, but the rate of acceleration has dramatically increased—from as little as nine miles per year in the early 1900s to roughly forty miles per year now.

Happily for modern travelers, this won't affect GPS systems, which rely on satellites, not magnetic north. Still, the common compass is an important tool, especially if your GPS crashes. As a result, the story said, aviation and marine industries are spending millions of dollars to upgrade their systems and charts.

My reaction?

Pffft! Don't worry about it.

Should you become a bit "bewildered" while hiking this summer, remember an important survival tip: Perrier and similar brands of expensive bottled water always flow away from civilization, never toward it. Guaranteed.

FISHING RECRUITING WARS

Oh, the injustice of being born too soon!

When I was an undergraduate at the University of Tennessee in the late 1960s, I was forced to cut class, and then lie my way out of it, any time I wanted to go bass fishing. To this day, my old journalism professor, senior advisor, mentor, and friend, Dr. Kelly Leiter, claims I hold the UT record for out-of-town grandmothers who died abruptly. Kelly says he lost count after seven.

My, how times have changed. Bass fishing is now a sanctioned sport at more than two-hundred colleges. The Vols have a bass-fishing team—complete with uniforms, boats, and school-sponsored road trips.

There's a College Bass National Championship, too. It recently was held at Brewer Lake, Arkansas. Eastern Kentucky won, followed by Georgia and Alabama. There's even a Top Twenty-five list of teams, as selected by FLW Outdoors.

And now there are scholarships. Tyler Wadzinski, a senior at Franklin High School, signed on the dotted line to trade his fishing skills for an education at Bethel University in McKenzie, Tennessee.

If this dizzying pace continues, we'll soon be bombarded with full-fledged recruiting updates along the lines of: "Hiram 'Wormy' Dunksford III, 6-2, 215, Bilgewater High School, Plowshare, Mississippi. Holds the high-school large-mouth record (eleven pounds, six ounces). A plastic worm virtuoso, Dunksford is equally proficient with Texas rig, Carolina rig, Shakyhead, and drop-shot. Also excels with buzzbaits and flipping pig'n jig. Has been plagued with nagging left-ankle injuries that restrict full use of electric motor controls, but shows great improvement after months of fish-oil therapy. Originally committed to Ole Miss, but recently expanded his options to include Tennessee and Auburn. Seeks a degree in aquatic biology."

You know what will come next, of course. NCAA investigations and sanctions, that's what.

The offenses might include overzealous alumni giving "graphite grip" handshakes to promising recruits. Or unreported use of live bait. Or off-campus contact by a sporting goods rep. Or the worst, which could result in the death penalty—sneaking onto tournament waters and surreptitiously practicing during the "off-limits" period.

I can close my eyes and hear the lies of the guilty: "C'mon, Coach! You gotta help me out! Tell the NCAA I was in class last Tuesday, not fishing!"

Proving that everything eventually comes full circle.

A PAIN IN THE BASS

I have pulled some incredibly stupid stunts in the name of "relaxation" by fishing for bass.

Once while jig-poling on Fort Loudoun Lake, I set the hook so violently (on a bass that apparently had just spit out my gob of worms), I wound up with an acute case of tennis elbow.

Once while floating Little River, I much-too-casually reached out to grab a pipsqueak bass that had inhaled my crankbait—only to have the fish shake at the wrong moment, driving a treble hook into the palm of my right hand. The float trip was delayed long enough for a visit to Blount Memorial Hospital's emergency room.

Once on Norris Lake, I eased my bass boat onto a large, remote island, intending to hop out and explore its woodlands for hunting possibilities later on.

> In 2010, the Tennessee General Assembly approved separate bills that would (1) make it illegal for athletes to sell fake urine and (2) require alarms in swimming pools. Speaking as a lap-swimmer of thirty-plus years, I wish our lawmakers would have combined both proposals and required an alarm to sound whenever there is placement of pee, real or fake, in pool water.

As I stepped off the deck, my shoe caught on something—maybe a rod, maybe a tackle box, who knows?—and I lost my balance. To avoid swan-diving into the water, I made a split-second decision to push off as hard as I could, hoping to arc safely ashore.

So done. Tah-dah!

Alas, physics being what they are, the energetic leap immediately slingshot my boat toward the middle of the channel.

I was alone, of course. There was nothing to do—after heatedly cursing for several moments—but swim for it. Mercifully, the wind shifted before I completely stripped down. I had to scramble a couple-hundred yards along the bank and wade into the shallows, but managed to grab the S.S. Venob before it got away again.

Yet nothing compares with the crime of aggravated stupidity I committed a few afternoons ago on Douglas Lake.

I tried to kick a bass and wound up busting my ass. Literally.

This occurred as I was fishing the muddy edges of a creek embayment, casting into schools of shad minnows for ravenous largemouths feeding below. Foot access was required because the water was too shallow for approach by boat.

I was standing and casting, quite awkwardly, on a mud-and-shale bank. If you've never tried to traverse one of these semi-liquid landscapes, imagine standing and casting atop a mound of pea gravel—except pea gravel affords far more stability.

Anyhow, I hooked a two-poundish bigmouth, played it toward the shore, and was swinging it out of the water in one motion when the bass made a final shake and threw my lure. The fish came tumbling back toward me, flopping helter-skelter. Reflexively, I kicked out with my right foot to stop it.

Not smart.

Muddy left foot went one way in the loose shale. Muddy right foot went another. In the process of cartwheeling into the mire, I stretched Ye Olde Gluteus Maximus from Dandridge to White Pine.

As we speak, I am hobbling around on a cane. It hurts to stand. It hurts to walk. It hurts to sit. It hurts to lie down. Hell, it hurts to blink.

Oh, and get this: On the drive home from the lake, I got pulled over for a defective brake light. Thankfully, the deputy let me off with a warning ticket.

What the officer should have warned was to quit fishing altogether. Before it kills me.

A FEW FOR THE FOLKS AT NYFU

Before you head to Neyland Stadium, before you gnaw the first piece of tailgate chicken, before a chorus of "Rocky Top" breaks out, before the Volunteers run through the giant T, one critical task remains.

We must offend everyone with jock jokes.

I used to launch these barbs toward specific schools, particularly Tennessee's opponents. Then one year it struck me: Why such a narrow approach? Why not paint everyone with the same broad brush? Thus were born the players, coaches, fans, and cheerleaders from good ol' NYFU—Name Your Favorite University.

Herewith is a selection of equal-opportunity offenders. Feel free to steal and customize as you need. What the heck. I stole and customized myself. Hut-one! Hut-two!

Why did the NYFU fullback run to the post office every ten minutes?

Because his computer kept saying, "You've got mail."

Why did the NYFU cheerleader place a distant last in the swimming competition?

She didn't realize she could use her arms in the breaststroke.

Why did the NYFU lineman bake his Thanksgiving turkey for sixteen days?

Because the instructions said cook one hour for every pound, and he weighs 384 pounds.

What do you call a beautiful girl on the NYFU campus?

A visitor.

How many NYFU freshmen does it take to screw in a light bulb?

None. At NYFU, this is a sophomore course.

Why did the NYFU coach have his players work in a bakery during the summer?

So they would get familiar with turnovers.

What do you call a NYFU player with a national championship ring?

A thief.

What serves as foreplay for a NYFU cheerleader?

"Git in the back o'mah truck, sis."

Why did the NYFU quarterback drive his truck off a cliff?

To test his air brakes.

Why did the coach at NYFU dress only twenty players for the opening game?

He assumed the rest could dress themselves.

Why did the NYFU center climb a chain-link fence?

To see what was on the other side.

What did the NYFU tackle name his pet zebra?

"Spot."

What is the definition of gross ignorance?

One hundred forty-four NYFU fans.

What did the NYFU alum do when he learned that 85 percent of accidents occur at home?

He moved.

Did you hear about the NYFU linebacker who bought an AM radio?

Took him six months to discover it would also work at night.

But, wait! There's more where those came from! Pile on, I say!

As the NYFU team filed onto the airplane for the first game of the year, a coach handed each player a stick of gum.

"What's this for?" asked a hulking lineman.

"It keeps your ears from popping," said the coach.

At the end of the journey, the kid said, "It sure worked, but how do I dig it out?"

NYFU just signed a triple-threat running back. On any given play, the kid can jump off-sides, go the wrong way, and fumble.

An NYFU player took his dog to class for four years but finally had to stop because the dog graduated.

"I got one-hundred today on two different tests!" the NYFU linebacker told his adviser.

"Great! Which ones?"

"In chemistry I got a forty-seven, and in history I got a sixty-three."

"But that's one-hundred ten."

"Yeah, I know," the player said with a sigh. "I flunked the math test completely."

The entire first string at NYFU made straight *A*s in writing class last semester. Next semester, they're going to start working on their *B*s.

An NYFU player was shopping in a department store one afternoon when a fierce thunderstorm rolled in, knocking out electrical power. The poor kid was stranded on the escalator for forty-five minutes.

One NYFU player approached another in the locker room and said, "I just heard a great knock-knock joke. Let me tell it."
"OK," said his buddy. "Knock-knock."
"Who's there?"
The two guys stared at each other for a moment. Finally, the first one said, "Wait! I was supposed to start! OK, knock-knock!"
"Who's there?"
The kid's face suddenly fell. "Aw, hell," he said glumly, "I forgot the dadgum punch line."
"Aw-hell-I-forgot-the-dadgum-punch-line-who?"

It was the first day of composition class at NYFU, and students were told to write a six-hundred-word essay on what they did over summer vacation. Immediately, the football captain began working furiously. His pencil fairly flew across the paper.
"Oh, not much," he wrote two hundred times.

A guy walks into a bar and blurts, "Hey! I've got some great NYFU jokes to tell!"
"You better watch your tongue," says the bartender. "I was a four-year letterman at NYFU. So was that bouncer over there. In fact, just about everybody in this bar is an NYFU grad."

"Not a problem," says the customer, "I'll speak v-e-r-y s-l-o-w-l-y."

And then there was the NYFU player who was so smart that he finished a two-week diet in three days.

The quarterback from NYFU was so dumb, he couldn't even pass remedial science. One day in class, the professor asked him, "What do you call a fish with no eyes?"

The kid answered, "A fsh."

Several players from NYFU were in their dorm room, watching a football game on TV. A fellow jock walked in and asked, "What's the score?"

"It's 14-6," someone replied.

"Who's ahead?"

"The one with 14."

What do you call a drug ring at NYFU?

The huddle.

The center from NYFU went into his dentist's office and said, "I got a tooth knocked out at practice today. Can you put me in a new one to match all my others?"

"Sure," said the dentist, "but it's going to take a little while to prepare."

"How come?" asked the kid.

"Because I've got to color it green and drill three cavities."

If four NYFU players are in a car, who's driving?

A police officer.

The blonde cheerleader from NYFU was walking along a street near campus when she was approached by a panhandler.

He began his spiel, "Ma'am, I haven't eaten in five days . . ."

The young lady was shocked. "Five days?" she exclaimed. "Wow! I sure wish I had your will power!"

And then there was the 435-pound lineman from NYFU who was so ugly, the only thing attracted to him was the force of gravity.

The running back from NYFU was trying on shoes at a department store.

"How do they feel?" asked the salesman.

"They're a little bit tight," the guy responded.

"Hmm," said the clerk, bending down. "Let's try pulling the tongue out a little."

"Nope," the kid said, "theyth sthill feelth a bith tighth."

The old coach from NYFU went to an orthopedic surgeon, complaining of water on the knee. The doctor made a thorough exam but could find nothing wrong with the coach's knees.

One week later, the coach was back. He said, "I'm tellin' you, Doc, I've got water on the knee." Again, the surgeon conducted a battery of tests. The knees checked out perfectly.

Nonetheless, the coach returned a few days later complaining about water on the knee.

The physician glanced at his patient, snapped his fingers and said, "Of course! Now I see your problem! And the cure is oh-so-simple!"

"Great!" exclaimed the coach. "What do I need to do?"

"Aim better when you pee."

And now, let the games begin!

PANCAKES, TOMAHAWKS, AND TROUT

If you're searching for trout in unspoiled wilderness, travel to Alaska, hire the services of a seasoned bush pilot, and fly hundreds of miles into the outback.

If your targeted territory lies closer to home and your financial means are a bit more modest, you might try some of the famous western rivers like the Madison and Yellowstone. Or perhaps the fabled northeastern flows of Au Sable and Letort.

Remote trout environments are decidedly more scarce in the Southeast. Yet if you're willing to invest sweat and boot equity, the national parks and forests of Tennessee, North Carolina, and Georgia offer miles of high-country streams where bears outnumber humans by a vast majority.

And then there is trout fishing in downtown Gatlinburg, Tennessee, the tourist-taffy-tomahawk-and-tawdry-T-shirt capital of Amurika.

Pristine boondocks this isn't. If all other trout venues are an Armani suit, this is a pair of size forty-four blue jeans with the knees worn bare, the butt ripped out, and a Skoal ring on one back pocket. But like eating raw oysters, you ain't lived until you've tried it.

Gatlinburg has honed put-and-take trouting to a bio-economic science. Customers put money on the counter, and the city lets them take five fish from the waters cascading through the heart of town. The only difference between this transaction and those at the Kroger seafood department is that here, patrons are required to actually wade, cast, set the hook, reel their trout to a dip net, and reduce it to final possession on a chain stringer.

I recently fished Gatlinburg with a couple of old friends. We had a ball—although as one quipped while we were ferrying trout from stream to the car, "This is like visiting a whorehouse and then claiming you're the world's greatest ladies man."

I have insufficient experience to grasp the full extent of his analogy. But I am now qualified to speak on the trout program here. Only in Gatlinburg do you:

Fish under the constant gaze of audiences milling along the sidewalks.

Inhale the bracing aroma of pancakes, hamburgers, hot dogs, pizza, and fried chicken instead of woodsmoke.

Receive rave reviews of each catch from above—ranging from "Geez, noice fush!" if the commentator is of Yankee extraction, to "Hale far, buddy, 'at's a damguddun!" from the locals.

Think twice about your old habit of biting off the tag end of a knot after reading all those downstream warning signs about "elevated levels of fecal (sewage) bacteria."

Overhear spirited debate about the relative merits and subtle advantages between salmon eggs, Green Giant canned corn, and nightcrawlers from Walmart.

Have a hard time discerning the laughter of running water over the din of cars, buses, fire engines, and Harleys.

Step from a real river rock to an artificial river rock to a concrete piling to a pipe casing, all in the space of twenty feet.

Duck under a bridge to recycle your coffee because that's the only "remote territory" available.

But what the heck. The folks in Gatlinburg, bless their capitalistic hearts, have been selling kitsch as handcraft for lo these many years. More power to 'em.

We'd do the same thing in Knoxville if we could figure how to charge tourists for the privilege of yanking carp from the mouth of First Creek. So take off your tweed jacket, set your crook-stemmed pipe aside, and join the fray. It's a hoot.

To paraphrase Jeff Foxworthy: "If you ever stole a biscuit from the breakfast bar at Shoney's and used it for trout bait, you might be a redneck."

And you sure could do it, yee-haw, in Gatlinburg.

A BARGAIN AT ANY PRICE

Larry Cook and I have three-fourths of a century of turkey-hunting experience between us. Still, we learn something new every year.

"How long did it take this bird to come in, once we got set up?" Larry asked a few mornings ago as he swung a Jefferson County gobbler into the bed of my truck. "Four minutes? Five?"

"Maybe six at the outside," I replied. "Just about ran over us, didn't he?"

I unscrewed the stopper on my Thermos and added, "Now, maybe we can finish our coffee break."

As is the case with most freshly departed spring gobblers, this one made the mistake of opening his mouth at the wrong time. Wrong for him, that is. It was perfect timing for Larry and me.

We had begun the morning on the same ridge where we each bagged a turkey on opening day. On cue, just after the first blush of dawn, the boss bird we figured was still prowling this territory sounded off. Perfect.

Right by the book, I quietly tree-called to him. Right by the book, he began gobbling fit to choke. Right by the book, I let the ol' boy build a head of steam, then gave him a dose of the kinkiest she-bird sex talk I could deliver. Right by the book, he flew down and walked off, showing no interest whatsoever in my torrid appeal. Whereupon the morning's silence remained unbroken.

Hoo-boy. Been there, done that. Many times. Will be, and do, again. Many times. That's why they call it turkey "hunting" as opposed to turkey "shooting."

After an hour or so of fruitless prospecting, Larry and I hiked back to my truck to drink some coffee and debate where we might next try our luck. We were standing there, sipping joe, plotting whether to hit Place B or Place C, when down in the valley to the east of us a county road crew began working.

Part of the job involved dumping and packing fresh gravel. Every time a truck backed up, it emitted a piercing "beep-beep-beep-beep."

On about the third series of beeps, a gobbler fired back.

This is a phenomenon known as "shock-gobbling." It's an involuntary response to any abrupt sound. I've heard turkeys shock-gobble to crows, owls, thunder, roosters, gunfire, car horns, car engines, peacocks, woodpeckers, even—I swear—loud sneezing. But until that moment, I'd never heard one shock-gobble to a dump truck.

I turned toward the general direction and cupped my ears. The truck beep-beep-beeped. The gobbler rattled. Then again. We grabbed guns and lit out.

It took us probably thirty minutes to close the distance. In that time, I lost count of the beep-beep-beeps and subsequent gobbles. But they were frequent enough that I only had to stop once and crow-call to keep us on track.

We approached as near as we dared in the open woods and plopped down beside a tree. I "cutt-cutt" two or three times on a slate, then covered it up with excited yelping on a mouth call. The bird answered immediately.

You know the drill from there: Propped on respective knees, both barrels pointed toward the source of the gobbling. I cutt again. He gobbled again. Closer. At times like this you wonder if the pounding in your chest isn't audible at fifty yards.

Perhaps sixty seconds later, there he stood, head aglow in breeding colors.

"Take him," I hissed—as if Larry needed coaching.

Boom. Thirty minutes of hoofing later, we were sipping that second round of coffee.

"We need to get us one of those gravel trucks," I kidded. "How much you reckon a good used one might cost?"

"Oh, around sixty or seventy grand," Larry said, grinning in response. "Pretty expensive gear."

"Yeah, but it could be worse," I said. "Back in the '80s, Ray Harper was hunting at Tellico when an F-14 streaked across the treetops. The sonic boom 'bout blew him out of his boots. Liked to have scared him to death. Ray told me he hadn't heard a gobble all morning, but then every bird in the Cherokee National Forest hollered at that thing. He went toward the closest one, called it up, and killed it.

"Compared to $38 million for an F-14, one of those gravel trucks is a bargain. And you don't need a runway, either!"

PUTTERING IN PEA SOUP

Mother Goose would not be pleased with three men who recently rub-a-dub-dubbed a tub across the English Channel.

At least they *thought* that's the mission they had accomplished.

The trio were in Great Britain and, surprise, had been drinking heavily. Someone suggested what a swell idea it would be to visit France. So they boarded a seven-foot, inflatable boat, equipped with a bottle of hooch and one paddle, and spent the next eleven hours navigating the channel.

Upon reaching what they thought was the other side, they greeted everyone with a cheery "bon jour!"—only to learn they were still in British waters, a mere two miles from where they had started.

According to a story in the *London Daily Telegraph,* the three were "lucky to have survived overnight with no protection and no lifejackets. It would have been so easy for the dinghy to have been capsized by the smallest of waves."

We shall leave it to others to address the foolishness of embarking in a tiny boat, packing nothing more than a snoot full of liquor. But I do know a thing or three about getting tee-totally lost on open water. So does anyone who hunts or fishes the reservoirs of East Tennessee.

Huh? Lost? Around here? Where you can easily see from one side of any lake to the other?

Absolutely. You can't fathom this predicament if your boating is limited to daylight hours or clear, moonlit nights. But once you've been enveloped in a pea-soup fog, especially after dark, you'll discover how quickly any TVA lake can turn into a vast expanse of aquatic wilderness.

One of the first times it happened to me was while duck hunting on Fort Loudoun. Well before dawn, I left the cove at Chota Marina, intending to cross the main channel and weave into the Ish Creek embayment, commonly known as "Prater Flats." The fog was thick enough to slice with a knife, but I thought—incorrectly—all I had to do was hold my boat steady and proceed slowly until I hit the Blount County shore.

I eased along in the void, barely able to even see Stormy, my Labrador retriever, in the bow of my boat. After twenty minutes, I spied shoreline ahead. I hunted Fort Loudoun regularly in those days and knew every square inch of the bank—which only compounded my problem.

You see, I thought I'd arrived on the Blount County side of the lake. Thus, I was searching for Blount County landmarks. But nothing made sense. Not until I saw a faint light and gunned my engine toward it did I learn the error of my ways.

It was the light at Chota Marina. The torque of my outboard had simply propelled me in a wide arc. I was right back where I'd started. End of duck hunt.

Sometime later, Claude Fox, now deceased but then a master mariner and head of the National Outboard Association, gave me a tip about navigating in fog:

Just tie a long rope to your stern. Tow it and watch it as you motor along. Soon as a curve starts to develop, realign your boat, and you'll travel in an arrow-straight line.

Indeed you will. Ever since then, I have "straight-roped" myself across miles of foggy waters. No GPS necessary.

True, this tactic will only work if you're familiar enough with the lake to know your starting point and where you're headed. In other words, you gotta know you're at Point A and wish to travel to Points B and C. Once you're lost out there in the mist, all the rope at Home Depot won't help.

One more tip sure to work anywhere in East Tennessee: If you do get lost and finally putt-putt your way to dry land, don't say "bon jour!" to the first person you see.

A heartfelt "Dah-yum, buddy! That fog is some kinda thick!" will suffice.

A COCKLEBUR CRISIS

I've just finished reading a big medical story from Texas, and my reaction can be summed up in two boring words: "Well, duuuuh!"

Maybe you've heard about this thing, too. If so, and if you're a native or long-time East Tennessean, you probably share my feelings.

First the facts, straight from a Scripps Howard News Service dispatch from Wichita Falls. The story, written by Judith McGinnis, describes a strange turn of events that occurred in the life of a twenty-six-year-old Wichita Falls man named Justin Martin.

In May 2007, Martin was ejected from his car during a wreck on a rural Texas road. He suffered a broken pelvis, plus arm and knee injuries so severe he underwent multiple surgeries and months of physical therapy. During follow-up treatment, a painful, marble-sized lump appeared on Martin's left arm. Surgeons removed it for biopsy.

That's when they discovered a tiny plant. It was a cocklebur that was sprouting.

Doctors concluded the cocklebur had jammed into a deep cut during the wreck. Undetected, it migrated six inches and eventually got close enough to the surface of his skin to find light. Then—*voila!*—it sprouted. Ever since, Martin has become quite a celebrity in medical and botanical circles. He was featured in the 2011 edition of *Ripley's Believe It or Not.*

Well, OK. Perhaps it is significant that a plant took root inside a living human body. If this had been a watermelon, a dogwood tree, tumbleweed, goldenrod, a muscadine vine—heck, even kudzu—I would have shouted, "Holy Luther Burbank!"

But a cocklebur?

Good grief. Cockleburs will grow *any*where—and if you don't believe it, I invite you to slog through the sterile mud flats of any TVA lake in late summer.

After decades of impoundment, the soil on the bottom of our reservoirs is as leached of nutrients as a chunk of chipped concrete. Calling it "dirt" or, more accurately, "mud" is a stretch of both language and agronomy. This stuff is stickier than fifty sheets of flypaper, gooier than condensed honey, and so poor it makes Job's turkey look like a Butterball. It will support no life whatsoever.

With one exception. Cockle-you-know-whats.

As soon as the tributary reservoirs start dropping in August, wade—I use the term loosely—onto the nearest mud flat and see for yourself. Water will hardly have receded before these vast expanses of barren wasteland are lush with green cocklebur plants. By the multiplied millions.

I'm amazed energy researchers haven't discovered this vegetative gold mine. Who needs switchgrass? Just turn cockleburs into biofuel, and the price of gasoline should drop to pennies per gallon overnight.

Green cockleburs are no big deal. But as soon as they die and turn brown, they evolve into a kajillion-billion itty-bitty, needle-pointed balls of Velcro that cling tenaciously to anything from armor plate on down. Ask anyone foolish enough to walk within touching distance of a mature cocklebur plant while wearing corduroy pants and a wool shirt.

But wait 'til they quit hollering first, or else you're bound to get an earful. Of cuss words *and* cockleburs.

HAIR OF THEIR "SKIN"

There must be something about the surname Skinner and hair that breeds controversy.

Leonard Skinner, the most famous gym teacher in the history of rock music, died September 20, 2010, in Jacksonville, Florida, at the age of seventy-seven. His claim to fame occurred in the late 1960s, when he sent several students to the principal's office because their hair was too long.

Among the shags was one Gary Rossington, who played guitar in a teenage band. In just a few years, the band would rocket to stardom and, bezillions of record sales later, remains one of the icons of southern rock. We're talking, of course, about Lynyrd Skynyrd, which mockingly took its name from the ol' coach.

Here in Knoxville, another Skinner and his hair were making headlines about the same time. That would be Bill Skinner, a track star at the University of Tennessee, the greatest javelin thrower of his day. In his first three years at UT, Skinner hurled the spear to record lengths throughout the United States and Europe. But as a senior, about to graduate with honors, Skinner committed a heinous sin.

He grew a mustache.

I know that seems tame today. But in 1971, it was high crime. The Athletic Department ordered him to shave. Skinner refused. Thus, he was banned from competition as a Vol.

Skinner won the national javelin championship under the colors of the New York Athletic Club. *Sports Illustrated* chronicled the entire affair in a four-page spread.

Oh, and speaking of hair and local musicians, you surely know about Phil Everly's well-documented encounter with West High School Coach Walter Ganz. This was shortly before he and brother Don headed to international fame in Nashville.

The coach gave him two choices: a haircut or a hair net. Next day, Phil showed up with a hair net. And wore it proudly.

Amazing, isn't it? In an era when athletes routinely sport chartreuse manes and are tattooed like road maps, it's hard to fathom that follicles would foment such furor.

NOT TOO TICKLED ABOUT THE TWITCHING BAR

I bought a new casting reel the other day. I needed it worse than the proverbial hole in the head, but the price was right and the brand was one of my favorites. Yet as soon as I got home and inspected the reel in detail, I packaged it back up and returned to the store for a refund.

The guy behind the counter didn't blame me.

"Nearly everybody is bringing them back," he sighed.

Why?

Because the manufacturer felt obliged to monkey with a long-proven design and include a "twitching bar," perhaps the most ridiculous fishing accessory I've ever seen. To paraphrase an old mountain saying, this thing is as useless as mammary glands on male swine.

A "twitching bar," for those in the dark, is a V-shaped piece of metal mounted above the spool. When you press it, the reel handle rotates a time or two. According to printed material that came with the reel, this is perfect for drop-fishing finesse lures.

It is nothing of the kind. It is a gewgaw that gets in the way.

The "V" stabs your fingers when you grip the reel in a conventional manner. Imagine trying to fish with the sharp point of a can opener in your hand.

"Why would anybody design something this nutty?" I asked the clerk. "Have fishermen gotten so lazy they can't twitch lures with a flick of their wrist and rotate the handle with their hands?"

The guy could only shrug and point to the large inventory of returned reels, still in the box.

Before you label me a fossilized croak who longs for the days when cane poles were state of the art, let me stress that I am a fan of fishing technology. Some technology.

Having been raised with level-wind reels that backlashed on every cast unless they were thumbed with a surgeon's touch, I nearly swooned when free-spoolers hit the market—starting with the red Ambassadeur 5000. Subsequent models, by a variety of manufacturers, became progressively smoother, lighter, faster, stronger, more reliable.

Then comes this nonsense.

Oh, well. I've seen it before. Thankfully, the marketplace speaks louder than designers. About twenty years ago, some genius decided open-faced spinning reels would be easier to operate if they had a "speed trigger" to open the bail. As if flicking it with your opposite hand was a loathsome chore.

Before you could say "pisces," all spinning reels were cursed with the hateful things. They were a royal pain in the, uh, hand. It was like trying to cast with

> In 2009, a commercial fisherman in England was sentenced to prison for fraud. Seems that one Derek Atkins sent his fake obituary to London's Marine and Fisheries Agency, hoping authorities would stop pursing him for various fishing regulations. It didn't work.
>
> According to the Associated Press, Judge Ian Pearson lambasted Atkins with this torrent of words: "You are a lying, cunning, calculating fraudster."
>
> Of course he is! He's a fisherman, for Pete's sake! Although this is one time when the big one didn't get away.

a Popsicle stick taped to one finger. In desperation, I removed the speed trigger from a new reel I'd purchased, only to discover the entire mechanism was now out of balance.

Apparently other anglers felt the same way. Check out the spinning reels at your local sporting goods store these days. The vast majority, especially better-quality models, have sent their speed triggers to the grave.

Perhaps I'm sensitive about goofball tackle innovations because one of them proved to be the final straw that convinced me to get out of outdoor writing after fifteen enjoyable years.

This occurred the summer of 1984, when I attended the American Fishing Tackle Manufacturers Association's trade show in Atlanta. I always spent a few days at the AFTMA bash. Everybody who was anybody in fishing was there. It was a gold mine of story material.

The big buzz that year was a computerized reel that "talked." It calibrated casting distance and retrieval speed. You needed a degree from MIT to fish with it.

Here's what I wrote at the time: "Looking around that room, I saw more than one hundred outdoor writers from all over the United States. Some of them were the dearest friends I ever had. Many of their names are among the most respected in outdoor journalism. They were taking notes and snapping photos and trying to digest every morsel of what was transpiring. All of a sudden, I felt very alone. When reels start talking, it's time to start walking."

I left the outdoor beat several months later and never looked back. I still hunt and fish with a passion. But I do so to relax and get away from computers—not take them to the woods and waters with me.

Chapter **10**

BEING A GUY

The last thing I'd ever do, especially here in the socially enlightened twenty-first century, is attempt to provoke rancor between the sexes. Or rancor between any diverse groups of people, for that matter. When it comes to the human interactions, I prefer to take the Rodney King approach: Can't we all just get along?

Frankly, there isn't a lot of difference between men and women, besides the obvious—which, for that matter, appears to be getting a bit less and less obvious all the time. Consider this example, which I offer with no hint of judgment in any way; it's just one of those weird situations you encounter from time to time.

It occurred more than a decade ago when I was attending a writers' conference in South Carolina. During an early evening mixer, I made brief, cocktail-table talk with another attendee. To this day, I couldn't tell you whether this was a guy or a gal. The "traditional" characteristics of clothing, mannerisms, and voice inflection could have easily fallen into either camp. Even "Pat" on the "Hello, my name is—" shirt tag refused to clarify the matter. I got drawn into another conversation shortly thereafter, as did Pat, and that was the end of that. The encounter has long-since filed under the general heading of "Things That Make You Go 'Hmmm'." Perhaps for Pat, as well.

I will, however, go on record with four areas in which men and women tend to strongly disagree, right down the line. My findings are not based on scientific research or academic studies. Instead, they have been formed over forty-three-years-and-counting of marriage to the woman I fell head over heels in love with during sophomore English in high school.

These decades have been delightful on so many fronts, they literally are too numerous to list. Suffice to say that Mary Ann and I have lived, loved, and learned together through our dual professions, our hobbies, our children, our grandchildren, and countless other facets of our wonderfully blessed lives. Sure, there have been bumps and dips along the way. Craters, even. But you work through them and keep plugging on.

In no particular order of importance, these three categories are: Buying New Underwear, Dressing to the Nines, Going to the Bathroom at a Party, and Riotous Redneck Recreation. Let's just hop right into the fray and take 'em from the top.

THE ABCs of BVDs: In September 2009, the venerable *Washington Post* filed a long dispatch (tee-hee, given the subject matter, you might call it a "long-handled dispatch"; then again, you might not) stating that men's underwear sales are a key indicator of the nation's economic situation.

The article cited stats by several business-tracking services. They said skivvies started sliding in 2008 as the recession began to grip America by the, uh, throat, and have continued to plunge into the nether regions ever since. Fortunately, the story said, the decline seems to be losing speed, a good indication that happy days are just around the corner.

With all due respect to these experts: Phooey! Baloney! Malarkey!

Men may have been using the recession as an excuse for not buying new undies, but the pure truth of the matter is, most of us would rather discuss aluminum siding than perform this chore. My own situation serves as proof.

Recently, Mary Ann has been nagging me to buy new undies. She claims mine are, in her words, "worn out."

They are most certainly not "worn out." They are "well broken in."

In a woman's world, underpants become "worn out" after several months of use and washing. Men tend to age theirs in terms of years, if not decades. Ours are not considered "worn out" until there is more material dangling off the elastic waistband than there is sewed to it. Only then will we consider replacements because this task is a pain in the butt.

The last time I broke down and subjected myself to the drudgery of shopping for new unmentionables—was it during the first Bush term or second, as in Bush the Elder or Dubya?—I was so confused by the vast array and multiple selections, I nearly stormed out of the store in frustration. Probably would have except my inventory had gone from "well broken in" to "Third World rejects."

Used to be, all a guy had to do was choose between boxers or briefs. Now, these things run everywhere from triple-XL mu-mus to gonad-grinding thongs that make a Speedo swimsuit look baggy. I found myself standing in front of one display after another, inspecting the body-builder image on the cover of each package and trying to imagine how I would look—and, more importantly, feel—while wearing the contents. (OK, true: if simply buying undies would transform my pot gut into one of those hardened, six-pack bellies, perhaps I would savor the process instead of loathe it.)

Even worse, these goods are sealed hermetically. Heaven forbid you'd actually tear open a pack and try on a pair, like jeans. So you wind up buying a multitude of three-pair or six-pair packs, carrying them home, selecting the one or two you actually will wear, and bringing the rest back to the store for a refund. Total and absolute waste of time.

Shopping for new camouflage clothes? Now, that's a different matter entirely.

Formal Duds: I cannot tell you how relieved I was in January 2009 when my wife and I failed to make the short list of invitees to the many festive dances and parties associated with the swearing-in of President Barack Obama.

Well, no. Now that you mention it, Mary Ann and I have never made an inaugural list—short or long, Republican or Democrat, during boom times or bust, in Washington, D.C., or Nashville, Tennessee. But why dwell on insignificant details?

The Obama festivities saw more than a dozen official inaugural balls, plus at least ten others that immediately sold out, even though they weren't sanctioned by inauguration committees. For politicians, lobbyists, bureaucrats, contributors, beautiful people, and wannabes of every stripe, these events were a huge deal. It was crucial for them to see and be seen. And therein lies an eternal conundrum, a dilemma that underscores one of the main differences between persons of the he and she persuasions.

At all of these events, the men dressed exactly alike. Right down to their cummerbunds, shoelaces, and handkerchiefs.

Not the women. They would rather discuss hemorrhoid ointments on Jerry Springer's TV show than walk into one of these balls, glance across the room, and see another woman wearing the same dress.

One of the more recent displays of this nuttiness occurred in 2006 at the Kennedy Center. First Lady Laura Bush showed up in a red Oscar de la Renta gown. Oops. Three other women also were wearing the same type of dress. Nothing would do but for Mrs. Bush's handlers to whisk her out of sight and change her into another outfit.

Frankly, my dear, I don't give a royal rat's rump if this is a problem in Washington, Nashville, Knoxville, Bulls Gap, or anywhere else. What does it matter if someone happens to wear the same outfit you selected? For Pete's sake, what does it matter if fifty other someones do the same thing?

I realize that as a guy, I'm not qualified—biologically or sartorially—to offer an opinion on this matter. Clearly, the rationale behind such nonsense is ethereal in nature. The Y-chromosome is incapable of comprehending it. And for that, I can only say, "Thank heavens."

But now that we have broached this delicate subject, there's something else I will never understand about men and women in fancy social settings.

When a man has imbibed enough punch and feels the need to recycle it, he will excuse himself and attend to business alone. He doesn't feel compelled to announce his intentions to the assembled masses and ask every other man at the table to join him beside the porcelain. Thank Heavens II. Which brings us to Item Number Three.

No Discussions Necessary: Since it's not my habit to frequent women's re-strooms, I don't know much about the protocol. All I can address is the men's side of the equation, and after sixty-five years of practice, I pretty much have the routine down pat. Especially the do's and don'ts.

In matters of interpersonal communication within these confines—aka talk-ing—less is generally better.

If two strangers of the Guy Persuasion happen to enter the room simultane-ously, it's OK for them to acknowledge the other's presence with a silent nod. If they do speak, it should be in a low, monotone, "How'ya doin?" or "Wha'ysay?" Or "Wha'sup?" for Gen-Xers and "What up, dawg?" among the twenty-some-things. Beyond that, silence rules.

Another truism is the business of visual contact. Specifically, the lack thereof. Eyes forward, straight ahead is the order of the day. If women want to look at one another and remark, "Why, that's the prettiest blouse I ever saw!" more power to 'em. Men prefer to stare holes in the wall.

This is particularly true if one man is standing at the time, taking care of business, and another Guy Person walks into the room, approaches the same general area (each spot separated by a chest-high partition) and also begins tak-ing care of business in a standing position. This is no time for conviviality.

And yet a Guy Person I know—country comedy singer-songwriter Jerry "Hogman" Isham of Rockwood—once was forced to break this cardinal rule in Nashville. Jerry was in Music City to record some tunes for his latest CD. Later, he performed at a couple of nightclubs. Shortly after midnight, he was about to start back toward East Tennessee and decided to visit the john first. He was minding his own business when another Guy Person sidled up on the opposite side of the partition and began talking.

"Right out of the blue, he says, 'How're you doin?' " Jerry told me. "I said, 'Fine, how're you?'

"Then he says, 'When did you get into town?' I said, 'About noon today.'

"Then he says, 'Are you gonna sing?' I said, 'I just did.'

"Then he says, 'Who are you with?' I said, 'My buddy, Jeremy Ball.'

"I gotta tell you, I was getting nervous. I didn't dare look over. Just kept starin' straight ahead. But the other feller wouldn't quit.

"He says, 'Are you comin' back to town?' I said, 'Next Monday.' He says, 'When are you leavin' town?' I said, 'Right now!'

"I went over to wash my hands and heard that feller say, 'Bye, I love you, too.'"

Curiosity finally took control, and Jerry glanced across the room.

"He'd been talkin' to someone on one of those fancy Bluetooth cell phones!" he exclaimed. "Reckon he was just as surprised as me, 'cause all he did was stare at me kinda funny while he was washing his hands."

In the parlance of show business, the two parties then exited—stage right and stage left.

Hold My Beer and Watch This: In the vast majority of our discussions, my wife is right. Like the mathematician she is, Mary Ann approaches every facet of life in a reasonable, rational, sober, well-thought-out manner. In other words, totally boring. I much prefer shooting from the hip. Or lip, as the case may be.

> I noticed in the L.L. Bean Christmas catalog that you can buy a freshly cut Maine balsam Christmas tree and have it delivered to your door.
>
> Shouldn't you at least be wearing an L.L. Bean lumberjack shirt, an L.L. Bean hunting cap, L.L. Bean wool pants, and L.L. Bean insulated boots when you take delivery?

Not long ago, a mutual friend forwarded to us a YouTube link called "Firehose Rodeo." If you have access to a computer, go Google it now—and be prepared to laugh your guts out. For the computer-deprived, here's what happens: This goober clings to the end of a high-pressure hose dangling from a boom. When the water is turned on, he gets violently slung in approximately twenty directions at once, hollering, cussing, and begging for relief. Finally the hose throws him, quite painfully, into the mud as his buddies howl.

Mary Ann looked at the video. When it was over, she said the same thing she always says in the wake of unmitigated recreational stupidity, especially versions fueled by equal measures of bravado and alcohol: "Why do you never see a woman doing something like that?"

"I reckon they don't share the same sense of adventure as men," I replied.

"Sense? Hah!"

See? Boring to the max.

Anyhow, a few days later Mary Ann and I were at the Melton Hill Dam access area, waiting our turn to put my bass boat back onto its trailer. Our wait became lengthy because of a show in the middle of the ramp.

Three bleary-eyed goobers had more or less gotten their boat onto its trailer—somewhat sideways, but "on" nonetheless—and were attempting to start their truck. Periodically, the driver would get out, wade into the water to check things, slip and bust his butt, then return to the cab to keep cranking an engine that refused to start.

Finally, they determined the truck was out of gas. So they fetched the boat's fuel tank, yanked off the fitting that attaches to the outboard, and attempted to squirt gas into the truck. No luck. That's when the Phi Beta Kappa of the crew announced loudly he was "gonna siffle it"—by sucking on one end of the hose while Phi Beta Kappa II pumped the bulb.

Mary Ann quietly wished for a magic carpet to carry us to safety. I loudly wished for a video camera so we could become famous YouTube producers.

It all ended without undue gagging. Somehow, enough gas was transferred into the truck for it to sputter away. As it exited, Mary Ann repeated her claim about women and common sense.

Happily, I can report that at least one woman has pulled a stupid stunt in front of the camera. I know because I've just watched another YouTube production, this one called "Redneck Circus Ride Horizontal Bungee."

This gem features a giant homemade slingshot that is "cocked" by a four-wheeler. When the long rubber straps are loosed, the female rider, strapped into a seat, gets hurled into the wild blue. Then she bounces back and forth like a ping-pong ball in the Olympics.

Wonders of wonders! I had to pinch myself. For once, Mary Ann agreed this did look like great drunken fun.

Next thing you know, she'll start dipping snuff while she "siffles" gasoline.

AVOIDING "THAT DETERMINED LOOK" AT ALL COSTS

Recently my wife retired after a long career in the classroom. From jock math to algebra, statistics to software—in elementary school, high school, college, and private industry—Mary Ann taught 'em all.

I'm delighted she has more time to spend in her gardens and flower beds, with our grandchildren, volunteering, and tackling various projects around the house.

But storm clouds loom over that last category. You see, Mary Ann's projects often involve her husband. I fear her retirement is going to work me to death.

Please understand that this woman and I haven't survived four-plus decades together without adapting to each other's personalities, wishes, and quirks—and let the record clearly show that when it comes to quirks, oddities, idiosyncrasies, and overall weirdisms, I've owned the patent since the day we were wed.

Rest assured she is making up for lost time. At a gallop.

M.A. is, by DNA, a neat freak. I, on the other hand, am wired to be more comfortable amid clutter.

Since retiring, she has examined, inventoried, classified, collated, sorted, reorganized, cleaned, moved, switched, dusted, adjusted, redone, changed, altered, indexed, and filed half the house. I break into fervid palpitations at the very thought of it all.

I have suffered only peripheral damage at this point. But lately, she has begun staring with That Determined Look at my closets, my office, and my side of the garage. Things could get dicey.

Far better that she involve herself with outdoor projects, for here is where our mutual skills shine. Both of us rather enjoy yard work—well, yes, I underscore "rather" on my part—but neither truly minds sawing, chopping, tilling, hoeing, mowing, clipping, digging, trimming, raking, hammering, hauling, and other facets of seasonal sweat equity.

Mary Ann's latest undertaking is an enlargement of her vegetable garden, complete with a staircase down the side. My most strenuous contribution thus far is stroking a Visa card through the machine to pay for railroad ties and then off-loading them from the truck.

I went ahead and bought the ties even though Mary Ann is still in the "eyeball" stage of this project. That's the beauty of working with someone with a math mind. She can simply glance at the area to be worked, make a few mental calculations, and determine how much of this or that will be needed.

I'm ready, even eager, to leap into this task. Because, Trust your Uncle Nervousness: As long as Mary Ann focuses That Determined Look on the garden instead of my office and the garage, all will be right with the world.

FIFTY YEARS OF WEIRD TREASURES

I have just exhumed a time capsule.

No, not in the literal sense. This thing's been in plain sight for five decades and has been opened and shut hundreds, maybe thousands, of times.

We're talking a black leather cuff-link case. It was given to me on December 27, 1960, by my first cousin, Frank Venable Jr., on the occasion of his marriage to Jane Hartman. At age thirteen, I was the youngest of seven groomsmen.

Digging through some old files at home, I came across a copy of the Venable family crest—yes, there actually is such a thing—and noticed our tribe's famous motto: "Nous persevons."

My French is rusty, but I think this means, "Eat more possum."

Exactly fifty years and one day later, nearly two hundred folks gathered at Cherokee Country Club to celebrate Frank and Jane's golden anniversary. Frank asked several family members to speak. He specifically requested "the biggest bull (shippers) in the bunch," and for some odd reason, my name topped the short list.

But that night I engaged in no bovine scatology whatsoever. I merely held the case aloft, pointed out the still-visible inscription "S.A.V. 12-27-60" and described how, for reasons unknown, it has followed me through apartments and houses from Knoxville to Chattanooga and back.

To the best of sartorial memory, it never held cuff links. Instead, it has become a top-of-the-dresser catch-all for the nuttiest collection of unrelated junk known to archaeological history.

The government needs to study this box. How such an itty-bitty space (seven inches wide, four inches long, one inch deep) can contain such a huge number of items is a mystery. Here is what, I swear, was buried inside:

Thirty-four buttons of various sizes; four Sigma Chi fraternity pins; seven paper clips; seven pocket knives; two wristwatches (neither working); parts to two and one-half leather watchbands; one wristwatch band clasp; one vest fob for a pocket watch; fifteen lapel pins (including Three Stooges, 82nd Airborne, Orange Bowl, U.S. flag, breast-cancer awareness, Quail Unlimited, National Wild Turkey Federation, and a twenty-year *News Sentinel* service pin); five keys for vehicles, luggage, and houses no longer owned; two nail clippers; a 1991 rabies-vaccination dog tag from Farragut Animal Clinic; one shirt-collar extender; one can opener (circa 1966 from my employment with the U.S. Forest Service); three money clips; seven Susan B. Anthony dollars; $1.67 in assorted change; two pennies flattened on railroad tracks; a 1916 British shilling piece; one safety pin; one tie clasp (inscribed "4-2-69," thus possibly what I gave my own groomsmen, but neither Mary Ann nor I could recall); one small sheet-metal screw; two shotgun front sights; two split rings from fishing lures; two newspaper bundle openers (circa 1960 from my *News Sentinel* paper route); a school picture, first or second grade, of son Clay who just turned thirty-eight; one brass fitting (or maybe a piece from the firing pin assembly of my muzzle-loading deer rifle, not sure which); three *teeth,* for Pete's sake! (one alligator, one baby tooth, either Clay's or Megan's, plus one of my own gnarled wisdom teeth); one yellow plastic shotgun base wad retrieved from the gizzard of wood duck killed on Fort Loudoun Lake circa 1982; handwritten instructions to myself for finding a 1997 roof leak; three key chains; one tiny diamond or piece of glass (Mary Ann wasn't sure but says I dang-sure better not be buying diamonds on the sly); and, finally and fittingly, one business card from a muscle and stress-relief therapist at Fort Sanders Health and Fitness Club.

Holy hoarding! Just imagine what can get crammed in there over the next fifty years!

EAT ONE EVERY FOUR HOURS

Somewhere in the Great Beyond, Jesse Butcher and Ronnie Merritt are laughing fit to choke. It's all because of some food researchers at Texas A&M University, who began digging into watermelons. Scientifically digging, you understand—with test tubes and microscopes, not forks and salt.

What they discovered might turn you redder than a slice of melon itself. To wit: Watermelon can produce a Viagra-like effect. I am not joking. I hold two news dispatches describing this revolutionary finding. One is from *The Associated Press,* the other from the website sciencedaily.com. Both quote the lead researcher, Dr. Bhimu Patil.

He says watermelons provide certain "phyto-nutrients," including one called citrulline. As watermelon is consumed, citrulline is converted to an amino acid known as arginine. It helps improve functions of the heart and circulatory system.

"Arginine boosts nitric acid, which relaxes blood vessels, the same basic effect that Viagra has to treat erectile dysfunction and maybe even prevent it," Patil said.

So what does this have to do with Jesse Butcher and Ronnie Merritt? Plenty, even though neither is of this realm. Jesse died in 1996, Ronnie in 2009. They were the originator and successor, respectively, of a watermelon festival that has been a mainstay in North Knox County social and political circles since 1992.

It started when Jesse grew a bumper crop and invited some old buddies over to share the harvest. One melon fest became two, then three, then four, five, six.

They eventually outgrew Jesse's barn. These days, Gibbs Ruritan Park is permanently reserved on the third Wednesday in August for the annual meeting of the "DP Club."

That's what Jesse, ever the comedic curmudgeon, named it. He even had membership cards printed for attendees down through the years. Yes, I proudly own one.

The "D" on these cards stands for "dead." The "P" stands for (uh, rhymes with "decker").

When the gavel fell at this year's feast and I showed members the aforementioned news stories, three things happened in succession.

First, there was silence.

Next, roughly two-thirds of the mouths dropped open wide enough to ingest half a melon in one swallow.

Then laughter erupted, and one-liners began firing like shotguns on the opening day of dove season.

"Gimme another slice!" James Chesney and Warren Rule hollered in near-unison.

"Another slice, my foot!" exclaimed Charles "Tud" Etherton. "I'm gonna start eatin' watermelon twelve hours a day!"

"This is sure gonna make the price of watermelons go up," Tommy Overby lamented.

"No wonder I feel like I'm eighteen all over again," Jerry Cheung testified, biceps flexed and a broad smile across his face.

"I'm gonna clear forty acres and start the biggest watermelon patch in Knox County," said Roger Jones. "I'll even try to grow 'em year-round. Make watermelon wine and watermelon pickles, too."

"I'd love to stay around and jaw with you fellows," guffawed David "Red" Clapp, who took the DP Club reins after Ronnie's death, "but I believe I need to get on home."

And just as soon as I quit typing this essay, I'll have a fifth serving myself.

QUITE A MANLY COLLECTION

I've heard of some strange museums in my time.

Such as the Museum of Funeral History in Houston. Plus the Barbed Wire Museum in Lacrosse, Kansas. Then there's the Sardine Museum in Lubec, Maine. Not to mention the International Museum of Toilets in New Delhi.

But after getting not one, not two, but three alerts from *News Sentinel* readers, I started digging into what surely is the most bizarre museum in the history of the genre. And before I type one word further into this essay, let me stress on an entire case of Bibles that I'm not making it up.

This would be the Phallological Museum in an Icelandic fishing hamlet named Husavik.

(Which, oddly enough, reminds me of the sound someone might make if he or she had a herring bone caught in the throat: *Husavik! Husavik! Husavik!* "Keep husavikking, Anges; you're bound to bring it up!" But I digress.)

The museum's claim to fame is that it houses what is believed to be the world's largest (276 units) collection of—how do I say this politely?—"thingies." You know: the body parts male mammals are born with.

Yes. Those parts.

You are free to say, "Eeeew!" or "You're kiddin' me!" as you see fit. But I kid you not. Indeed, I quote directly from an Associated Press dispatch, written by Raphael G. Satter, and filed from London on April 12, 2011: "The Phallological Museum is an important part of the region's tourist industry, bringing in thousands of visitors every summer. Highlights of the museum's collection include a 170-centimeter (sixty-seven-inch) sperm whale penis preserved in formaldehyde, lamp shades made from bull testicles, and what the museum described as an 'unusually big' penis bone from a Canadian walrus."

In addition to its unusual theme, the museum has been in the news lately because of its latest acquisition: The last mortal remains—or "remain," as the case may correctly be—of a ninety-five-year-old Icelander named Pall Arason. Again, I quote from the AP story: "Several people had pledged their penises over the years, including an American, a Briton, and a German, but Arason's was the first to be successfully donated."

Arason died in January 2011. In accordance with his wishes, the specimen was surgically removed by a physician—I suppose Lorena Bobbitt wasn't available for duty—and presented to the museum.

Said director Sigurdur Hjartarson of the generous donor: "He liked to be in the limelight, you know? He was a funny guy. He was a boaster, a braggart."

I like to think of myself as a somewhat funny guy, too. But there are certain lines this ol' boy ain't gonna cross. Even in death. But what the heck. If this endeavor pumps renewed vigor into Iceland's ailing economy, so be it. Even if it gives every man from Knoxville to Timbuktu a frightful case of the nervous twitches.

And it sure puts new light on a popular football motto at the University of Tennessee. When guys on the gridiron pledge to "give my all today," I hope this isn't what they have in mind.

Trust one who once played the game: Football isn't worth *that*!

A MATTER OF HEART OVER MIND

The big news on the medical front these days is . . .

It's, uh . . .

Hmm, let's see . . .

Oh, yes: It's whether cholesterol-lowering medications cause memory loss in some patients.

These developments have been at the top of the news page lately. And they seem slap-dab contradictory.

The *Wall Street Journal* recently carried an article suggesting a link between memory problems and Lipitor, the world's best-selling cholesterol medicine. It quoted Dr. Orli Etingin, vice-president of medicine at New York Presbyterian Hospital, as saying, "This drug makes women stupid."

The paper did not indicate whether the good doc was a finalist for the Archie Bunker Sensitivity Award. But it did go on to note that Etingin later said, "I've seen (memory loss) in maybe two dozen patients. This is just observational, of course. We really need more studies, particularly on cognitive effects and women."

On the heels of that story, ABC News aired a report discrediting Lipitor's alleged link with reduced brain function, stressing that its role in heart attack and stroke prevention far outweighs any possible risk.

"You can never make policy based on one case," said Dr. Timothy Johnson, the network's medical editor, "and when you look at the overall evidence, it does not appear that problems with cognition are a common or serious side effect. In general people should not worry, but if they're having a problem, they should talk to their doctors about switching the drug they are on."

Excellent! This works for me either way.

Like millions of fat-blooded Americans, I take Lipitor under prescription from my doctor. Have for several years. It's because I only did a fifty-fifty job of picking my parents correctly.

On my father's side, cholesterol has always been elevated. Not so coincidentally, the folks in Big Sam's tribe also tend to be built rather low to the ground, have a constant craving for sweets and fried foods, and buy the farm at early ages.

On my mother's side, cholesterol runs low. Again, not surprisingly, Maw's people tend to be taller and slimmer, eat lots of veggies, and live into their eighties and nineties in relatively good health. I can only hope that during a certain session nine months prior to May 24, 1947, Maw's DNA claimed the upper hand.

In any event, Lipitor—in conjunction with a semblance of exercise and dietary prudence—seems to be working. Instead of being known in Knoxville medical circles as Señor Grease Ball, I am now referred to merely as His Oiliness. I take it as a badge of honor.

Conversely, if Lipitor is turning my noodle to mush, it provides me with the perfect excuse whenever something slips my mind.

It's just like I was telling my wife the other day, "I know you asked me to . . . er . . . huh?"

Anyhow, what was it you and I were talking about?

HIKING THE HIGH-PRICED WILDERNESS

I first realized the planets were out of alignment when cell-phone pockets became standard issue on bib overalls. This condition worsened when Lincoln, manufacturer of executive cars, rolled out a pickup truck.

Now my tiny universe of normalcy has come completely unglued.

Gucci, the company that makes outlandishly expensive clothing for the Beautiful People, is offering men's hiking boots. I'm talking high-topped, lug-soled, leather clodhoppers normally associated with deer camps, country stores, and the Appalachian Trail.

> **Hoss Wyatt of Crossville just had knee replacement. Four years earlier, he went under the knife for back surgery—and two years before that, he got a new shoulder.**
>
> **"I have reminded my wife, Anne, that she can honestly tell her friends I'm not the man she married,"** he said.

Except these high-topped, lug-soled, leather clodhoppers will set you back $795–$995 per pair. Of course, that's only $397.50–$497.50 a whack if you buy them one at a time, which should ease the pain on your billfold—although you will look rather silly hopping through the forest on one foot until the second installment arrives. But that's your business.

I was alerted to this haberdashery news via a blurb in *The Week* magazine. It described these Guccis as "a finely crafted pair of boots meant to be durable enough for the trails and sleek enough for the streets."

I assume they mean streets in the Big Apple, not Knoxville. But I'm so out of touch with high fashion, local or otherwise, half the members of the City Council and County Commission could be wearing Gucci hiking boots and I wouldn't know it.

But the point is, these highfalutin folks have no business infringing on the sacred purview of good ol' boys. What's next? Brown Mule chewing tobacco in $175 designer plugs? If so, they'll probably change the name to Broywne Mullé.

Agreed, I have pedestrian tastes. When I peruse an outdoor catalog—such as the fall Cabela's tome in my hands—and see top-of-the-line Danner boots advertised for $269.95 per pair (or $134.98 apiece, if you insist on the one-foot plan), I need smelling salts.

Nonetheless, I know whereof I speak in the matters of footwear for field and forest. I own in excess of a dozen pairs. In fact, when Imelda Marcos was making headlines for buying hundreds of pairs of shoes when most Filipinos lived in poverty, a friend glanced at my inventory and said, "Don't you *ever* write a word about her."

The most I ever paid for boots was $150 for one fancy pair advertised as the thickest-insulated, most-waterproof model on the market. Could be. Soon as I walked out of the carpeted salesroom and laced them up in the woods, they morphed into high-topped bricks with all the comfort of a steel-jawed trap. Currently they are on a shelf in the garage, layered in dust, not mud.

Oh well. If you want to spend $795–$995 on Gucci hiking boots, be my guest. Surely they're durable enough to repel any Grey Poupon you might encounter in the wilds of Sequoyah Hills.

NEW AROMA SURVEY SURE SMELLS NUTTY

My nose must be in terrible condition. Either that or I don't know the first thing about (*ssshhh!*) s-e-x.

I've come to this bizarre conclusion after reading the results of an equally bizarre research project at the University of Pennsylvania, which I promise I am not making up.

Thirty-one men, eighteen through sixty-four years of age, were rigged with delicate sensing devices and subjected to a variety of aromas. Then their reactions to sexual suggestions and romantic situations were recorded.

Do you know what appealed to these guys the most?

A combination of lavender and pumpkin pie.

Cross my heart. There was a 40-percent positive response to that blend of scents. I'm holding a printout of the results as we speak.

Second (31.5 percent) was a mixture of doughnut and black licorice. Third was pumpkin pie and doughnut (20 percent), followed by orange (19.5 percent), lavender and doughnut (18 percent), and black licorice and doughnut (13 percent).

On the other end of the spectrum (2 percent) was cranberry. Next lowest (9 percent) was buttered popcorn.

The way to a man's heart may be through his stomach, but this is ridiculous. As a longtime fan of pumpkin pie—doesn't matter if it's Thanksgiving Day or the Fourth of July—I can appreciate this pleasing aroma. But it makes me want to pull up a chair to the table, not yank down the sheets on a bed.

As for lavender, either by itself or in combination with any other smell? Bleech!

Lavender reminds me of a funeral. In its presence, I'm more likely to hum "Nearer, My God, to Thee" than "Come on Baby, Light my Fire."

Clearly, my idea of an aromatic turn-on differs radically from the fellows in this test. If pumpkin pie, doughnuts, and licorice send them into fits of romantic ecstasy, I'd hate to think what puts 'em in the mood to go through the buffet line at Shoney's. Chanel Number 5?

About our only area of agreement would be a low level of amorous response to cranberry. Upon detecting the aroma of cranberry, the only thing I'm reminded of is the frustration of trying to extract a column of jellied cranberry sauce from the can. Surely the military can find a use for this gelatinous stuff. It sticks better than industrial glue.

The researchers said they are going to test the same thing with women. I'll be interested in seeing the results. Given the epidemic of obesity in America, it wouldn't surprise me to see pies and pastries high on that list, either.

But if I start seeing pricey bottles of "Eau de Punkin" and "Olde Krispy Kreme" in the perfume section of department stores, I won't know whether to have my sinuses bored out or swear an oath of celibacy.

DISTRACTIONS APLENTY OUT THERE

Two random motoring situations of the "whew!" variety we've all seen too many times:

John Jordan of Clinton was following an Escalade on U.S. Highway 25W and noticed the vehicle speed up, slow down, and swerve from lane to lane. Jordan passed carefully. Then he glanced over and scored the trifecta.

"She was talking on a cell phone, reading a newspaper, and waving one hand, all at the same time," he said. "I guess that's what you call multitasking."

I was walking through the parking lot of the Walker Springs Walmart and witnessed the driver of a van pull into oncoming traffic without looking or paying attention. A millisecond later, she was nearly struck by an oncoming driver who was traveling too fast and talking on a cell phone.

I nearly jumped out of my skin. Fortunately no collision occurred, but I daresay adrenaline levels were elevated all around. I know mine certainly was.

Both of these instances involved female motorists, but you can chalk that up to coincidence. When it comes to DWD (driving while distracted), men and women are equal-opportunity offenders. And the highways are jammed with them.

Of course, they're always the "other" drivers. "We," thank you very much, are perfectly capable of safely operating a vehicle and simultaneously talking on the phone, checking a road map, changing a CD, switching radio stations, taking in the scenery, munching a cheeseburger, sipping coffee, combing our hair, arguing with a passenger, or any of two dozen other potential distractions. Right?

Don't look for things to get better anytime soon. The business of potential driving distractions is getting more complicated, and I wonder when the proverbial last straw will be dropped upon the camel's back.

In addition to your everyday burger-and-cell-phone hazards, we've now got those "rolling billboards" on trucks, plus pesky new automotive radios that flash messages from the station. Both are terribly irritating intrusions.

Larry Hutson feels the same way. Hutson drives eighty-four miles daily between his home in Loudon County and his hospital job in Knoxville. That gives him ample exposure to images that could grab his attention.

"If you've ever been caught between two of those 'rolling billboard' trucks on the interstate, which I have, it's dang-near impossible not to look at them. I try to get around them or lay back so I'm far behind them. They're very distracting. I don't know which is worse: an electronic sign you will pass in a matter of seconds or rolling signs you might be forced to look at for ten minutes."

How about having neither? Driving is demanding enough as it is.

THE PITTER-PATTER OF MANY FEET

Here's a nugget of Father's Day trivia that's too bizarre to ignore: The man believed to have sired the most children in this era is named "Daad."

I kid you not. His full name is Daad Mohammed Murad Abdul Rahman. He is sixty-four. He lives in the United Arab Emirates. At last count, he had seventy-eight children ranging in age from thirty-six years to twenty days.

"At last count" is quite important to this discussion. You see, the most current information I could find about Daad the Dad was an August 20, 2007, story in the newspaper *Emirates Today*. At that time, two of his three wives were pregnant. And he has intentions to add several more children. By 2015, Daad told the newspaper, he expects to reach one hundred.

It takes more than a few mamas for such a feat, of course. The guy has accumulated fifteen brides. But in order to conform with the Muslim limit of four wives at any given time, he takes legal steps to end the extra unions.

Which also makes him Daad the Divorcer.

According to the *Emirates Today* story, this chap lives on a military pension, "plus the help of the government of Ajman, one of seven emirates that comprise the UAE."

I reckon he would need help. For Pete's sake, he ain't got time to work! Probably takes him twenty hours a week just running back and forth to the store for Viagra.

Seventy-eight youngin's. Let that figure settle into your gray cells for a moment.

That's seventy-eight names you gotta remember. Plus seventy-eight birthdays. Not to mention birthdays of sons- and daughters-in-law as the kids start families of their own.

And that doesn't even touch the matter of refereeing squabbles between seventy-eight children. Or inspecting seventy-eight report cards. Or doling out seventy-eight allowances. Or driving seventy-eight kids to the mall. Not to mention sitting through seventy-eight piano recitals. And to think he intends to add twenty-two more to the flock!

I can just imagine Daad the Distraught as he strolls through fifteen houses—that's how many the newspaper said are needed to keep a roof over everybody's head—shakin' and howdyin' with the troops:

"Omar, my son. So good to see you."

"I'm not Omar. I'm Raheem. Omar lives on the second floor, three doors down."

"Oh, yes. How silly of me. Anyway, are the math grades picking up? I remember talking to your teacher about—"

"I make straight As in math. You're thinking of Haashim. He lives across the street."

"Of course, my son. But enough about you. How is your mother, Abida?"

"Huh? My mother's not Abida. My mother is Qameer."

"Certainly. How could I forget. Qameer had you right after your sister Mahveen was born."

"Mahveen? My next-oldest sister is Afreen. Mahveen's next-closest brother is Aleem."

On and on it goes until Daad the Delirious hobbles out holding his head.

While shopping at the Fairfield Glade United Methodist Church's rummage sale, Gary Nelson discovered the secret to perpetual motion. He forked over two dollars for a grab bag—and inside found a pair of pants he had donated to the cause.

But if you think that's bad, imagine being Daad the Dude on Father's Day. How many expressions of surprise and glee can the guy come up with when he opens his seventy-eighth bottle of Old Spice?

GIVING CROOKS AN EARFUL

When I read about Banshee II, one question immediately popped out of my mouth: "Where can I buy one of these babies?"

In case you missed my colleague Frank Munger's story, the appropriately named Banshee II is a handheld noisemaking device. It may be small in size (five inches by four inches), but it emits big sounds.

And I mean *biiiiggg*. Something on the order of 144 decibels. That's like a rock concert or jet engine taking off. It's being designed at the Y-12 nuclear weapons plant in Oak Ridge.

Ever the spoilsport, Frank threw cold water all over my ownership intentions. First, he said the Banshee II is still in developmental stages. The one Frank wrote about was merely a prototype.

Furthermore, Frank said something this powerful should never be allowed in the hands of the general public. Too much danger of misuse, he said.

To which I replied, "And your point is?"

Of course I'd want to misuse it! So would every Eddie Haskell wannabe!

(We pause here to elaborate to readers under fifty years of age. Eddie Haskell was a character on the old "Leave It to Beaver" television series. He was a syrupy nice guy in front of adults but a complete jerk when their backs were turned. If "Beaver" were on the tube today, Eddie would be saying something like, "Well, hello, Mrs. Cleaver; I was just introducing young Theodore here to the wonders of the Banshee II." And as soon as Mrs. Cleaver walked out of the room, Eddie would stick Banshee II into the Beav's ear and blast his brain cells into an adjacent county. Geez, why can't they make quality television programming like that these days?)

Banshee II—which came on the high-volume heels of the original Banshee— is being touted as an anti-terrorist tool and handy, non-lethal weapon for law enforcement officers. According to Frank's story, one short toot is so loud and so painful "a person has no choice but to drop whatever's in his hands and cover his ears."

Cool! And just think of the self-protection opportunities.

I'd love to be packing a Banshee II next time some kid pulls next to me in one of those open-windowed cars with the stereo turned to Quad-Max and the bass cracking plaster walls all the way to Nashville. Like Clint Eastwood's Dirty Harry, I'd calmly walk over to his car and say something intelligent. Like, "Loud enough for'ya, punk?"

Then I'd whip out my trusty Banshee II and splatter his ear wax all across the dashboard. I break out in prickly rash just thinking about it.

Oh, sure. There would be a bunch of namby-pambies like Frank who would wring their hands at the very thought I might defend myself this unique way. Wimps. They probably wouldn't want me packing a Banshee II into public parks and recreation areas, either.

And I'd have to be the first to remind them: If God hadn't meant for us to have Banshee IIs, he wouldn't have put ears on the sides of criminals' heads.

ON THE SHARP EDGE OF HISTORY

I was massaging computer keys a few nights ago, ordering replacement blades for one of my electric fish-filleting knives.

Typically, I prefer to make all of my purchases—hats to hardware, jeans to jelly—in person, in front of a real, live salesclerk, at a brick-and-mortar retail store. Trouble is, retail stores can't match the inventory of a warehouse the size of Neyland Stadium located half a continent away, yet conveniently linked to my house via the Internet. Thus the occasional need to cyber-shop.

Everything was going along swimmingly until a message, spelled in red letters, popped up on the screen. It said I had to confirm that I was at least eighteen years old before the sale could proceed.

Huh? I didn't have to give my age when I bought this knife. Or any other knife, electric or manual, that I can recall.

Perhaps this regulation only applies to online sales. If so, it makes no sense because there was no way to verify my claim.

For all I know, the computer would have taken it as gospel truth if I had listed my age as four score and seven years—although considering how digitized advertisements magically appear in bunches, this likely would have exposed me to a screen full of campaigns for Depends, motorized chairs, and beeper devices that blare, "I've fallen and I can't get up!" the instant I attempted to log-off. But I digress.

According to the sales confirmation and information sheet that came sputtering out of my printer, these knife blades were set to arrive on a specific date. Soon as I saw the date, I couldn't help but think, "Holy $#@! What are the odds?"

No, not that some cyber sales machine could predict the shipment of a product hundreds of miles away. It was something much more coincidental than that.

My blades were set to arrive on March 15. The Ides of March. This is perhaps the most famous date—or infamous, depending on your perspective about assassinations—in cutlery history.

On March 15, in 44 B.C., Roman dictator Julius Caesar found himself on the receiving end of many blades. Accounts differ on the exact number of stab wounds Caesar suffered, from as few as twenty-three to as many as thirty-five. Suffice to say that Marcus Brutus, Cassius Longinus, and their fellow conspirators were determined to render the ol' boy into a wedge of Swiss cheese. And they did.

Being of French descent, the Venables in that era probably were rather pleased with the events of March 15, 44 B.C. That's because only a few years earlier, Caesar and his merry men had sliced our Gauls into three parts with blades of their own.

Nonetheless, I doubt any of my ancient ancestors participated directly in the bloody activities that sent Caesar to that big empire in the sky. When it comes to deft knife work, we Venables are far more likely to inflict damage to ourselves than anyone or anything else. I will be happy to show you scars on my fingers as proof.

Plus, we've always found a way to bungle organized operations. I'll guarantee if some Platonius Silvanius Venabulus had been part of the plot to carve

Caesar, he would have wasted ten full minutes running around the Roman Senate trying to find an electrical outlet to plug in his knife.

GIVE ME THE GOOD NEW DAYS

Along with a bunch of other *News Sentinel* staffers, I got my annual flu shot the other day. We lined up in a meeting room on the first floor, rolled up our sleeves, got zapped, and had the obligatory Bandage of Honor pasted onto our shoulders.

Ooohh, the pain! The misery! The suffering!

Not from the inoculation itself, you understand. Maybe they make better (translation: sharper and thinner) needles than I remember from my youth. Or maybe shot-giving techniques are much improved. Or (most likely) childhood fear caused the perceived pain to ratchet far higher than it actually was. Whatever the case, this was a piece of cake.

But that itty-bitty bandage strip? Holy $#@! I swear six layers of skin, not to mention half an acre of arm hair, came off with it the next day. What do they use for adhesive in those things—Gorilla Glue?

I tease, of course. This is a minuscule price to pay for gargantuan protection. A flu shot's the cheapest medical insurance policy money can buy. If you've ever come down with influenza—the honest-to-gosh, equatorial-fever, arctic-chill, ache-till-you-moan, sick-for-two-weeks, please-Lord-let-me-die variety—you know what I mean.

Anytime I hear someone shrug, "I had the flu yesterday, but I'm fine now," I'm reminded of "Mannix," a private-eye television show from the 1960s.

In nearly every episode, the bad guys would beat poor ol' Joe Mannix into lifeless pulp, shoot him full of holes, and shove him off a cliff inside his car—which would invariably explode at the bottom. But by the next scene, Joe would have fully recovered, with only a junior-sized bandage over one eye. Ten seconds later, even the bandage would be gone.

They don't make good guys, or bandage strips, like that anymore.

Ah, but medical treatments certainly have improved—even if you're unlucky enough to meet up with the flu bug or some other noxious cootie.

I keep at my desk a book called *East Tennessee Lore of Yesteryear*. It's a long-out-of-print tome by Emma Deane Smith Trent and is full of odd procedures once used around here to cure the sick. That many of these remedies include directions to "continue until the patient improves or dies" should tell you something about their basis in scientific fact and effectiveness. A few gems:

"To cure a fever blister, kiss a dog."

"For frozen feet, apply roast beefsteak."

"To cure chicken pox, go to the chicken house after the sun goes down and let a black hen fly over you."

"Take new nails, put them in a bucket, and pour water over them. When the water is rusty, take it for blood medicine."

"A pan of water placed under the bed will prevent night sweats."

"For sore throat, cut slices of salt pork or fat bacon, simmer a few minutes in hot vinegar, and apply to the throat as hot as possible. When this is taken off, wrap with a bandage of soft flannel."

Strange, for sure. Ineffective, perhaps. But at least I bet that bandage peeled off easier than the ones we have today.

LESSONS LEARNED BY THE SEA

Every time I vacation on the North Carolina coast, which I've been doing thirty-something years and counting, I learn new lessons. Some are intellectual, some practical.

Once it was the life cycle of sea turtles. Another time, how to catch pompano on a bottom rig in the surf. Another, the history of lighthouses. Another, which footpath to the ocean presents the best opportunity to avoid painful sand spurs.

Also, which newspaper boxes down by the pier sell out first every morning. Or how coastal humidity alters cooking time in a charcoal smoker. Or which restaurant has the tastiest grouper sandwiches and which gift shop the goofiest souvenirs.

But the last few years have provided the finest education of all: I've been learning how a grandfather is supposed to behave at the beach. According to the lesson plans I have studied in earnest, a beach grandfather is required to:

- Empty the Atlantic Ocean, one bucket of water at a time.
- Each bucketful is delivered to a sieve previously filled
  with sand and poured out slowly, revealing a cache
  of shell fragments to be studied intently and deposited
  into a second bucket. Then the grandfather is dispatched seaside once more. And please be faster
  this time.

- Lead a parade of marchers across pasty, wet sand at low tide, stopping only to splash vigorously in every shallow pool left by the ebbing waves.
- Purchase a nonresident fishing license but never make the first cast because castles must be constructed and a moat dug to protect the sandy kingdom against an overnight tidal onslaught.
- Blow chardonnay bubbles in a wine glass—or milk bubbles in a sippy cup, depending on age of the bubbler—halting the session abruptly when a certain brown-eyed grandmother cuts one of her patented evil stares from the kitchen. Fortunately, grandmothers are easily distracted by stove-top duties, and the bubbling may then resume. Only *ssshhh,* quieter this time.
- Point out pelicans in flight, alligators in freshwater lagoons, deer in pine-palmetto forests.
- Carry wee ones to their beds at night while limp arms envelop his neck and gentle breaths flow softly across his shoulder.
- Play "Blue's Clues Shapes and Colors" in the car's DVD 6,215 times while driving to and from the coast. Plus 6,215 times more if requested. Without complaining.
- Pray for a repeat of these lessons every summer far into the future.

That last one is of the utmost importance. Because until now, I never realized what slow learners beach grandfathers can be.